FOR ALL IT WAS WORTH

A MEMOIR OF HITLER'S GERMANY - BEFORE, DURING AND AFTER WWII

BERNHARD R. TEICHER

Edited and Published by
BIOCOMM PRESS

FOR ALL IT WAS WORTH

Copyright © 2016 by B. R. Teicher.

All rights reserved.

Published by BioComm Press

http://biocomm.eu/press

CONTENTS

EDITOR'S NOTE

The Germanic linguistic subject-object-verb (SOV) typology of the Author has deliberately been retained, to authentically reflect the "voice" of the Author.

PROLOGUE

For most of my life I have been a passionate stamp collector. When all my material had finally been disposed of, I started compiling a *Timeline of Geophysical/Paleontological Parallel Developments from the Big Bang to 3 000 B.C.* which our son published on Amazon for me. Being an e-fossil myself, that sort of thing was way beyond my abilities.

After that, a collection of rocks and minerals was started. But after a few years this also came to an end, because we were now living in a retirement village, and there was just not enough space to extend these collections any further and, therefore, interest waned. A compilation titled *Rock Identification* rounded up this endeavor and will be published at the same venue in 2018. A veritable dumping ground for my hobbies, it appears.

What now? Sitting idly around was simply not an option for me. Talking to an old friend about my dilemma of how to spend my time now, he suggested that I write something, just to keep busy, as he himself had done quite successfully. I laughingly dismissed the idea, because I knew that I could never write the 'novel of the century', not even a halfway decent story. All I had ever written were management reports. Accordingly, when I eventually had followed his advice, that was what the embryo of this story looked like as soon as the first few lines appeared on the white paper, or rather the white computer screen.

There is, however, one consolation for the poor readers: at least they don't have to suffer wading through pages and pages of boring conversations, because there won't be any.

But I thought that an entire post-war generation – and in particular my family - might be interested in what went on and what went wrong in Nazi Germany, since they had no personal experience of these dramatic and traumatic, but also interesting years. I have endeavored to present a balanced view, which is based on my personal experiences and impressions.

Events following this period are probably of less general interest, but once I had started with this story, the memories and impressions simply continued to pour out. Some experience developed like "Fun and Games" and memories and impressions continued to pour out.

In March 2015, into my nineties by now, I started to jot down reminiscences and ideas as they popped up in my mind. Soon I realized that this would rather be a *curriculum vitae* (as we Romans used to say) or, even more likely, would resemble a report like I used to write as a management consultant in the dim past. After I had painfully filled six pages, I thought: that's it, there is nothing else to report. Yeah, well!

But as soon as I started formulating the first sentences, I realized that the real purpose of my writing would be to create an *aide memoire* for the time when I would tell my great-great-grandchildren about my life but had forgotten what to say next. Therefore, no romantic interests, not even a tiny bit of hot sex. To document how old-fashioned this book is going to be: in addition to the omission of this vitally important ingredient of modern literature, there will additionally be a total lack of expletives! Therefore, you have been warned. Entertainment value will be zilch.

It was amazing for me to experience how much I remembered from these long past years. But it was equally amazing to realize, in how many instances my memory had failed me. An interesting observation I had made, in the process of clicking on the computer keyboard, was the fact that the more I wrung out of what went for my brains, the more reminiscences and forgotten snippets of information popped up in my mind. This will probably mean, that this opus never gets completed. Unfortunately, since I am of a competitive nature, so I foresee that I will pressure myself to finish the job as quickly as possible. Which counteracts the reason for doing this, namely, to have something to do!

I have tried to record to the best of my knowledge and of what I remember, what has happened. But I also have recorded, as honestly as possible, my emotions and my thoughts at the relevant times. This has had several unintended consequences. Memories have floated up, obviously from my sub-conscious, which I had thought were lost or suppressed a long time ago.

In addition, I had to face some questions which I had never asked myself before. In many ways it was a cathartic process for me. In order to be able to record a true and complete picture I had to abandon, at least to a large extend, my ingrained refusal of showing emotions.

In some cases, I had doubts about the accuracy of my memory and therefore have checked my recollection of facts and dates with the 1938 edition of 'Ploetz', our high school history book, which had a specialized detailed section about the Nazi party up to this year, their organizations and their leaders. Other facts I checked against Google and Wikipedia, the Internet encyclopedia. If I had recollected the facts correctly, I made no relevant comment, but if I had things wrong and had to make corrections, or if I noticed interesting additional details of which I had no recollection myself, then I quoted the source thereof in brackets behind the statement concerned.

In the unlikely event that you find any mistakes or inconsistencies in these pages, I must plead as usual my utter innocence, since any such accidents were clearly the proof-reader's fault, in the person of my wife. She has helped me very much by her proof-reading efforts to avoid the most stupid typing mistakes.

It is quite unbelievable, what silly mistakes I made in the excitement of digging up one more morsel of my reminiscences. She spotted most of these mishaps (each discovery did cost me dearly!). She also spotted quite a few more serious oversights or mistakes on my part. Ash on my gray head! But despite her heroic efforts, the odd mistake probably escaped her eagle eye. In which case it is, of course, my fault.

There is one important point I would like to make here: This story, and its South African sequel, *A Zulu under my Bed* do not pretend to be scientific history books because they are merely observations and reminiscences of a witness of the respective times. It is only natural that mistakes due to my faulty memory may have crept in, for which I apologize.

PART I

THE PRE-WAR YEARS

1924 TO 1939

1924 Was A Remarkable Year

- In the Soviet Union Lenin dies. Stalin, the Secretary General of the communist party, and Trotsky differ about future policy direction for the party.
- The Greek monarchy ends. A republic is proclaimed, but soon after the monarchy is re-established again.
- The German Zeppelin Z.R.III flies from Lake Constance to Lakehurst near New York, as part of the reparations for World War I, which Germany had to furnish in line with the Treaty of Versailles.
- In the aftermath of the devastating 1923 earthquake, the Japanese capital of Tokyo is largely destroyed and burned down.
- The last Ottoman sultan and caliph is deposed, Kemal Ataturk is now the de-facto ruler of the newly established Republic of Turkey.
- Mahatma Gandhi is released from prison in India, and he tries to defuse the frictions between Hindus and Muslims.
- All over China the civil war is spreading. In Southern China Dr. Sun-Yatsen rules in Canton with his revolutionary Kuomintang Party.

―――

In Germany, other important events took place

- In this first year after the 1923 hyper-inflation a tax law is passed, but never enacted as far as I know, to re-establish the monetary values lost in the inflation, when the German middle-classes lost most of their wealth.
- Numerous parliament closures and re-openings, continuous verbal and physical battles between members of up to 30 political parties create complete chaos in Germany.

- No new housing had been built in Germany during the war, and not much afterwards either, because of the inflation. The result is a serious shortage of affordable accommodation.
- A substantial number of babies and toddlers suffer from rickets, caused by nutrition deficiencies. This illness is called by the German people the English Sickness, blamed on the British blockade of the German harbors for many years, even after the war had ended.
- Adolf Hitler writes during his incarceration his bestseller '*Mein Kampf*' (My Struggle).
- In Hannover the *Welfen* party demands a separate state Niedersachsen. The name of this party refers to a local dukedom in the High Middle Ages. The formation of this state only came about after 1945, with the help of the British occupation authorities.

This also is the year in which I made my appearance. All these events, except for the last one, had a decisive influence on the further developments in Germany up to 1933 when Hitler took over, and even thereafter.

1

INNER-CITY OF DRESDEN

1924 TO 1928

Every respectable autobiography starts with some very early reminiscences. But not this one, this starts with a Black Hole. I know absolutely nothing about the early years of my parents. Which type of school did they attend? Most likely primary school only. In this case, what has my father done, in the three years after school, before he joined the army? And has he also been a volunteer, like so many others?

My father was born in 1897 in Dresden. After four years as a member of the infantry in the front lines and trenches in France, including at Verdun and at the battlefields of the *Somme*, he luckily was only slightly wounded for his efforts. He was demobilized in 1918 when the war had ended. Eventually he found a job with Dresdner Bank in Dresden, after having survived for a while as a returned veteran by playing the piano in bars in Dresden's entertainment quarter (to name it politely).

He was a proper party animal and he always was the 'Soul of the Party'. His imitation of a gesticulating preacher was wonderful, as long as one was no bible pusher. But such people were for sure not to be found amongst his friends and acquaintances.

In 1921 he had married my mother, who was born in 1900. She had been in charge of a satellite office or shop of some unknown firm. Their first child, my would-have-been sister, died in 1923 in the first year of her life of the English Sickness, or rickets.

When I appeared panic was palpable, I was later told, this happened because I had been diagnosed with the same affliction. My chest was, and still is, somewhat caved in and my chest X-rays showed shadows of encapsulated tuberculosis bacteria in my lungs. They are still there, I am proud to report. Obviously, this was not a very good start, but my parents spent a lot of care, time and money to see me through.

Because of the shortage of affordable living quarters all over Germany we lived at this time in one room of the apartment of my grandparents (on my father's side) in Dresden. I could also have talked about my paternal grandparents, but I did not want to be pretentious.

Their apartment was on the fifth floor of the building they owned at 60 Ammonstrasse. We could see from the kitchen window most of the inner city of Dresden, particularly, of course, the church towers. Outstanding was the *Sophienkirche* with its filigree bell towers. The *Schlosskirche*, the church of the pre-war catholic Court of protestant Saxony, was clearly visible, next to the tower of the former Royal Palace.

For me as a little boy it was particularly interesting to get an almost aerial overview of a typical inner-city block. One could see on all four sides the uninterrupted rows of five-story apartment buildings, with the backyards containing smallish and medium-sized factories, warehouses and storage sheds of all descriptions.

My earliest recollection is of my great-grandmother, but only as a gray shadow against the window looking out over the roofs of inner Dresden. Was she the mother of my grandfather, or of either one of my grandmothers? I don't know. I assume that she also had her room in this apartment.

My grandfather was originally married to the mother of my father, a Miss Severin, a descendant of the Huguenots who had fled France after the 'Bartholomew Night', when many of the French protestants had been murdered on the orders of the French king and the catholic church. She had died early, well before my time, and she clearly had passed on to my father her French good looks, which I only remember from photographs. With his black hair he had to shave a second time if my parents wanted to go out in the evening. Our son seems to have inherited some of her and of his genes.

After my grandfather's first wife *née* Severin had succumbed to a herpes infection, he later married the sister of a house painter colleague who had turned blind from lead poisoning, caused by the lead-containing paints in use then by these artisans. A common occurrence in this trade in those days.

The poor man had received a generous financial compensation from some sort of Workmen's Compensation insurance, which enabled him at a later stage to grant a large bond to my grandfather, allowing him to buy his second block of apartments, after he had sold the original one.

My grandfather's first wife was most likely a sister of my uncle Carl Severin, who will make his appearance later in this *saga*. His daughter and his granddaughter will also take later their places on this stage. At some time before the first war or shortly thereafter, but before he met my mother, my father met uncle Carl's daughter (her first name has slipped through the cracks of my memory), and I suspect that she was his first great love.

This assumption is based on what happened to me eighteen years later, in connection with her daughter. Now, don't push, details can wait for their turn in the sequence of reminiscences. As will also be revealed later, my family luckily kept in close touch with her family. Obviously, there were no hard feelings involved.

Several other memories are also connected with the Severin family. Uncle Carl was co-owner of Severin & Zeh, a factory for fasteners, which was producing nails, screws etc. He was not only of obvious Huguenot ancestry, but looked every bit the French *bonhomme*, with his pronounced beer belly, and his *barbe-en*-pointe, the characteristic goatee of the French gentlemen of that period.

His family lived in a typical *Belle Époque* two-story villa in one of the best up-market pieces of real estate above Dresden. I don't know how many rooms they had, but when my parents visited for a typical *risqué* party night, I always found myself put to bed in a large spare bedroom. These were, not to forget, still the Wild Twenties, with Jitterbug, Boogie-Woogie *et al.*

Maybe you noticed my perfect mastery of *La Langue Française?* OK, never mind!

He, or his company, owned a Maybach luxury car, which together with Horch was one of the two luxury car *marques* of the time in Germany, placed, maybe, even above the Mercedes star. Shockingly by today's standards, the car had neither heating, nor an electric starter motor. I still remember the driver trying to start this top-of-the-range car, wildly cranking the starter handle.

One day in winter we were invited on a journey into the *Erzgebirge*, the Ore Mountain, forming there one of the boundaries between Germany and Czechoslovakia. We drove to Zinnwald, near the border and close to the ridge of the mountain, and nearly froze to death, despite heavy blankets and a genuine animal pelt to keep me warm.

The floor of the car consisted of wooden planks (surely very expensive imported timber), with the wind whistling through the gaps, despite the expensive fur floor coverings. A tiny 20 x 30cm view panel with electrically heated wires was attached to the windscreen, for the driver to be able to more or less see the road when the window was iced up or when it was snowing heavily.

My grandfather, vintage of 1871, was a master house painter. This master qualification was very important in Germany, allowing the employment and training of apprentices. Since he had his own business, he clearly belonged to the established middle-class. He was spared the losses associated with the 1923 hyper-inflation because he had no bank or savings accounts to speak of, only his firm and his apartment building. At this stage my own family was in the lucky position to own practically nothing, so they also lost nothing.

He was, however, more than a mere house painter, because he also had studied painting at the famous Dresden Art Academy and he painted in his spare time some beautiful oil pictures which he also successfully sold. A few I have salvaged over all these years. Often, I looked at them, reminiscing about the times with my grandparents, and the memories of Dresden as it was then, before the 1945 fire storm and the virtually total destruction of the city.

Recently our son had sent us an e-mail message with a picture of a painting of the Dresden *Frauenkirche*, signed B. Teicher. He had found this on the internet in an advert by a local art dealer. This large painting used to be the pride of my parent's lounge in Dresden. We offered him that he should try to buy this picture, as a gift from us. He was able to report some time later that the transaction had been successfully completed. This heirloom is now safely back in our family.

Grandfather's first apartment building of five stories, naturally without a lift, had been built in the late 1870's, when, after the victorious 1870/71 Prussian/German war against France, a building boom took place in Germany. It was a typical *Mietskaserne* or Rental Barracks, decidedly a bit less than comfortable and definitely not a 5-star establishment, but it provided a roof over the heads of our family.

The ceilings in the apartments were very high, and the rooms, therefore, difficult and expensive to keep warm. The absence of a lift created huge problems for older people, who often lived higher up, because the rentals were somewhat lower. Most of the apartments were as crowded as that of my grandfather, and for the same reason: the crippling shortage of affordable accommodation.

The toilets were situated between two floors of three parties each. I make this out as six families per facility. My grandparents, living on the fifth floor, had their own private toilet. I cannot be sure, whether this was a long-drop, or already a modern water installation, but we did not have the luxury of using toilet paper. Instead, we used square-torn pieces of newspaper, as was the general habit in those days. Much cheaper, and eco-friendly as well. Sorry, I forgot that this eco-business had not been invented yet.

My next memory is of my mother taking me one afternoon for a walk in my pram. I stuck out my arm and let my hand glide over some iron railings. Unfortunately, this happened near the main railway station, and these railings were covered with a couple of inches of the soot produced by the steam railway engines. I seem to remember that there were some harsh words uttered. At the time I wondered what all the commotion was about?

Going anywhere was always a lot of fun for me, but rather annoying and frustrating for my poor mother. In those days I was sporting a knitted all-in-one suit. As soon as I was packaged into this receptacle, plus fitted-out with socks, shoes, knitted cap, gloves and a knitted shawl, I declared that I had to go. Modesty prevents me from being more specific as to where to. This procedure was repeated every time the occasion arose, according to my mother, but I prefer to think that she was very much exaggerating there.

The municipal tram line number 26 ran along our street on its way around inner Dresden on both sides of the River Elbe. It was thus providing easy direct access to most parts of the inner city. Additionally, it also connected to all of the tram lines serving the suburbs, thereby providing a perfect transportation hub. We made extensive use of this public transport. Tram lines, and to a lesser extent the bus services, were of great importance to the people at a time, when ownership of a car was a rare exception, reserved for the very rich.

My mother often took me in my pram to the *Grosser Garten*, the Great Garden. This was a so-called English Park, with numerous well-spaced huge old trees and lawns and paths between them. The number 26 tram would have delivered us within walking distance to the entrance. The center of the park was taken up by a relatively modest Royal Sommer Palace, with a large pond containing ducks and huge carps, which always looked starved and had to be fed by little boys. But much more important to me was there the existence of a Punch and Judy show next to the park's garden restaurant.

The Dresden *Vogelwiese* was a huge (according to my infantile memory) amusement park, open for, as I seem to remember, two weeks every year in July or August. My recollection regarding the fares and other attractions is rather vague, not surprising when considering that I was only 4 on our last visit, and we probably had only been there maybe twice, as far as I can remember.

One of the war comrades of my father lived with his wife and his son of my age in Rabenstrasse in Dresden, in walking distance from where we lived. He worked as a compiler of timetables for the German government railways. We often went there, and I remember a *Fasching* (carnival) day early in February of probably 1928. There was still some snow in the streets. My friend was dressed as a Red Indian and I was camouflaged as a cowboy. I carried a so-called 'hundred-bullets' toy gun, with concussion-strip 'ammunition'. On this day I saw for the first-time men on stilts. This was an advertising gimmick for *VIM*, a new household cleaning compound, which is still around in Germany today, I believe.

Some days my mother took me to the *Güntzbad*, an indoor swimming pool named after its founding (and financing) patron, to meet there the wife of our friends from Rabenstrasse with her little boy. I was still small enough to be able to crawl underneath the door of their change room to visit my friend, while his mother was changing. When I was told not to do this again, I simply could not understand what the fuss was about. After all, I was only three or four years old, but by now I guess I understand why she was not too happy about my friendly visit.

One of my early unpleasant memories is of cod-liver oil, which I had to take for many years on a daily basis because of my rickets affliction. For the same reason I received, probably weekly and for several months, UV radiation as another treatment for this condition. But this was much more pleasant, because it involved the visit to a pediatrician in another part of the city, and therefore a ride on a different tram line. There I got to wear black protective glasses, very cool!! Mumps and diphtheria also required visits to this same doctor.

Yes, I enjoyed almost the full medical bouquet of treatments by a pediatrician. This included medical attention for a bilateral inflammation of the middle ear, which provided me in my old age with occasional tinnitus and a certain loss of balance, as well as some hearing problems.

My next memory is the Kindergarten. There we were taught to crochet with colored wool, using cotton-thread holders with four small nails added around one of the holes. The result of our endeavors was a multi-colored wool sausage. A very impressive achievement for a 4-year old, I figured. This was also the place and the occasion where I decided and announced my future profession: driver of a red fire engine. Apparently, I completed this first out-of-the-house adventure without any remarkable complications, and all the Kindergarten gaolers (minders) survived my attendance undamaged.

It was usual for little boys to be called by some other than their proper first name. My pre-teenager moniker was Bubi, a name which at the time appeared to be fine. But as a teenager I had a serious problem with this childish name and made great efforts to avoid its use. Probably quite unnecessarily, because in the late '40s and early '50s we had a famous boxer in Germany, Bubi Scholtz, who obviously had no issue with this name.

My first toy I remember was a sturdy wooden push cart. I never received a machine pistol or a sword, which I never missed anyway. My first book told the story of a bunny, or rather a baby hare. I could recite the whole short tale, but I don't know whether I could read at this stage or simply had memorized my mother's many readings.

In about 1928 my grandfather had acquired a detector radio. This was a contraption the size of a large cigar box, with what looked like a silver wire on an arm touching a crystal, a quartz most likely, and a dial to select the wavelength of the desired radio station. In his case this was somewhat theoretical, because the only station he could receive was Radio Dresden, and this only very scratchy. But a lot of fun was had by all, as I remember. After all, this was for this generation the first really new technological adventure, after electric light, cars, Zeppelins and Flying Machines.

It must have been in 1928 or thereabouts, when my grandfather took me to a tiny flea-bite cinema next to the Dresden power station in Könneritz Strasse. It was incredibly primitive, showing only silent Black-and-White flicks. On this occasion we saw a Western, starring the famous Tom Mix. I soon learned that the good guys wore the white Stetsons (I obviously did not know this name then), and the baddies wore the black ones. When I asked my grandfather why the wheels of the mail coach turned backwards, I was instructed to concentrate on the story. He must have had a bad day, or he just did not know. This moving picture invention was, after all, very new to him as well.

Later we enjoyed a proper small cinema at Freiberger Platz, also in walking distance from Ammonstrasse. Some late afternoon, probably in November, we were both standing in front of this 'moving picture' place, waiting to be let in. It was bitterly cold, and I was wearing my thick winter coat. My shoulders were hurting badly from the weight of the overcoat, but possibly also because of the cramping of my muscles due to the freezing cold. This was the first time I remember my painful shoulders. I have no idea what we saw that day.

Around the corner from my grandparent's apartment building in Rosenstrasse was the chocolate factory of Hartwig & Vogel. Their most famous product was the *Tell Apfel*, an apple-shaped packet of chocolate slices. I'm not sure, whether I ever had any of their products, or even whether I ever saw any of their chocolates. But the shiny brass plate with their name at the entrance to their premises had always had a peculiar fascination for me, whenever I walked past, probably thinking of their products.

Since we were just talking about food: a Dresden cheese specialty, which my grandfather regularly bought, were the 'corpse fingers'. This macabre designation referred to elongated cheese sticks, approximately sized like fingers, and which were covered in a white cheese mold. Their taste was close to the French *Camembert*.

And there was another, less gruesome, specialty of his to report: dried bananas. These were not the shriveled remainders at the fruit and vegetable shop, but an industrially peeled, sliced and dried product. They had their place on his nightstand, ready to be nibbled in bed.

Quite a different memory relates to the yellow trucks of the Post Office parcel deliveries. Eat your heart out, Mr. Musk, these were fully electrical vehicles without a combustion engine! When these trucks had to traverse a somewhat elevated bridge over the railways, they were just crawling along, at less than walking speed.

What we also could marvel at in about 1928 was the green Opel *Laubfrosch*, the 'tree-frog' car. These small 4 PS cars were the first assembly line cars built in Germany, and they sold for RM (*Reichsmark*) 4 500, then the equivalent of one thousand US Dollar, or the cost of a small cottage (Wikipedia). I remember about them a somewhat rounded silhouette, a little bit like the later *Volkswagen* Beetle.

2

OUR NEW APARTMENT

1929

Next came a major upset: moving to a new house, or rather moving apartments. In early 1929 my father was able to find us a brand-new three-room apartment at 17 Prohliser Strasse in Dresden-Reick. This was an average Dresden suburb, which was neither fancy nor neglected, about seven kilometers from the center of town. Our apartment was in the middle one of three identical blocks of eighteen apartments each: ground floor, first and second floor.

We lived on the first floor, in US parlance: the second floor. We were proud owners, or rather tenants (apartment buying had not been invented yet in Germany), of a so-called three-room apartment, with sitting room or lounge, two bedrooms, living-in kitchen, a separate combined bathroom and toilet, as well as a balcony, our own cellar and attic compartments.

The monthly rental of forty-nine *RM* for this apartment must be seen in relation to my father's then monthly salary of about three hundred *RM*. To show the relative value of the *Reichsmark* at the time: a loaf of rye bread cost 54 Pfennig, a double scoop on an ice cream cone set me back 10 Pfennig, a single tram ticket in Dresden came to 18 Pfennig and the return ticket was 22 Pfennig. An inland letter cost twelve Pfennig. The value of 1 US Dollar was RM4,20. These prices did not change at all until the end of the coming World War. The Germans had learned their lesson and were terrified of inflation!

In my grandparent's apartment the kitchen had looked like a squeezed-in afterthought of the builder. Our new large kitchen was therefore an absolute novelty for us. The stove had in addition to the fireplace a built-in hot-water tank and two gas rings.

There is, unfortunately, an unpleasant story connected with this kitchen stove, involving myself. One winter day, when I was alone at home, I decided to investigate how such a coal fire actually functioned. I had opened the fire-door and with the poker moved the red-hot coals a bit around to see what would happen.

All of a sudden, and all by themselves, some of the coals decided to make a dash for the open door and freedom. Somehow, I managed to confine them to their quarters again, but by then the linoleum in front of the stove had acquired some black smelly discolorations.

As soon as my mother had returned home again, the same type of discolorations was to be found on my completely innocent bum, but at least they were not smelly. This was the only time I remember, when I really got my backside warmed. But I also should record here, that a 'cat-of-nine-tails' was hanging somewhere, which however served only as the symbol of a final warning.

We had in our kitchen also a washing-up table for the dishes. This had a pull-out section on rollers, containing two sunken basins. Next to it was the sink with the cold-water tap. Presumably, hot water pipes had not been invented yet, or, at least, were not as common in Germany as they are today. All in all, a very modern kitchen for these times, and a huge improvement over our previous abode in the inner city.

It was even more amazing for us to have a *chaise-longue* in the kitchen, in line with the then prevalent habit in German middle-class households of using one's kitchen as a so-called *Wohnküche*, a live-in kitchen or a quasi-living room. The advantage of this arrangement was the fact that in winter one had to heat only one room, a very important consideration for any German middle-class household of the time, since the period requiring heating lasted in Dresden some nine months of the year, and the level of living standards was very much lower than it is today.

That brings me to what was called the *Kalte Pracht* or Cold Splendor, namely the living room or lounge. 'Cold' because the magnificent *Kachelofen* stove, constructed of glazed tiles, was heated, and the room was used, only at Christmas and Easter festive days. 'Splendor' because this is where the best pieces of furniture were to be found. Absolutely crazy, but such happened to be the conventions and aspirations of the middle-classes in those days in Germany. One had to compete with the 'Joneses' and ascertain one's self-esteem.

Needless to say, that I was forbidden to ever enter this room on my own. It was strictly out-of-bounds! Fat chance that I would obey and forgo the mysteries maybe to be found there! Alas, there were none.

That leaves the main bedroom, which was facing the back lawn, with a double bed and a large white wardrobe and a crib for His Excellency, yours truly. A special memory of mine is attached to this latter item. My parents had what was called a theatre subscription. Once a month they would go to the opera or the playhouse in downtown Dresden. Nowadays, this would make a babysitter mandatory, but in those days people's attitude in this, as in so many other aspects, was different: less emotional and more realistic and practical. So, I was lying in my crib, all on my own, anxiously waiting for them to return, and of course I promptly fell asleep.

Finally, there was the so-called *Kleine Zimmer*, the small second bedroom facing the street. This served as a substitute for the out-of-limits sitting room, because it was smaller and had an efficient small stove and could therefore be heated more often and more economically. Soon a second-hand piano appeared there, which later served as a torture instrument for me. My father could play the piano very well but was not able to read music.

He had a small wall cupboard hanging in this room, containing some paraphernalia extremely interesting for a small boy, such as his empty 6,35mm pistol, obviously a left-over from the war. I do not remember, whether he had some bullets as well. In this cabinet he also had some tools to deal with electrical installations.

In my grandparents' apartment we, like most other middle-class families in Germany at the time, had our bath once a week in a galvanized tub, filled with water heated on the kitchen stove. Our new bathroom was a really exciting and luxurious new experience for us. For myself it was particularly the heating contraption for the bath water: a tube of galvanized steel of about thirty centimeters diameter, a sort of geyser, and underneath a fireplace as in the kitchen stove.

What was missing, however, was a shower. Apparently, this piece of ablution equipment was either not available in Germany at the time, or it was practically unknown to the majority of the population, so nobody missed it. This room also contained our very own WC. And we now had the use of civilized toilet paper rolls as well!

My father had screwed some sturdy hooks into the ceiling of the passage which supported a swing, to keep me busy and out of trouble on rainy days. In this passage stood a white cupboard which obviously previously had been located in someone's bedroom. In there I had one or more shelves to store my toys and other treasures. This was also the storage facility for the eight 100g slabs of milk chocolate which will be mentioned later in conjunction with my first day at school.

Also, to be found in this passage was our *garderobe*, or coat stand, to hang one's overcoats, umbrellas and hats. *Apropos* hats: in those days no man, and definitely not any woman, would ever have left the house without wearing a hat. Even the kids had most of the time something on their heads, a knitted cap, the kepi of the *Hitler Youth*, or a *Schülermütze*, if they attended a High School. I will come back later-on to this last piece of boy's apparel, after I had joined college.

We also had a spacious cellar compartment. Over the winter season my mother stored there a hundred-weight or so of apples from my maternal grandparents' orchard. We also kept in our section of the basement a few hundred kilograms of briquettes and household coal, which the Germans called 'stone-coal', because they looked like pitch-black stones.

I was always fascinated by the numerous fossil plants I could find among the stone-coal: leaves, parts of branches and seeds and such. Unfortunately, I did not know anything about fossils then, and not much now, either. And now I am a fossil myself.

Three guesses as to who had to haul up the coal from the cellar to the second floor. It was my job to carrying them up to feed all the fireplaces in the apartment. No protection then for exploited and overworked little boys! In those days no laws existed against child labor, as far as I remember.

Also, to be found down there were jars of jams and numerous *Einweckgläser*. These hermetically sealed glass jars were an invention by somebody called Weck, which operated on the vacuum principle to sterilize the contents. After the jar had been filled, alcohol in a tiny scoop was ignited and the burning of the oxygen in the air pocket created a vacuum, and a red rubber ring provided the sealing insulation. These jars contained all sorts of fruit and vegetables, such as strawberries, cherries, gherkins and the like.

Each tenant in addition had quite a useful walled-off separate section in the attic of the apartment building. There we kept the usual paraphernalia which one does not really need, but is not prepared to throw away, yet.

The useful large balcony had space for two rattan easy chairs, a table and some flower boxes with red geraniums. Always red geraniums, never any other colors or plants. From the balcony we looked down on to the lawn behind the apartments, and then on to a large field of a nearby farm, and beyond that to a storm water drainage canal, further fields and finally the next suburb.

This balcony also gave us a clear view of the *Borsberg*, with the moderate altitude of 300 meters above the sea. The level of the city of Dresden was just above 100 meters. Next to this landmark, and high above the Dresden skyline, we looked at some up-market select residential Dresden suburbs. Principally that of the *Weisser Hirsch*, the 'White Stag' area.

As I only found out sixty years later, there was in the '80s, during the days of the DDR, a very prominent Russian visitor residing in this luxury residential area. He was a resident *KGB* boss, in charge of recruiting suitable new agents at the Dresden Technical University (Wikipedia) for the secret service of the Soviet Union. He is nowadays known as the friendly and peace-loving Vladimir Putin. You may have heard of him, perhaps.

We also could clearly see in the distance the *Sächsische Schweiz*, the 'Switzerland-in-Saxony', with Mount Lilienstein and the fortress of Königstein on top of one of the typical sandstone table mountains. This area near the border with Czechoslovakia was about thirty to forty kilometers away from us as the crow flies.

The River Elbe had cut not only these amazing flat mountains, but also steep cliffs and towers like the *Bastei* (Bastion) out of this yellow sandstone formation. This mountain had provided virtually all of the material for the work of the stone masons for the old representative public and prominent private buildings in Dresden, long before bricks were available in the district.

3

LIFE IN THE SUBURBS

1928 TO 1930

My health started to improve with the healthier living conditions in our suburb. I developed more or less normally as a boy, and I do not remember any particular problems, apart from the usual childhood ones, like measles, mumps, tooth ache and the like. The only thing worth mentioning that I remember in this regard is the fact that my mother had to cook rice soup for me, only in plain water and without any animal fat, because I was allergic to it (another one of those fancy words we had to survive without). I also had to eat a lot of calf liver with the rice soup, both of which I liked very much

As a result of the German living standards being much lower than today, eating habits were quite different from the present. We ate things which middle-class people nowadays would not even look at and which are unheard of in Western Europe now. Tripe, brain and lung hash were standard fare, together with plenty of potatoes and soups, of course. Many working-class families also ate horse meat and horse-sausages, but we did not.

In those days the German housewives generally did not bake at home but prepared their cakes and brought them to the baker to finish the job. Except in the villages, where often no bakers existed, because most farmers baked their own bread in communal baking ovens.

One of the local cake specialties was the *Dresdner Weihnachts*

Stollen, a Christmas cake full of butter, raisins, almonds, orange and lemon peels, sugar, cinnamon, and cake flour, of course. To be ready for Christmas, they would already be baked in the middle of November, and there were always enough large *Stollen* loafs to last us for the Sunday afternoon coffee until Easter.

The winter of 1928/29 was particularly severe in Eastern Germany, and especially early and long-lasting in Saxony. Near our place there was a small plantation of maybe fifty to sixty peach and apricot trees, and they all died of frost in this terrible winter. I remember quite well helping my mother to bring our *Weihnachts Stollen* to the baker on my sled, because there was in the middle of November already enough snow in the streets to be able to do so, which was unusual so early for this time of the year.

Every two or three weeks a disreputable-looking man would appear in our streets, the *Scherenschleifer* or scissors sharpener, with his push-cart-type contraption. This contained a grinding wheel which was turning in a basin full of water. He was selling a service which is not existing anymore: sharpening of the housewife's knives and scissors.

A similar-looking chap made his appearance maybe also every two or three weeks or so. He announced his arrival with a voice reminiscent of a roll of barbed wire. He was the *Lumpensammler*, the rags-and-bone-man. As far as I remember, he did not want bones, however. A further service offering, which already has disappeared a long time ago, due to our raised living standards. We were warned off both of them by our mothers, as they were considered to be highly suspect individuals. But I assume now that both were harmless and simply members of the unemployed millions, who tried to earn a few Mark.

Another service, which has disappeared for the same reasons, was the weekly visit of the horse-drawn cart of the *Gurkenhändler*, the cucumber merchant. He sold many sorts of cucumbers, gherkins and similar stuff. Not being properly household-trained, I knew very little about the subject then, and that little I have forgotten by now. What I do remember are only the *Senfgurken*, the mustard cucumbers, the *Sauregurken*, the vinegar-soaked cucumbers, and *Sauerkraut* in a huge barrel. I seem to remember that all these goodies came from the *Spreewald*, a large marshy area southeast of Berlin.

The fronts of our three apartment buildings faced on the far side of our street a farmer's field. In most years he used to grow wheat there. In the middle distance we could see a rubbish disposal site and next to that a large suburban apartment development which appeared to be a few years older than ours.

Our street had sidewalks on both sides, but at this stage only the one on our side was surfaced. This was not at all standard in developing suburbs. This meant, that our street was in an interme-diate planning state, from a rural road to a city street. But someone at the Dresden city council had planned well ahead, because even-tually the far side of the street was built-on as well.

Like any proper city street, ours also sported gas streetlights. Every evening a workman came along on his bicycle, and with the help of a long pole he switched on the lamps. Presumably the same thing happened early in the morning, but I do not recall to ever have observed this reversal of the procedure.

This sidewalk on the far side of the street became the dedicated playground for us boys. Our principal entertainment was playing with our marbles. Most of these were colored and consisted of baked clay, but some lucky boys possessed the odd fascinating glass marbles. It was worth a 'Red-Indian's scalp' to win one of these. There will be coming a sting in the tail of this part of the story, as will be seen later-on.

I still remember vividly a particularly pretty glass marble with swirling colored lines, which I had won in one of our many games. While typing this section I was just wondering what may have become of it. Rather a silly thought, really. But I was nevertheless contemplating, who might be the lucky chap owning and playing with this marvel now.

The lawn behind our apartment building was serving as the drying area for the tenants' laundry. About a dozen four-sided concrete posts enabled the housewives to string their washing lines from post to post. One afternoon us boys were chasing each other around on the lawn, and yours truly ran full steam and headfirst into one of these posts, naturally hitting one of the edges. Much blood and quite a few tears were shed, and at least one shirt had to be decommissioned. The concrete post survived undamaged.

The assortment of clothing items on the drying lines was enlightening. The underwear items of the ladies' (we used slightly less elevated terminology, I am afraid) were quite mysterious for us boys. Some of the knickers looked rather like tents and bore no resemblance to the present-day stamp-sized panties. The brassieres on show seemed to have belonged to the big sisters of Brunhilde and appeared to have been made from bleached tarpaulins. All housewives in those days were wearing substantial but rather plain petty-coats, and most of the wives also squeezed themselves into a corset, at least whenever they left their homes.

By far the most intriguing items, however, were the *Monatsbinden*, the sanitary towels. My engrained modesty makes it difficult for me to talk about this subject, particularly since at that time I did not know what their exact purpose was. Only much later were we informed about such subjects by some older brothers of members of our gang. Let us therefore just say that they were mysterious female items of unknown purpose and function.

There were on show also many different items of gent's underwear, in particular the famous long-johns, which were clearly centuries removed from modern Y-fronts, boxer shorts or jockeys. Other common items in those days were the men's shirts with detachable snow-white collars, which had to be starched to the consistency of *Plaster of Paris* or the iron neck-rings for criminals which were fashionable in the Middle Ages. Relatively new were the just invented sweatshirts, which nowadays not even a garbage worker would be seen in. But by far the best item in this collection was the toupee hanging on one of the lines, but this was only seen once. The owner remained unknown, unfortunately.

Next to the lawn was our playground, consisting of a sand pit with a concrete surround and, for us small boys, a large concrete bench. Why all this concrete? Did the owner maybe not trust our good behavior? We also had a medium-sized fruit tree there, which we climbed again and again, sometimes even harvesting a miserable excuse for a plum.

Boys and girls of my age group were surprisingly numerous in our apartment buildings. Most of the tenants were in their twenties or thirties. One day, an older girl in the neighborhood of maybe ten to twelve years roped in about half a dozen of us four to six-year-olds into attending a medical examination.

She had somehow organized some blankets, or a tarpaulin, and she was the doctor and told us to lower our pants. In view of her authority, represented by the huge difference in age, we complied. Also, because all of us had been to the doctor before, and we knew the drill. As far as I remember, the visual inspection was all that happened, but afterwards there had been some stink about this in the community. Somebody must have snitched and spilled the beans!

This reminds me of something else. There was a rumor flying around that a girl of our own age group in the neighboring block had a penis (called something more descriptive by us, of course). And a boy of the same age in our block was rumored to have an additional vagina. I don't remember what we called this unknown thing, but the older brother of my friend called it 'a sex thing under plaster'. As neither of these two children attended our instructive and educational medical inspection session, I am not able to comment further. But one thing is clear: there must have been at this stage in our development quite some interest in discovering the differences between boys and girls.

The farm field we looked at from our balcony was a source of much fun and adventures for us boys. Some years the farmer had planted potatoes there. After their harvest we would swarm over the field, collecting the potatoes the farm labor had missed. Some of those (of the potatoes) we roasted over a fire we had made with our solar lenses from the dried-out potato leaves left lying on the ground. The others we took home. Our mothers certainly appreciated these no-cost vegetables.

If the farmer had planted cereals, wheat, rye, corn (maize) or barley this year, after the field was cleared, we would go and search the stubble field for hamster holes. Somehow, we had figured out that the hamsters would dig a number of escape holes around their burrow. By locating these holes, we could work out approximately the burrow's central position, which was about half a meter underground. Once we actually caught one of the critters, but I don't remember what happened to him afterwards. I doubt very much that he is still around after all these years. Is it not typical that I have used 'him' and 'he' instead of 'it'?

Beyond the fields we looked at from our balcony was an open storm water canal. It discharged any flooding into the River Elbe eventually, but before that could happen, it had to go underground, to cross a major suburban road. A substantial concrete structure provided the open mouth to accept the flood waters. After severe thunderstorms there would be substantial and very dangerous water flows. We often played there, with the resulting wet shoes and socks. However, the canal was ruled off-limits by our mothers after one of the boys was swept away into this open mouth. He was never seen again.

In those days nobody in the suburbs bothered with garages, except for luxury cars. At night a grand total of two cars, both of them DKW models of these basic vehicles, were parked in our street. They had 2-stroke engines and the gear shift was attached to the steering wheel. They did therefore not run on petrol but used the same petrol and motor oil mixture as motorcycles, and nowadays the lawn mowers. This resulted in a melodious noise like empty tins and bottles rolling down the street. The smell out of their exhaust pipes was also rather uncivilized.

One of these two cars was owned by the director-general of a small Dresden insurance company. The other belonged to a chemical engineer, who was often on the road for his employers. Not even the owner of our three apartment buildings could afford a car then, but years later he also bought one of this type. As mentioned before, a typical middle-class neighborhood. Even though we could not afford a car, a few years later we all three of us had our bicycles, but even this was not at all very common then in Germany.

One part of our suburb was a development of what would nowadays be described as social housing. It was called the *Vogelsiedlung*, the Bird Housing District, because all the internal streets were named after birds. For Germany the unusual and peculiar point was that all these double-story houses were constructed of wood. The fact that the inhabitants were poor, and in most cases had large numbers of children, confronted me for the first time during my primary school years with the substantial differences in living standards within our suburb, and within Germany.

In our neighboring suburb of Prohlis we had an aristocrat's *Rittergut* and *Schloss*, somewhat above an English lord's manor. The small castle even had an astronomical observatory in the tower, which must have been quite well equipped, because Herschel, at the time a famous Jewish/British astronomer, had worked there for some time in the eighteenth century.

An adjacent pub, not surprisingly called Schloßschenke, the 'Castle Pub', was the source of a weekend's jug of *Dortmunder* beer, which I sometimes had to collect for my parents. Drinking a beer brewed in faraway Dortmund was a bit of a sacrilege, because we also had two famous beer brewers in Dresden: *Feldschlösschen* and *Waldschlösschen*, and not to forget the nearby *Radeburger* brewery. They all brewed the famous *Pilsner* beer, like the Dortmunder did, but maybe theirs tasted better to my parents. As usual, I was discriminated against, and was not afforded a chance to determine the veracity of such claim for myself.

A road cutting, reminiscent of the stories and films about the classical English highway robbers, skirted a brickwork, where a huge pit had been dug to extract the loam required to bake the bricks. These were fired in large ugly looking kilns. Eventually the excavation was flooded, which spelled the end of this enterprise.

Next to it was the abandoned relic of quite a large restaurant-cum-guesthouse, which probably was a victim of the 1929 economic meltdown, but it was possible that it was much older. As was to be expected, some very scary stories were connected to this fearsome and ghoulish ruin, some more unbelievable than others. Naturally, we boys did not believe any of these, but every time we passed there, some furtive side-ways glances could be observed.

In those days we did not all have bicycles yet. On Sunday afternoons it was tradition for our family to go for a walk through the fields in the neighborhood, which was half suburban and half rural. There were some large farms in our and the next suburb very close to ours. Some of these farmers even had already cars, so they must have been rather well off, but we had no contact with any of them. There was, however, one farmer's daughter......, but let us not digress from much more interesting observations.

Close to our apartment building there existed also some nurseries and many *Schrebergärten*, the small allotment gardens for playing at growing flowers and some vegetables. But I must not joke about this. Most of these people were dead-serious about their horticultural endeavors. Many of the allotment lessees were for the first time able to have the feeling of owning some real property. Even those who had only leased their few square meters.

Another nearby establishment was a landfill site, which at my time had just been started. Occasionally, we received a whiff of a rather foul smell from there, but it was not a serious problem.

When the hole was eventually full, which only happened after the coming war, apartment buildings were constructed there for some of the thousands of families who had lost their abodes when Dresden was burnt down in February of 1945. These buildings had many problems because the site had not been compacted properly prior to the start of construction.

Probably around 1930 my parents acquired a marvel of modern technology: a proper Mende radio. This was a huge progression from my grandfather's primitive detector radio. To be able to listen to any radio station, my father had first to rig up an outside aerial. A wire had to be strung from a long pole, tied to a fruit tree propitiously growing at the correct place in the lawn behind our block, to the top of our apartment building. A cable led down to our bedroom window and from there to our living-in kitchen and the finally the radio.

The largely improved technology allowed us now, in addition to listening to Radio Dresden, also to receive its parent station Radio Leipzig, about a hundred kilometers away, as well as the long-wave and short-wave stations of *Deutschlandsender*, the national radio station, which could be received all over Germany, and in most places abroad as well, even in overseas countries.

What we did not have, in common with most other middle-class families, was a telephone. I guess there were probably no more than two or three of these in our three blocks of fifty-four apartments, and these were owned by some businesspeople. We actually did not really need a telephone, because nobody amongst our family and friends possessed one, with the notable exception of my previously mentioned uncle Carl Severin, who seemed to have everything a well-to-do family could possibly possess then.

Also, at around this time, my father became the proud owner

of a DKW 200cc motorcycle. Apparently, financial conditions were moving in the right direction for the family. The fly in the ointment, however, was the economic situation in Germany, and in the world generally. The meltdown, which had started in 1929 in Wall Street with the New York Black Friday, had by then become an economic catastrophe also in the rest of the world, and in Germany.

There were two other gadgets my father owned, which were intriguing for a small boy. One was an obviously old, but still functioning camera, which operated with glass plates of about 6cm by 10cm. It had a flashlight attachment of sorts, which worked with the help of an external timer. The other item was of course much more interesting to me. A 6,35mm automatic. (With ammunition as well?) I only saw this once as a boy, because it was locked up in the small wall cabinet in what later became my room.

A further item of interest was his collapsible top hat which, to the best of my recollection, he only wore two or three times in his life for funeral attendances. And there were his dentures, of course. They were similar to modern ones, except that they were joined together, obviously with some spring mechanism between the two parts. He had needed these, because he had lost all his teeth in the flooded trenches of France during World War I.

Our apartment neighbor, a senior police officer, had a daughter Ursula, of my own age. We spent a lot of time together as kids. But no more of that, in line with my chastity pledge in the Introduction pages. One of their family's more interesting possessions was a wind-up record player, something I had never seen before. But I have no recollection which types of records they had, nor if we ever played any.

Actually, we had quite a few policemen living in our three blocks. In the neighboring section (entrance) of our block stayed Uncle Erich. He was quite famous for his playing of the French Horn in the police music corps. At midnight of every New-Year's-Eve he beautifully played some sentimental tunes from his balcony, and I remember my mother and some others crying. Not me, of course! In one of the other blocks lived uncle Kurt, the brother of the musical uncle. As the Chief of Detectives in the Dresden police department, he was considered a big shot in the neighborhood.

In that same block we also had a police constable living, who was sporting two sleeve bands on his tunic, stating that he spoke English and French. In those days it was quite unusual for people to speak any foreign languages beyond school level. And even this capability was an exception, because most kids never went to High School, in contrast to today's situation. I do not know where and how he acquired this knowledge, since he appeared to be not particularly well educated. But maybe he had travelled extensively as a young man. Up to the end of 1933 he was also the only one in our street to hoist the flag of the KPD, the communist party, whenever there was an election, and this happened often enough.

It escaped me at the time why it was my father, and not my mother, who taught me how to tie my shoelaces correctly: a double crossing of the laces, and a double knot of the bows. Now I can see the reason. In WW1 the German soldiers were wearing lace-up ankle boots and only the officers wore proper long boots. So, he was talking from experience. Also, when he showed me how to warm my hands in freezing weather: two chaps rub each other's hands to prevent them from turning blue. I soon enough found out how valuable these simple instructions were. They probably saved me from a lot of trouble later on.

4

FURTHER DEVELOPMENTS

1930 TO 1933

The owner of our apartment buildings had started in about 1930 with a new development of about eighty more of his apartments on the other side of our street, opposite our blocks. I suppose he must have secured his financing before the stock exchange crashes of 1929 in Wall Street, in Germany and all over the world.

An about thirty meters wide strip of the farm field adjacent to our marble playing ground became an unfenced builder's yard. In addition to all the usual paraphernalia, the builders had established there a rail line for the use of a small fleet of trolleys. Since the property was being developed in a ninety degree 'dog-leg' along two streets, they needed a turntable. A round steel plate with rails allowed the trolleys to proceed from one part of the builder's yard to the other.

One day this steel plate had become dislodged, by the workmen or by us well-behaved boys, I don't remember. I believe 'suppressed memory' would be an adequate description of this state of my mind. In any case, about fifteen to twenty shiny steel balls were exposed to the very interested eyes of the members of our gang. Instead of studying the basic principles of a ball-bearing, because that is what it was, we appropriated these wonderful 'marbles' for our games.

Next, we found ourselves at the local police precinct. A stern uniformed policeman read the riot act to us, regarding stealing these shiny balls. I have to admit, this made a lasting impression on myself, and as far as I could observe, also on my fellow criminals. We never, ever, again stole steel 'marbles' out of a turntable, I swear. For accuracy's sake: no other turntables happened to be available near us.

I still remember that about in 1931 Dresdner Bank took over (willingly, or nudged by the Central Bank?), the collapsed *DANAT* (*Darmstädter und National*) Bank. My father one day brought home a shiny silvery piggy bank, stamped with the *DANAT* logo. Did we have here an early example of insider trading? But no, it was empty! I had to fill it myself with my weekly savings of 10 Pfennig, which I duly did over the next few years.

A few weeks later, Dresdner Bank in turn had to be rescued by the *Reichsbank*, the German Central Bank. All German banks remained closed for a few days. The bank rate went from 8% to 15%, later to 20% (Wikipedia). All salaries were reduced by up to 10%, including my father's. Not surprisingly, not those of the politicians, however, as far as I remember.

For us, these problems of my father's employer had the sad result that my poor mother dreaded daily the possibility of my father coming home early one day, as had happened to a few men in our neighborhood. This would have meant that he had lost his job. The pressure must have been terrible for my parents.

One thing I missed very much was the fact that we did not have a dog. The horn-blowing policeman uncle next door had an Airedale Terrier. Once or twice a week I took him (the dog) out for a long walk in the fields and meadows. The dog was quite clever, and I was able to train him, sort of. I really loved this chap and spent a lot of my free time with him.

The purchase of a green female budgerigar was all I could wheedle out of my parents. I taught her to speak quite well, and she loved to babble into the lid of our silver (actually alpaca) sugar bowl standing on the breakfast table, which produced some sort of an echo. Probably she considered this as a kind of answer.

When we thought she was feeling lonely, we bought her a blue male companion. He was too stupid or lazy to learn to speak, so he forfeited the chance to talk to her. But maybe he was sly enough to have found a way to avoid any marital arguments or dressing down?! He loved to bite my ear lobe when he was sitting on my shoulder, but nevertheless I did not warm his bum.

Once a week I had piano lessons, originally taught by my uncle Hans, the son of the Chief-of-Detectives uncle in the neighboring apartment building. His remuneration was a pack of, maybe, ten or twelve *Salem* cigarettes, a product of the famous Dresden cigarette factory of *Yenidze*. It was one of my jobs, to go and buy these from one of the small shops in the neighborhood. I have been trying to remember what their cost was, but this information is lost, just as tragic as the whereabouts of the sunken continent of Atlantis.

Neither of my grandfathers was ever seen in the kitchen. This was the domain of the housewives. My father was already much more domesticated in this regard. Preparing the Sunday afternoon coffee was his substantial contribution to the weekly household chores, but this was the only one. No need to over-do things! His advancement to domestic science was his secret addition of a pinch of salt to the freshly ground coffee beans, before he added the boiling water.

Two or three of the neighborhood's housewives shared some of the heavy household work, such as the fortnightly job of doing the laundry. They were busy all day in the laundry room, with heating the coal-fired round tub, washing, installing the clothing lines between the concrete posts (remember my collision with one of them?), squeezing the wet washing through the hand-operated wringer, and finally placing the laundry on the drying lines in the backyard.

I have a terrible memory of these laundry days. No, I escaped forced labor, but because the standard meal for supper on these occasions was a horrible thick soup of white beans. Aaagh!

Virtually no married middle-class housewives were working then, except in an enterprise owned by their family. The historically high unemployment rate had possibly something to do with this. But I rather suspect the archaic attitude: the place of a married upper- or middle-class woman was in the kitchen, and to attend to the upbringing of the children.

Notwithstanding the fact that there were some career women and other female employees, mainly office or sales staff, this held true for the majority of the population other than the working-classes. And even there only some of the married women were employed.

In case one wonders about my incessant references to the economic classes: the distinctions between upper-, middle- and working-classes were quite definite, and much more pronounced than today. The term 'working-class' was understood to imply that the upper-class was not working at all, or were just playing at working, such as being directors and chairmen of companies. And the middle-class was perceived to be working only in white collar positions and the professions, in the trades and business. Something which the working-class people generally did not consider as 'proper working'.

There was more than a grain of truth in these perceptions of the working-class, because neither of the other two classes were generally working physically, and a very large percentage of the upper classes were really not working at all, living off family fortunes and the interest on their money. But this was at the time the situation in other countries in Europe as well, I suppose.

This idea was further reinforced by the fact, that the percentage of jobless laborers was much higher than for those of the other two classes, because the employers always shed the jobs of the unqualified laborers first, whenever there was a squeeze on turnover and/or profits.

Probably sometime in 1932, we visited the *Zirkus Sarrasani* in Dresden-Neustadt for the first time. This enterprise was the proud owner of their own permanent circus building. A huge cupola, which was meant to be reminiscent of a very large circus tent, was the center piece. If I remember correctly, this was the only such building in Europe at that time. The vast majority of the other circuses were housed in a typical circus tent, which one could observe in many places during the year.

We saw there, amongst many other attractions, the famous Buffalo Bill. Actually, it had to have been an imitator, since he was long dead at this time (spotted by the proofreader!). His real name was William Cody. How come that I remember his name, I don't know. Probably a case of typical disconnected bits and pieces of more or less useless information.

An interesting point is the fact, that at this time there were no supermarkets yet to be found in Germany. There were General Dealers everywhere, not only in the rural regions. They were later called *Tante Emma Läden* (Aunt Jane Shops), a name which was only coined after the second war, when the first supermarkets had made their appearance and started to squeeze out the small family run shops.

Numerous more or less specialized small family owned and operated shops also attended to the requirements of the people. Bakers, butchers, dairy shops, greengrocers, shoemakers et al. were found everywhere. I well remember being sent to go shopping, with a cloth shopping bag (no plastic bags yet) and a slip of paper listing the items to be purchased. The wife of the shop owner, who served in a dual capacity as a saleslady would note the cost behind each item for my mother to check, and probably to have a beady look at the change I brought back home. In those days I went shopping for something or other almost on a daily basis.

Only the very modern butchery had a proper electric cash register, together with a modern electric scale, a Dutch one (Berkel, I think). However, there was already developing a new form of shop at this time as well, named *Görlitzer*. This probably belonged to a new chain and combined the sale of many different commodities, mainly in the food sector, but still without self-service. It could be termed a sort of supermarket forerunner.

But this marvel of progress left us boys cold. A much more exciting prospect was the next Saturday afternoon, when our local baker sold paper bags full of *Kuchenränder*, the cut off margins of the large square cakes they had baked that day. They sold at the reasonable price of 10 Pfennig, which one was usually able to wheedle out of mother dear.

Maybe once every two months my mother went with me by tram to inner Dresden, to buy things she could not find in our suburb. First, we usually went to the *EHP* or *EinHeitsPreis* department store in Wilsdruffer Strasse. There everything, in specific sections, sold uniformly for 5 Pfennig or 10 Pfennig, for instance. I think the most expensive price group was 50 Pfennig. They only sold hardware, neither clothing nor foodstuff.

Next stop was the Woolworth emporium. I remember my father explaining to my mother a peculiarity of this business. He was not sure, whether the firm had started in England or in the USA. But the firm had split later into two completely different enterprises, a British one and a US one, with vastly different business cultures.

The British business was high-class and with correspondingly high prices, which spread quickly all over the British Empire, whereas the US firm was low-key and branched out into Europe and Asia. Our local Woolworth was part of the US group, a paradise for the cost-conscious German housewives, whereas the Woolworth, which we encountered decades later in South Africa, was decidedly British, with high quality and the concomitant higher prices.

Later we inevitably landed in the Renner department store on Altmarkt. This was the only real department store in Dresden, because almost everything was available there, but probably without a food section. Later, in 1938, this Jewish enterprise would be 'arianized' and sanitized by giving it to the "proper" people with the correct political connections.

Most importantly, they had a toy department, which was huge (?), at least in the pre-Christmas period. At this time, from early November onwards (not from September like nowadays), I would have loved to spent hours of browsing but, naturally, was not allowed to do so.

During one of our visits there, I encountered an amazing sight: a toddler having a tantrum, and his mother giving in to his performance. This behavior by the woman was then in Germany highly unusual.

On our way home, we stood packed like sardines in the streetcar, and if it had rained, the smell of most of the workers returning home was fit to be bottled. Personal hygiene was something not much appreciated by the working-classes in those days. But to be fair, they did not have bathrooms and the modern sanitary equipment and goods we are today accustomed to. And even the middle-classes would not have appeared 'smelling like roses', if present day standards would have been applied.

In those days we read with much satisfaction in the papers, and heard in the radio newscasts, about the flights of our *Zeppelins* to South America, to Chicago and across the North Pole. Particularly the stamp collectors like myself, because commemorative *Zeppelin* stamp sets were issued by the German Post Office for each of these flights. Needless to say, the face value of several *Reichsmark* for each of these sets made them unobtainable for me, and for most other people as well. Not surprisingly, they are now worth a small fortune because of their resulting scarcity.

Another proud accomplishment for Germany in this period was the establishment of the so-called *Katapult Flüge, the c*atapult flights, across the South Atlantic. An airplane was installed on the upper deck of a *Schnelldampfer*, an express steamer, and was catapulted into the air on the high seas, to start its flight long before the steamer reached its destination harbor. Proper scheduled transatlantic flights over these huge distances were not feasible yet, but this system shortened the time for the mail crossing the Atlantic from Europe to and from the USA and South America by a day or more each way.

1932 was the year of the Lake Placid Olympic Winter Games and the Los Angeles Summer Games in the USA. All I remember about these events is the fact that Germany earned quite a good number of medals, but very few gold ones. And, of course, that the US Postmaster issued a blue 5c stamp to commemorate the sporting triumphs of the USA.

One of the things which appear strange now, but which was quite normal then, was the fact that the uniformed police force, to the best of my recollection, did not include a single policewoman. There was relatively little serious crime then, apart from political disturbances and killings, and consequently the police force was of only moderate strength.

This allowed a strict selection as to competence and thus assured a force of a high quality. After all, there were thousands and thousands of unemployed former soldiers and officers willing and available, and there was no need to lower the standards by employing policewomen. Yes, I know, I'm a fossil and a Male Chauvinist Pig as well. But at these times, this was the prevailing attitude in this regard, at least in Germany. Nobody would have seriously considered to utilize females in the traditional so-called male professions and occupations.

That serious crime was reasonably contained had, in my opinion, something to do with the fact that the death penalty was still very much alive. This retribution was, quite differently from today, not seriously questioned at all in those days. People were convinced, rightly or wrongly, of the deterrent effect of executions. In any case, all religious bodies in Germany agreed with these views, so they could not possibly have been wrong! Furthermore, this was the policy followed all over the world.

In February of 1932 a violent riot broke out when youngsters of a neighboring suburb met with the hooligans of our own, to engage in a street fight with bicycle chains, knuckle-dusters and other assorted tools. When the same thing started again in 1933, the police was ready and broke up this nonsense for good. It was never allowed to happen again.

5

MY PRIMARY SCHOOL TIME

1930 TO 1934

In 1930 I started my educational career at 45th *Volksschule*, our nearby primary school in Herrschelstrasse. But just now I discovered, thanks to Google Earth, that the correct name of the street was actually Hülsestrasse. Und I had been dead-certain of my facts! This just shows again, how fickle and unreliable one's memory can be.

The best part of this event was the fact, that the new pupils received a *Zuckertüte*. This was a cardboard cone, about 60cm high (how high was I?), filled with plenty of sweets and chocolates. This was presented by the family of the newly convicted kid to suffer an education, probably as a form of institutionalized bribery. I remember that as a result I hoarded at this time eight slabs of milk chocolate, at 100g each, on my previously described shelf in the cupboard standing in the passage of our apartment.

Primary schooling was free. We were, I think, about 45 more or less eager starting packages of what should eventually become young men. Yes, you got it, no co-eds for the German educationalists. That was considered, if not immoral, but definitely too dangerous. Accordingly, all our teachers were male, too. Probably just as well!

In this uni-sex picture lies a mystery, wrapped in a conundrum, being a riddle regarding my memory: on the one hand I was sure we only had boys in our class, and a survived class photograph proofed it. On the other hand, the question remained: where did the girls go to school? Yes, we were an enlightened country (in 1930!) and provided also schooling for girls.

Our suburb was well populated, and I doubt that the girls would have had to go to school in another area. But I cannot fathom where their school could have been. And I would have thought, that even at this early age, I would have remembered a situation of some interest like that. Is it possible that classes full of girls in my own school could have been completely evaporated from my memory?

For the first time I came now in close contact with a large number of other boys from various backgrounds. Many were from families with numerous children and/or were rather poor. But we also had in our class a pair of twins, which nobody could distinguish one from the other, and which were rumored to be distant relatives of the pre-war *Reichskanzler*, the German chancellor *von Bülow*. And much later I thought that maybe one of them was the then in Germany famous caricaturist *von Bülow*, signing as *Loriot*, but this was proven to be no more than wishful thinking (Wikipedia).

I remember that I could read when I first attended school, which gave me a starting advantage. One of the few details I still remember from this period was the method how I found my way around the four directions of the wind rose. Somehow, I was familiar with North and South, but had originally a problem to distinguish between East and West. We had a large-scale map of Saxony hanging on the wall of our classroom, and the small country town of Wilsdruff was, and presumably still is, clearly located to the west of Dresden, thus establishing the geographic West for me. Even today I sometimes have to envision a map to be clear about East and West. Rather peculiar, this.

The school yard of this only recently built school was immense (as remembered by a six-year-old!). But even when I saw it again eighty years later, I must say it was large. Particularly, if compared with the tiny and awful one, later at our high school. This primary school yard was covered by something yellowish, probably rounded quartz sand, which made crashing down bearable.

On one side of the yard a strip, about five meters wide, was dedicated to some common garden plants: vegetables or herbs. We were taught by a teacher, male of course, something about gardening. What a complete misinterpretation of young boy's priorities. Who needs stuff like that! An impromptu soccer game would have been much more appropriate, or some discussion about fire engines, maybe.

Now I am surprised how little else I remembered of these first four years at school. There was only one teacher I could recall, and I even remembered his name and what he looked like (a bit like my father), but all the others (if there were others!) were not even hazy shadows. They were simply not there. Probably an indication that I must have been under semi-permanent shock during these initial four years! But, seriously, I suspect that we only had this one class-teacher. On the other hand, I do remember a few of my class-mates, even though only vaguely.

There was, however, something like a negatively charged reminiscence: the absence, at this early stage in my life, of the opposition to existing or claimed established authorities or tenets, which became so obvious in my later years. Another thing I remembered in this connection was the fact that in addition to my pronounced political activism, I was also prepared to share my meager pocket money for a good cause. Both of these attitudes have evaporated since the end of the war and its connected disappointments, dissolutions and bitterness. It appears that in my primary school days I must have been an idealist of sorts!

As an example, there was the *VDA, the Verein für das Deutschtum im Ausland*, the society for the support of German culture in foreign countries. For 10 Pfennig per month we could buy a small lapel needle with the emblem of this society, which served both, as a cultural as well as a political body.

In retrospect, this is amazing to me. Nowadays I would generally not dream of spending time or money on political or cultural causes.

And what could have resulted in such a change in my attitude, if not in my character? The only reason I can think of is the dehumanizing experience at the end of the war, to see one's idealism betrayed and sullied by politicians one had previously admired.

However, I remembered another aspect in this regard. In 2002

Dresden suffered substantial damages by a flooding of the River Elbe, which was termed by the media a 'Century Flood'. Shortly after this catastrophe we happened to be in town, and everywhere they were soliciting donations. And completely unexpectedly, particularly for myself, I signed up to donate 500 Euro.

At the same time, money was being collected to finance the reconstruction of the bombed-out and collapsed Frauenkirche in Dresden. Either through a mistake by myself (impossible to envisage!) or by the Bank cashier, my contribution landed up with the fond for the destroyed church. Ten years later, when we were in Dresden again, this time with our son and our grandchildren, we were able to admire the marvelous result of this renaissance. A beautiful example of unintended consequences of a decision.

In 1934 some changes took place in my life. At the end of the first four-year tenure at primary school, two or three of us (about 5% to 8%) were promoted, after an entrance exam, to one of the *Höhere Schulen* (high schools or colleges) in the city center of Dresden. Another one or two of our class were promoted to a *Mittelschule*, a type of school in-between the primary school and high school.

The remaining majority of primary scholars would have received their completion certificate at age fourteen, at the end of the eight-year primary school cycle. The *Mittelschule* pupils received theirs at age sixteen, and the college students were awarded their *Abitur* certificate at age eighteen. In all cases, with the proviso that they had been promoted each year. This, however, was by no means automatically the case. Each year one or two members of the class had to repeat the course again.

The *Abitur*, or *Baccalaureus*, was the pass to the inscription at a university, but I don't remember, whether there were further entrance exams for specific faculties, because I never made it to university, due to the (lost) war. More about that later.

6

EARLY POLITICAL MEMORIES

1932 TO 1933

My recollection of the period just before the Nazis took over, and of the following early years of their reign, is deeply etched into my memory, even though I was very young. This resulted partly because I was so very young and impressionable, and partly because I took an early interest in politics and in many other developments of the period.

After the lost First World War and the ravages of the 1923 hyper-inflation, all German governments had a difficult task to govern this country efficiently. Considering all the difficulties, the country coped reasonably well under these dire circumstances.

The most decisive improvement happened at the end of 1923: the introduction of the *Rentenmark*, which was later renamed the *Reichsmark* or *RM*. This decision normalized the economic life of the country and enabled the central bank to terminate the crippling hyper-inflation.

To give an idea what the hyper-inflation meant for the people: in the final months of 1923 the fee for an inland letter was 20 Billion Mark, for a newspaper 50 Billion. Salaries were paid out every morning and had to be spent in the forenoon, since they were almost worthless by late afternoon. It is obvious, how the less sophisticated suffered, and that the sharpies enjoyed a string of field days.

The concept for the restoration of monetary order was created by Hjalmar Schacht, the President of the *Reichsbank*. This financial genius realized that the main problem was one of confidence into the currency, and he had the revolutionary idea to declare that the total of the German real estate would from now on guarantee the new currency. Strictly speaking was this a confidence trickster's ploy, but it worked, because the people believed him, and they did so because they desperately wanted to believe.

One of the brave and politically dangerous decisions of government had been to legislate mandatory employment quotas for the disabled, in particular for the victims amongst the war veterans. And there were huge numbers of these, of course.

This was one of the few positive results delivered by the '*Weimar System*'. Overcoming the legacy of the authoritarian pre-war Empire and creating a viable democracy, however, was clearly outside their competencies or priorities.

The subsequent economic meltdown of 1929 to 1931 created further problems and hardships for everybody. This latter phase was actually a period of deflation, a term which was and still is not generally understood by the public. Only now do the economists begin to really grasp what deflation in practical terms means for the economy of a country suffering from it. Prices came down, a very welcome development for the impoverished householders, but salaries were also cut (also wages?). Investment atrophied, resulting in the unemployment figures increasing dramatically.

An early strong memory of mine centers on what I read in the *Dresdner Anzeiger*, our local conservative (right wing) newspaper, about the 1931 Bad Harzburg agreement. It established the *Harzburger Front*, the coalition of the Nazis with the nationalistic and conservative *DNV*, the *Deutsch Nationale Volkspartei*, and the *Stahlhelm*, the party of the frontline soldiers of the recent war, which grouping won the 1932 parliamentary elections. Probably the reason, why I remember this event so well, was the fact that the *DNV* was part of this arrangement, because this was the party my parents voted for. And also, because my father was a member of the *Stahlhelm* organization.

In the autumn of 1932, my father took me to a Nazi rally at the Dresden *Velodrome*, the bicycle racing arena. Hitler was campaigning for the coming elections, which saw his Nazi party emerging, for the first time, as the strongest one in Germany, but without achieving the absolute majority. He crisscrossed the country in a large Mercedes cabriolet and, and this was a genuine political novelty, by plane. Either his driver or his pilot was called Baur, as I still remember.

The magnetism and charisma of this man was phenomenal. The enthusiasm and facial expressions of the attendants of his election rallies was clear proof of that. And this magnetism was probably largely responsible for the electoral outcome. Hitler was an outstanding, and dangerous, populist and demagogue, who clearly voiced what the vast majority of the voters wanted to hear.

The Nazi election victory was, among many other reasons, the result of the very strong feeling among the electorate that anything would be an improvement over the existing democratic '*Weimar System*', with up to 30 political parties producing lots of hot air, but few tangible benefits for the people. That was the general perception, at least of the middle- and upper-classes. And as usual, perceptions were more powerful than facts.

For many years after World War 1 and before 1933, there reigned absolute political chaos in Germany. One parliamentary election was followed by the next and a provincial election happened almost monthly, somewhere or other. MPs engaged in fisticuffs in parliament because of the political hatred between communists, social-democrats and the Nazis. An interesting aside: all three of these violent organizations claimed to be pure socialists!

The *Sozialdemokratische Partei*, the *SPD*, had for most of the time ruled Germany, alone or in coalitions with other parties, since the end of the war. Political violence was forever escalating. Many social-democrats, communists and Nazis were murdered or wounded, for purely political reasons.

The Nazi party was temporarily prohibited, then legalized again, and afterwards prohibited again. Then the *SA*, the Nazi *Sturmabteilung* received this same treatment and their uniforms were outlawed, and then this was also reversed again.

No wonder that the voters were confused and fed up with this as ridiculous perceived democratic system. One could argue that these were signs of a vibrant democracy (including the violence and murders?), but all this was above the horizons of the proverbial man-in-the-street. This chaotic behavior gave democracy a bad name in Germany.

The politicians did not manage to convince the population of the benefits of this political system. As some very clever and insightful gentleman has put it: it is admittedly a louse system, but it is the only one we have which works, or something to this effect.

Before the Nazi party took over, the country was morally, politically and economically devastated. The people just could not understand what had happened to them after the end of World War I in 1918. The predominant feeling was, that Germany somehow had been cheated out of victory, after losing two million fallen soldiers.

Because at the end of this war the German armies were still standing deep in occupied enemy territory. It is immaterial that the war was genuinely lost at this stage, militarily as well as economically. As usual, perception was the all-important consideration, the facts were not understood or simply ignored by the population.

Another nail in the coffin of German democracy was the Allied war propaganda, about the German 'Huns' raping nuns in the occupied countries and butchering babies and women, particularly in Belgium. Since men in virtually every family in Germany had served in the front lines, the people knew that these were lies.

But this propaganda was never, even after the war, retracted by the Allies, and remained as vicious accusations, without a possibility for the German soldiers and their families to defend themselves against these propaganda lies. And the German politicians stayed mum! They were so far removed from the political groundswell, that they simply did not understand the emotions of the German population.

Isolated war crimes can and do happen in any war or armed conflict, but any modern army knows how to deal with this threat. If there had been any truth to these claims, there would have been at least some amongst the millions of German soldiers to have aired such facts.

After my wife had had a look at the draft of this chapter, she justifiably queried how I could know that the reports of German atrocities in Belgium had just been enemy propaganda. After all, she correctly pointed out, there were plenty of men anywhere, who were prepared to act like this. I explained to her, that in fact several British sources after the war had confirmed this propaganda agenda of deliberate horror lies. Lord Beaverbrook, the publisher of the 'Daily Express' in London, was the main culprit. He had been appointed the British Propaganda Minister (Wikipedia).

It should be remembered here that in the perception of the majority of the German people, democracy had brought about the loss of the war, or had at least contributed to it, as demonstrated by the example of the social-democrats voting repeatedly during this war against the military budget allocations.

Even worse were the memories relating to the 'Reds', the social-democrats and communists, who had instigated the rebellion of the sailors of the German navy, which was seen as the final straw breaking the back of the German war effort. Again, perceptions were more powerful than the unwelcome facts.

The democratic system was also perceived to have been responsible for accepting the shameful and crippling 1919 Versailles Treaty, and the subsequent excessive Allied reparation demands, which in turn caused the 1923 hyper-inflation, which directly lead to six million unemployed in Germany. Again, it was immaterial that the German politicians had no choice in the matter, and that these events had very little or nothing to do with the German democratic system.

Germany had become a member of the League of Nations in Geneve, but despite many friendship treaties, which were signed with former WWI enemies after the war, conditions did not improve much for the German people. Also, the Germans were relentlessly hammered with the accusation that they had started World War 1, ignoring the fact, that it was Austria-Hungary, which first declared war on Serbia, which started the domino-effect of all the subsequent declarations of war.

In any case, these unfair and misleading accusations were not accepted by the German people, because it was postulated, by the Nazis amongst others, that it was never any population which started a war, but that political power systems had always been the culprits. In the specific case of that First World War it was clear enough that all the large states in Europe were more or less guilty of warmongering, or at least of playing with the matches next to a barrel of gun powder.

The operative word in the *'Weimar System'* was 'compromise', whereas the Nazis stressed the necessity of 'authoritarian decision making', like in the military. In other words: action instead of talk, decisions instead of negotiations and following orders without questioning them. This appealed to the people as a convincing case for an 'efficient' totalitarian state.

The Germans were literally down and out, and without hope. This was the main reason, why they were prepared to 'sleep with the devil' to escape from this hopeless situation. Indirect proof that this *'Weimar System'* was seriously flawed, can be seen in the fact that the new democratic dispensation after 1945 took care to avoid most of the shortcomings of this discredited *'System'*.

We also should remember that after the war Germany did not become the only dictatorship in Europe. Abandonment of the democratic idea was widespread. Most of the European states in the '20s and '30s were ruled by dictators and/or one-party systems, who all routinely arrested their opponents and did away with human rights and trampled on the freedom of the press with their jackboots.

Starting with Lenin and then Stalin in Russia, through Marshall Pilsudski in Poland, Admiral Horthy in Hungary, Dollfuss in Austria, Mussolini in Italy, through to General Franco in Spain and Salazar in Portugal, they were all dictatorships. Apart from France, Switzerland, the Benelux and Scandinavian countries, democracy during this period was not exactly popular and flourishing in continental Europe.

Another point to note in this connection was the fact that the *'Zeitgeist'* and the aftermath of Spengler's *Untergang des Abendlandes* (Decline of the Occident) reinforced all these negative basic feelings. I remember, for instance, a drawing in a 1932 edition of the *Berliner Illustrierte*, a weekly illustrated magazine, which showed an early '30s view of a German *Mietskaserne*, a large sub-prime apartment building (yes, even a fossil can still learn the odd new word), with most apartments in the building shown as occupied, and another drawing of the same building in the projected 40's, with half the apartment windows boarded up, implying the relentless move towards annihilation of the German people.

The Nazis were helped by the fact that almost all army and police officers supported, or at least tolerated, the Party. A large segment of the intellectuals and a substantial percentage of the nobility also sympathized with them and their ideology. So, it was not really surprising that the German people eschewed democracy in favor of a totalitarian regime, which promised them jobs and national recognition and redemption.

The *'Weimar System'* was certainly in need of extensive improvements. But it should also be remembered that Germany did only have a relatively short experience and culture with a functioning democratic state, from 1870 to 1918. I am convinced that without the lost war, and without the inflexible, brutal and short-sided attitude of the Allies afterwards, democracy would not have been abandoned so easily by the German people. There would quite simply have been no compelling reason to do so.

There is one other point I battle to understand. After the Napoleonic Era there were many efforts in the German States to improve the feudalistic ruling structures. By 1830 some progress had been made: a few of the states had introduced a constitution, giving limited rights to some segments of the population, mostly based on property and wealth, but largely preserving the privileges of the ruling class.

Particularly the students in many of the universities all over Germany demanded a softening of the harsh rule by the aristocratic establishment, and the introduction of democratic rule. In 1832 at the *Hammbacher Fest* wide support for these demands manifested itself, but the ruling aristocracies held firm. But since then the establishment had re-asserted and reinforced their dominant role, and the token advancements of a democratic spring had been harshly suppressed and most of the constitutions had been rescinded. Press freedom had largely disappeared again, and the prisons had filled up with 'revolutionaries'.

Again, in 1848 these demands came to the fore even stronger, and resulted in the *Frankfurter Paulskirche* assembly, demanding democratic reforms. An additional element at this time was the additional demand for a united German Empire. This time German intellectuals were in the forefront, and men like Richard Wagner, the famous composer, found themselves in prison or had to emigrate to save themselves. Far reaching plans had been made but came to naught in the end. In all these struggles there had never been any suggestion to abandon the monarchies, or to limit the privileges of the two churches, an indication of the conservatism of the times.

Considering these historical events, and despite all the elements, which contributed to this fundamental change in the German political attitude, it is even more astonishing for us now to comprehend why democracy was abandoned like that in 1933.

After all, Germany had a reasonably well functioning, albeit rather short, democratic system up to 1914, if we ignore the foolish interferences by the last *Kaiser*. But this line of reasoning ignores a basic fact: attitudes of nations do change as well as that of individuals!

7

NIEDERFRAUENDORF

UP TO 1934

From about four to about eight years of age, I spent every summer school holiday with my mother's parents in Niederfrauendorf. My parents brought me to the bus depot of the *Kraftwagendienst des Freistaat Sachsen*, the bus service of the Free State of Saxony, next to the main railway station in Dresden. There they handed me over to the bus driver who, after a two- to three-hour drive and a lengthy stopover at Dippoldiswalde, deposited me on stopping at my grandparent's village. My grandmother came to collect me at the bus stop, pulling her 4-wheel hand cart for my luggage, most likely a carton box. I hope I helped her pulling this jalopy up the steep incline of the village road during the half-hour trip back home.

Next to the bus stop was, what we would later in the rural backwoods of South Africa ironically have called the 'regional shopping center'. This was a small single-story cottage, with one room of about fifteen to twenty square meters converted into a General Dealer's trading-store. This shop carried or ordered almost everything the villagers needed.

A relative of the owners, an elderly lady, used to speed-walk, for a kilometer or two, along the bus route talking loudly to herself, and sometimes angrily arguing with someone unknown and absent. And all this with her arms and hands wildly gesticulating. A remarkable sight for a little boy of five or so, from the big city.

On long weekends, early in the time we had moved to the

suburbs, my father usually took us on his DKW motorcycle for the thirty to forty kilometers drive to the property of my maternal grandparents. I used to sit between my parents, probably mostly on my mother's saddle, and the trip would have been quite uncomfortable, but I have no actual recollection of this.

We often met there the family of my uncle Walter, the husband of my mother's sister, who also was riding a motorcycle. I don't know whether this was maybe a case of inter-family rivalry.

My grandparents' double-story house had probably been built in or shortly before the year 1830, because that was the marking on a single sandstone slab, which was serving as a bridge over the creek flowing between the property and the village gravel road. The upper story had huge exposed wooden roof timbers, and some were simply tree trunks. They were twisted like they had been made of putty and had only later taken on their peculiar forms.

There was also a small stable inside the building, providing at different times living quarters for one or two sheep or goats. For a little boy one of the more unpleasant memories of these vicious animals was the unwanted side-effect of being fed goat's milk. I was seriously told how wonderful the taste was, and how I would love to have this milk each morning.

Attached to the house was my grandfather's workshop as a wheelwright. His business consisted of two different occupations: on the one hand he worked as a wheelwright, manufacturing for the farmers of the surrounding area the large wooden wheels with steel rims for their oxcarts and their horse-drawn carriages, but also producing wooden farming implements like scythes and rakes.

But he also had adapted his workshop to the manufacturing, for some distant factories, of wooden forms to press felt hats for the ladies.

In his workshop he had, in addition to all the usual woodworking tools, a large wooden work bench and an electric band saw. An overhead transmission was powering the band saw and some other pieces of power equipment.

I cannot make up my mind about the situation regarding the electricity supply on this property. On the one hand, my grandfather must have had power from the beginning, probably 380V, in his workshop for his heavy equipment.

On the other hand, I clearly remember in the early years petroleum lamps in the sitting room. Later they had electricity definitely in the living quarters as well. Is it possible that originally only the workshop had electricity? I cannot quite figure out this discrepancy in my mind.

A large shed was also on the property, housing his apiary, with something like twenty to thirty bee *Voelker*, or 'tribes', each with its own queen. The protective closing my grandfather was wearing while working with his bees would have easily qualified him for a visit to Mars.

During autumn the removable honeycombs of the beehives, which contained the honey, were removed by him from the apiary. The honey produced by the bees during spring and summer was extracted from the honeycombs by a centrifuge (electric or cranked with a handle?). During winter the bees had to be fed with sugar water, to compensate them for the honey that had been stolen from them earlier.

His obvious expertise with stinging insects resulted in him being called out, probably by the *Bürgermeister*, the burgomaster or mayor of the village, whenever there was a problem with these fellows. I recall one incident, when he had to remove a swarm of bees near the village school, which threatened the teacher and the school kids. Another time a swarm of wasps had started building a burrow in a bank next to a frequented byway. Their removal required lighting a fire to produce clouds of acrid smoke, an operation much to my delight.

Sheep, goats and bees were not the only wildlife on the premises. In addition to an abundant population of house flies, some kind of mosquitoes and some horse flies, there were also about two dozen chickens in the grounds. They were scratching around all day somewhere on the about one-acre property, but in the afternoon, a few minutes before five o'clock, they were all assembled in front of the house, waiting to be fed by my grandmother, or in the summer holidays by myself.

My grandmother was also the vet-on-call, if one of the hens, when laying her egg, had pushed out her intestines too far. She (my grandmother) simply pushed them back in and the hen ran off, and presumably lived happily thereafter, until she was slaughtered, eventually.

Yes, none of these animals were kept or treated as pets. Except for a terrier, who was as grumpy as my grandfather, and whose farts (the dog's) were something to behold. It was claimed by grandfather that a diet of bones was responsible for the odorous mishaps, but considering the dog's general nasty dis-position, I'm inclined to believe that not only did he do this on purpose, but that he enjoyed himself thoroughly.

Sometimes my grandmother got busy with her sickle, if she needed just a small quantity of cut grass or some herbs. She had a small vegetable garden next to the building, which was out-of-bounds for everybody else.

She was also surprisingly well read regarding general knowledge, even though she only had a primary school education. No crossword puzzle was safe from her. She knew everything, or so it seemed to me, and she taught me how to go about solving puzzles. I still remember that gin is the alcoholic beverage produced from *Wacholder*, the juniper bush, and that Lena and Dnepr are rivers in Russia, amongst many other such essential tidbits.

Next to the house they had a small meadow with an orchard of about two dozen fruit trees, where my grandfather got busy with his scythe to cut grass for the goats or sheep, or to make hay for the same customers. I wanted to try to copy his sharpening of the scythe with a wet-stone, but he considered this, probably correctly, as too dangerous for me, or maybe for his scythe.

He was also often busy pruning and grafting his fruit trees, to improve the quality of the harvest. I observed enough to remember how this was done. I have the technical English terms probably all wrong, but hopefully the procedure is understandable, never-the-less.

He started on the inferior species of the fruit tree, by carefully lifting a square of the bark covering five by two centimeters, without completely separating it from the trunk. Then he slightly roughened the exposed part of the stem. Next, he selected a small twig of the superior tree species, which had to have at least two or three leave nodules. Then the inner wood of this twig was also exposed, the two exposed parts were fitted together, and finally the loosened bark was folded back into the original position and secured by some twine.

Maybe tape would also have done, but this could have been dicey because the air would have been cut off. But come to think of it: tape had not been invented yet, as far as I can remember. Finally, some tar was applied to disinfect the wound inflicted and to keep away the insects, who would have loved to get to the sap of the poor tree. But who wants to be beautiful must be prepared to suffer.

Another thing I learned on this occasion: how to harvest fruit correctly. One does not tear it from the branch, but carefully turns it, until it comes loose. Otherwise, the tree will require two or three years to repair the damage, before fruit will form again. Yes, these old-timers had to have a wide spectrum of practical know-how. They could not just contact an expert or look things up on the internet.

His orchard consisted mainly of apple and pear trees. This selection of fruit trees also provided our family with apples and pears for the whole of the long winter season. My grandfather also collected the apples, which had been stung by insects and prematurely ripened and fallen off, and he sent them to Donath's, a nearby factory which converted them into apple juice.

For some reason we never had any of this at our home. Only when we were visiting my grandparents did we get a glass or two to drink. It was presumably the same story as with the 10-Pfennig-eggs, years later in Quohren, when my grandparents had moved there.

In the creek, running between the village road and the property, there were Rainbow trout to be found. I learned only later, that these were actually 'invaders', as we would say nowadays. My grandfather taught us boys how to catch them with our bare hands, but we only succeeded once or twice. The use of primitive, jerry-made fishing rods was not much more successful, but it had always been fun to try.

One day, when I was about 6 years old, and while playing with a group of small village boys and girls, one of the little girls fell and exposed the fact, that she was not wearing her panties. This was apparently accepted by everybody as nothing special, but nowadays I realize, that this was most probably an indication of the abject poverty of the farm laborers. Almost all the children were in summer without shoes, and quite a few of the adults also seemed not to wear any. Their work clothes also looked shockingly poor. This, however, must be seen in the general context of the then much lower level of living standards in Europe.

This incidence reminds me of the local primary school. It served two villages, Nieder- and Oberfrauendorf. This was a small building on the border of the two villages, and it contained a grand total of two classrooms: one for the six to ten years old, and the other one for the eleven to fourteen years class. No separation, of course, of the sexes. This probably meant that the school also had only two teachers. When I visited the place with my family in the 2010s (funny, how this looks and sounds) it appeared that the school was still in use as before, but since we were there during school holidays, this observation was not very conclusive.

In one year during spring a tornado-like storm had swept through this part of the *Erzgebirge* and resulted in thousands of trees being uprooted, broken and damaged. A large swath of forest plantations had been flattened, leaving the fallen trees like match sticks on the ground. Several square kilometers of forests had been devastated, and yet, a few hundred meters further on, there was no trace of any storm damage to be seen.

During the following summer my grandfather developed a frenzied activity to buy up some of this damaged, and therefore cheaper timber for his workshop. He even borrowed a large sum of money, with my father somehow involved in the negotiations. He was, after all, a banker.

In the neighboring cottage, a hundred meter down the valley, resided a glass worker. He blew glass the way I saw it done many years later at Murano, near Venice, in Italy. He created many varied items, from glass deer and other animals to flowers and naked dancing girls. I was, however, only interested in looking at the deer and flowers. He also worked with crystal-glass. We had a beautiful crystal fruit bowl of his at home, but I never saw any fruit in it. It probably was considered to be too valuable for such prosaic usage.

Eighty meters in the opposite direction there was the large farm of the burgomaster, who seemed to hold this position in perpetuity. During the Nazi years he was also additionally the chairman of the local farmers organization of the party. Afterwards, he probably was a true Anti-Fascist. But this last remark is to be deleted, since my grandparents left the village already in 1934, and I therefore could not have any knowledge about this.

Opposite the mayor's farm the blacksmith had his forge. When I was a bit older, my grandfather often sent me there, to have some iron parts manufactured, which he needed in the wheelwright branch of his work. Especially for the iron hubs and the rims for the wheels of the ox-wagons of the farmers. Being allowed to operate the bellows was an interesting experience for me and watching the red-hot iron parts being worked on by the blacksmith was fascinating. I usually spent a lot of my time in this magic world.

One of the highlights of rural life in Saxony was the annual *Vogelschiessen*. This autumn festivity saw on a weekend a large wooden image of an eagle (?) with spread wings, which was mounted on a tall pole, demolished by crossbow bolts. Each of the wing feathers was detachable and had to be hit in turn to bring them down. Finally, only the body of the poor bird was left, and to knock this down ended the contest.

I don't remember the details of how the various hits were valued or counted, but I think the competitor who brought down the last part was declared the winner. He was crowned the *Schützenkönig*, the king of the marksmen for the year, with an impressive chain to show for it. But he also was expected to sponsor for the participants a round, or more likely a dozen rounds of drinks at the open-air pub. And this was obviously the main purpose of the exercise. My grandfather won this trophy several times, as I recall.

Especially at this occasion, but also at some other weekends, the women of the village prepared, and the resident baker had baked for them, typical rural German cakes. These were prepared on black tin-plates measuring about 50cm by 1m. Mainly crumble cake (like apple-crumble but without the apple component), sugar cake with plenty of cinnamon, potato cake and plum or cherry cake with fresh fruit.

My grandfather was an early member of the Nazi Party and somewhat of a big shot in these rural surroundings. He was the dedicated speaker of the Party for the district, rushing from one election rally to the next, praising the virtues of the Nazi ideology. He had also run for the position of *Bürgermeister* of his village, and for that of district chairman of the Party as well. I don't remember any details about the outcome of these efforts, but I know he did not make burgomaster, because that position seemed to be nailed down in favor of the neighbor on the opposite site to the glass worker's cottage.

Apparently, grandfather had always been a bit of a rebel. In 1906 he was involved in violent demonstrations of the Social-Democratic Party in Dresden and, as I suspect, found himself afterwards for a while in prison. But this subject was never discussed at his home. He rather preferred to tell us about his time as the secretary of a bicycle touring club. Or about his experiences as a *Wanderbursche*, when he traversed many of Europe's countries as a journeyman.

In pre-WW1 Germany, and in many other European countries, existed certain customs dating back to the Middle Ages. Strict rules governed the artisan world, for instance. Young boys (there was no place for girls as artisans) at the age of fourteen, after completing primary school, entered as apprentices into a contract relationship with a *Meister*, a master artisan. Only these masters were entitled to train the future artisans.

Originally the apprentices, or rather their parents, had to pay for the privilege of the young man being apprenticed, and no wages were paid. This slowly changed eventually, but when these apprenticing payments had fallen away, and later wages were paid, these were rather miserly, not much more than pocket money.

Usually the apprenticeships lasted for three to four years. Often there were complaints, that these boys had to perform household chores for the master artisan's wife, instead of being trained. In all cases, they had in their first year to attend to the menial tasks connected with their chosen trade, such as to fetch the beers for the artisans, before the proper on-the-job training even started.

After completing their apprenticeship, these young men were certified as *Wanderburschen*, and the 'journeymen' translation describes this position correctly. They were required to go for some years on a working and learning traveling existence. They had to journey from town to town, and in most cases from country to country. This required them to work for a number of different master artisans on the way. This gave them vast exposure, not only to many different bosses, but also to local customs and local-specific secrets of their trade, as well as to general trade and social conditions in different countries.

All their travels and their working stints in between were documented in a combined passport and record book. Whenever they arrived in a new location, they had to obtain the stamp of the local police or the signature of a local dignitary, such as a priest or lord of the manor house. In those days the people did not have much, but they had plenty of rubber stamps! Some of these important stamps were actually wood cuts, to be more accurate.

This life lasted quite a few years, and after completing this stage successfully, they would now be called a *Geselle*, an artisan or craftsman. After some further years of working in their chosen trade, they finally could apply to become a master artisan.

This was rather a tricky exercise, because one of the conditions to succeed in this endeavor was the endorsement by the guild and by an existing master artisan of the same trade in the town. Not surprisingly, such endorsement would only materialize, if the guild of this trade and the town in question felt the desirability to appoint another master artisan in the trade in question. One was careful not to create unnecessary competition, after all.

Curbing the competition in the trades was a tradition in Europe, which was upheld at all times during and after the Middle Ages. This was the main purpose for the existence of the guilds. This attitude appears to be an inborn and ingrained reflex of human nature, as documented by the often-unsuccessful battles by the competition authorities against monopolies and anti-competitive behavior.

PART II

NICE WHILE IT LASTED

A TEENAGER'S LIFE (1933 TO 1942)

The title of this part clearly can only refer to the majority of the German people of that period, the famous "man-in-the-street", but obviously not to the German Jews, and also not to the active opponents of the Nazis. Virtually all thinking people agree on what has happened in and what was done by Germany during World War II, and they condemn the atrocities committed by the Nazis.

8

MY POLITICAL MEMORIES

1933 TO 1938

From here on I will identify the Nazi party simply as the Party, with a capital P, in order to avoid confusing this one with any other political parties (I promise to refrain from bothering you with tales about my own private parties. It should be clearly understood, that during the Nazi period the Party and the German government were practically congruent and were tightly interwoven. This was so, even though the Party had its own organization at all levels, from the top in Berlin right down to the smallest village.

Early in 1933 four important events took place in Germany:

- the takeover of the government by the Party,
- the arson of the *Reichstag* building, the German parliament,
- the more-or-less voluntary dissolving of all other parties,
- the scrapping of the Weimar post-war constitution.

Firstly, the takeover of the government on 30 January 1933, through the appointment of Hitler as *Reichskanzler* by the *Reichspräsident* was a perfectly legal and constitutional act, since the Party, after the elections at the end of 1932, had the largest number of seats (but not the majority!), and Hitler's coalition had become the largest grouping in the *Reichstag*. Therefore, there never was any *coup d'etat.* The fact that the Nazis took power quite legally later served as an important ideological and psychological support basis for Hitler.

It is necessary to remember here that the animosity between SPD and KPD was absolutely virulent, preventing any possibility of a coalition or cooperation between these two large parties.

Van der Lubbe, the claimed communist from the Netherlands and suspected arsonist of the parliament building, was arrested red-handed. Later a Bulgarian member of the *Komintern*, the Communist International global organization, was also brought to court, together with some colleagues. They were all tried before the *Reichsgericht*, the German Supreme Court, located in Leipzig. Van der Lubbe was found guilty by this court and executed forthwith, but the Bulgarians were acquitted, due to lack of evidence.

The immediate result of the verdict was the rounding-up of four thousand communist functionaries and MPs, Members of Parliament (Ploetz), and the prohibition of the KPD, the Communist Party of Germany. This had the 'welcome' side-effect, that this action gave the rightwing parties now an even stronger majority in the *Reichstag*.

After World War II the German news magazine *Der Spiegel* claimed in numerous articles, that it was in fact Hermann Göring, effectively the number two in the Nazi government, who was responsible for this incendiary happening. As far as I can remember, they could not provide conclusive proof, one way or the other. Göring had shortly afterwards been appointed the Governor of Prussia, the largest of the German States.

At the time we did not doubt the accuracy of the accusations tabled by the prosecution. But what has occupied my mind, starting right after the court proceedings, was the question, why the case was brought direct to the Supreme Court, where neither appeal nor revision was legally possible. Maybe that was the real motive for deviating from the normal course of justice, where the case would have been heard by one of the High Courts. It is possible that this procedure was quite legal, but of course it opened wide the door for later conspiracy theories.

The third drastic event was the 'voluntary' disappearance of all the political parties, except the Nazi Party, of course, which is difficult to understand today. This applies in particular to the question, why the SPD, the Social Democratic Party, had given-up so easily, after so many of their members had risked, and often had lost, their lives in bloody fights against their political opponents.

Most of the parties dissolved (more or less) voluntarily, but the communist party had to be prohibited. This previous act, and the incarceration of most of their functionaries was strong motivation for this surrender. But, as usual, it is easy to afterwards question this decision by the leaders of the SPD, which for many years had been the largest party in the *Reichstag*.

The fourth event, which finalized the dismantling of democracy in Germany, was the abolition of the Weimar constitution and the *Gleichschaltung*, the integration into the *Reich*, of the nominally semi-independent German States. I don't remember their number, but there were many of them. For all practical purposes, all the individual *Länder* (States) were now ruled by the Nazi Party, with the result that the German state administration had become as centralized as the one in France, particularly as the local authorities by now were also firmly in the hands of the Party.

The next 'achievement' the Nazis created (and they were really proud of it!) were the first concentration camps, intended to incarcerate and thereby isolate all political opponents. The idea was probably copied from what the English had done to the Afrikaners at the turn of the previous century in South Africa.

One of these prisoners was my uncle Walter, who was a bricklayer and, as far as I knew, just a simple member of the Social-Democratic Party. He was kept there for a few months without any charges or trial, and then he was released as 're-educated'. Later he re-trained as a technical draftsman and was employed by Göring's air force to help design their new ministerial buildings and the numerous regional command complexes of the Air Force, which were needed in conjunction with the now starting remilitarization of Germany. He never ever talked about his time in the concentration camp, nor about any political subject at all.

Going the other day through one of our old photo albums, I came across a picture of this uncle from the late '30s or early '40s. To my consternation, and to my utter surprise, I noticed the Party pin on his lapel. I never knew that he had become a *'Parteigenosse'*, a Party member. As far as I know, he was the only one in the family.

This reminds me of another reminiscence in connection with these concentration camps. During the early Nazi time the best known of these was the camp at Dachau near Munich. One of the entertainers on the state-owned radio station, famous for his risky political jokes, was a few years later sent to Dachau, because of something he had said, which was a bit too close to the truth. But a few weeks or months later, he was back and plying his trade again as before. Conclusion for everybody to arrive at: toe the line, or you get 're-educated' for a while, but nothing too serious will be happening.

The point I'm trying to make here is the vital, but often over-looked, difference between the concentration (holding) camps starting in 1933, and the extermination camps, which only came in existence after 1942. Everybody knew about these holding camps, and no serious effort was made by the Party or the state to keep them secret. Surely, there were crimes committed in these earlier camps as well, but this was not their main purpose, and nobody ever mentioned any such occurrences in public.

At this point it might be illustrative to talk about another one of my uncles, whom I had mentioned earlier. This one living in a Berlin suburb, with his small house-painting business, was a communist. As a young man in the 1920s he had won a medal at one of the *Spartakiade*s, the 'Olympics' of the *Spartakus Bund*, the sports organization of the communists. As far as I know he never was in trouble during the Nazi time, but he also never changed his political views – he just kept them to himself, at least in public.

My parents did not vote for the Nazis, but for the DNVP, *Deutsch Nationale Volkspartei*, the German National People's Party, a moderate nationalistic and conservative rightwing party, which was part of the coalition, together with the *Stahlhelm* (Steel Helmet), the frontline soldiers' party, which had won the 1932 elections, which brought the Nazis to power in 1933.

In May of 1933, at the ripe old age of not even 9 years, I joined the *DJ, Deutsches Jungvolk* (German Young Folks), the Nazi youth organization for boys under fourteen years old. My parents did neither object nor encourage my decision. If one wonders about my tender age at becoming a political animal, please remember, what the German newsreels of April 1945 showed from Berlin, when the Russians had begun to penetrate the capital city and when the war had already long been lost by Germany.

Dozens of young and very young *HJ, Hitlerjugend* (Hitler Youth) and *Jungvolk* members, armed to the teeth with rifles, grenade throwers and the like, received medals as volunteers from Hitler personally. Their facial expressions clearly showed their pride and dedication. They were as convinced and fanatic as we were in 1933, despite of all that had happened by then. Which proves the power of political brainwashing and indoctrination of the youth by a dictatorship.

One of my earliest memories of this very early period was a ride on a flatbed truck in May of 1933. There were a few members of the *SA (Sturm-Abteilung)*, the paramilitary unit of the Nazis, on board and about a dozen *HJ* members of all age groups, all in uniform. We were demonstrating for some election or referendum, and we were driving along Tornaer Strasse, through a working-class quarter of our suburb, which at this time was still a communist and social-democratic hotbed.

This action of the people who had authorized this provocative show-off was highly irresponsible, because in those days it was not unusual at all to demonstrate drastically one's objection to any other political party. Firing an automatic handgun or rifle was almost as common as attacks with knives and knuckle-dusters. Milder forms of political discussions consisted of throwing bricks or pavement stones and getting into some fisticuffs. Many activists of all the major parties had been wounded or killed in the years following the war. Luckily, all we were bombarded with at this occasion was abuse and the odd rock.

Our new radio was heavily utilized at this time. One of the events eagerly listened to by my father was the 1933 boxing world championship bout in the USA between Max Schmeling, who only recently died at an age of 99 years, and Max Baer, a half-Jew (Wikipedia). My father had been sitting in front of his technical marvel until two in the morning, due to the time difference. The German heavyweight champion lost this fight. This was quietly considered by the Nazis a major political set-back, because of Schmeling's popularity and the un-palpable fact that a Jew had overcome an Arian German.

This latter consideration had been downplayed in Germany but was of interest and a rallying point in the States, due to the beginning of the campaigns against the anti-Semitic Nazis (Wikipedia). This boxing match was for me the first occasion when I was confronted with the race question, which acquired such huge importance in the later years for Germany.

Equally important to my father were every Sunday morning the radio emissions of the *Hamburger Hafenkonzerte*, the Hamburg Harbor Concerts, and the performances by Richard Tauber, the famous tenor. I was, however, his bad luck to be Jewish, and he was therefore replaced in 1933 or 1934 by Benjamino Gigli, who had the right religion and the correct nationality of Hitler's idol, Benito Mussolini.

I have just come back from my after-lunch snooze and have noticed that I had forgotten to shut down my computer. This poor fellow would surely have liked to have had a break as well.

In July of 1933 it was decreed by Rudolf Hess, Hitler's Deputy as Leader of the Party (in modern parlance Secretary General), that the minimum age for the *Jungvolk* was to be ten years. Consequently, my membership was suspended until July of 1934. I could hardly await the arrival of this important date, allowing me to rejoin my *Fähnlein* (the equivalent-size organization of a company in the army), when I was considered an old hand by my comrades. If you have formed the impression that I was a proper little Nazi by now, you would be perfectly correct.

It is not generally known that the membership of the *Hitlerjugend*, which was originally a sought-after privilege, later became compulsory. 98% of the German youth was organized there (Wikipedia). This fact of the compulsory membership of the *Hitlerjugend* was completely unknown to me until I started this book. It appears, therefore, that this measure was only introduced after I had joined the army in 1942.

I have few other memories about my time in the *Deutsche Jungvolk*, apart from one memorable Saturday morning at the tram depot in our suburb. That must have been in the summer of 1935 or maybe 1936. We were allowed to ride a light 80cc motorbike in the yard of this depot. Most of us were used to riding our bicycles, but this was something new and fantastic. Much more exciting than the usual weekly Boy Scout-like meetings.

Actually, there was a very important additional aspect of the Saturday mornings, which were our regular meeting times for duty: on my return home there was a huge (?) bowl of either chocolate or vanilla pudding waiting for me on the table. During the war years they were prepared with water, since milk was not available anymore, but this did not detract from the pleasure had by me.

But there was also another minor consideration regarding these Saturday mornings: membership in one of the *Hitlerjugend* formations resulted in the automatic dispensation from having to attend school on Saturdays. As I said, a minor point (if you believe that, you will believe anything!)

My unreasonable mother insisted that during the winter months I had to wear long brown stockings with my uniform shorts, just because we had minus fifteen or twenty degrees Celsius. This was most humiliating, because said stockings had to be anchored by suspenders. A double discrimination for a teenager and, additionally, most un-manly!

When I had become a *Jungenschaftsführer* in charge of a *Jungenschaft*, a group of ten to twelve boys, our *Fähnlein* organized at one of our Saturday morning outings a competition between about ten such groups. The aim was for the complete group to arrive first at the winning post, after covering a distance of about three or four kilometers. My group won, after I employed a system, which I had remembered from one of the *Karl May* books about the *Red Indians* (that is what they were called then in Germany). We won by alternating between marching for one hundred paces, then jogging (another word not yet invented) for one hundred paces, and so on.

Probably around 1935, the leader of our *Fähnlein* decided, that the 'corporals' in the organization should have nick-names. My friend landed up with *Geigei* (his surname being Geissler) and I became *Bimbo*. Neither of us liked this idea, for obvious reasons, but discipline and obeying orders had to be maintained at all costs.

In the spring of 1938, the *Jungenschafts-* and *Zugführer* (the military equivalents of non-commissioned officers) of our *Fähnlein* went on a march from our suburb to Königstein, about thirty kilometers or so away. For part of the march I was delegated to carry the *Fähn-lein's* surprisingly heavy flag. This caused me a rather bad pain on my shoulder. As I had found out earlier, and again years later, there was something wrong there. Any pressure on my clavicles was and still is uncomfortable, to put it mildly. We stayed overnight at the youth hostel in the Königstein fortress, and on the next day we returned the same way to Dresden.

In July of 1938 I had turned fourteen and consequently was automatically transferred from the *Deutsche Jungvolk* to the *Hitlerju-gend* proper. I always found it peculiar that the proverbial German bureaucrats allowed such an inconsistency in their terminology. The term *Hitlerjugend* was used for the composite group of all the Nazi youth formations. This organization consisted of the *DJ*, the *Deutsche Jungvolk* (boys 10-14), the *BDJ*, the *Bund Deutscher Jungmädel* (girls 10-14), the *BDM*, the *Bund Deutscher Mädel* (girls 15-18) and the HJ, the Hitlerjugend proper (boys 15-18).

Reaching eighteen years of age, the young men were in the beginning automatically transferred into the Party. The young women, similarly, but in their case at age twenty-one. This practice was stopped early in 1935, but was later re-instated, but with certain conditions (Ploetz). I had always thought that young women were further advanced in their development as young men of the same age, but the reason for this differentiation was probably the simple fact, that women were not taken quite seriously and equal in those days.

One other amazing thing, at least for me, was the Nazi tendency to continuously change the names of organizations and official positions and titles. The *Hitlerjugend* and their subsidiary organizations had their names and structures changed at least a dozen times between 1926 and 1942 (Ploetz), when I lost track of matters due to my military service.

But then, I became a management consultant in later life, specializing in organization and systems. This probably explains this early nitpicking attitude, regarding illogical or misleading terminology. Now, stop mumbling "Pedant". The correct word you were thinking of is "Perfectionist".

When the time came for my transfer, or as we saw it then, for my promotion to the almost-adult *Hitlerjugend* organization, I decided to join the *Motor HJ*. The disappointing thing was, however, that in this special organization we came not once to ride a motorbike, nor were we ever taught to drive a car. We never progressed beyond our bicycles.

But, of course, by then the war had started. Petrol was just about the first thing which became scarce, and almost all motorcycles, cars and trucks were immediately requisitioned by the *Wehrmacht*, the German Armed Forces.

It was in September of 1938, when a group of about twenty of us *HJ* members marched with our flag to Nuremberg for the *Reichsparteitag*, the annual national Party rally. On the way we slept at youth hostels or in farm barns. I don't remember much about this *shindig*, except that I acquired some large blisters. We were disappointed that we did not understand much of Hitler's speech, particularly because this, as usual, went on, and on, and on. Did good old Fidel Castro study perhaps here, or in Moscow, where the 'brass' also had the same bad habit on verbal diarrhea?

9

PEACETIME TEENAGE YEARS

1933 TO 1939

My collection of toys slowly progressed, via the annual Christmas gifts, over a period of ten years or so, from my early wooden cart, to first a simple tool-box with a hammer (very important), then to a train set with the engine having a wind-up drive (electric locos being too expensive). To my surprise, I never received a drum. Then I progressed to an airplane assembling set. Later was added a working model of a steam engine, with a number of operating pieces of miniature machinery screwed onto a wooden platform. In between, of course, the despised pseudo-gifts of socks, shirts and underwear, instead of the hoped-for toys or, at the very least, of plenty of chocolates and sweets.

Later a simple electric train set was added. The last one of my toys was the best: a *Stabil* building set. This consisted of many different elements, all in stainless or chromed steel, with holes of standard dimensions and distances. The screws and nuts supplied with the set allowed me to build quite sophisticated models of equipment, a tram or an airplane, for instance. I learned in this way how to fix two nuts on an axis in a certain position, which would not be undone when the vehicle I had built would move on the tabletop or on the floor.

I remember, and cannot forget, some recurring dreams I had as a small boy. The first of these nightmares occurred quite a few times, whenever I had a fever, and this happened relatively often. I dreamt that I was moving in a sort of vortex, spiraling deeper and deeper downwards. The last time this dream happened when I had contacted malaria during the war, therefore I seemed to have outgrown this particular affliction.

In another dream of this nature, which was also often repeated, I was climbing an external staircase without a banister, coming to a dead stop against a blank wall. No door, not even a bricked-up one. Nonsensical, but disconcerting, nevertheless. A further repeat performance saw me walking up the stairs in our apartment building, only to find myself in front of our entrance door, but which showed a strange name on the name plate. These nightmares faded away over time and I do not know when they last occurred, but they are still very much alive in my memory.

A final instance sees me repeatedly walking in a town which I remember clearly, but which has changed very much. Taking a short-cut, I try to get from A to B, and lose my way completely, and always in the same part of this town.

At other times I am walking in the countryside and I decide to take a short-cut, with the result that I get again completely lost. I'm not sure whether in these dreams I finally arrived at my destination or not. One or the other version of this one still happens to me occasionally today.

Only as a late teenager did my political fervor cool down somewhat. There were now other things to employ my mind. At this early stage I already had decided that I would later study jurisprudence at the university. At this juncture I spent hours studying the basic German legal statute books, which I had borrowed from my uncle, the chief of the Dresden CID: the *Strafgesetzbuch*, the penal code, the *Strafprozessordnung*, the criminal procedure code, the *Bürgerliches Gesetzbuch*, the civil code, the *Zivilprozessordnung*, the civil procedure code, and the *Handelsgesetzbuch*, the commercial law code.

I even remember quite a bit of this stuff today, but after seventy-five years much is now outdated, and even more has been forgotten by me in the meantime. However, due to the lost war this dream never materialized.

As a teenager I had no idea what old age or being old really meant. A man in his late thirties was old, a woman in her forties was quite old. All four of my grandparents, in their sixties, were very old and would soon be gone. But then, maybe once a month, the radio would announce that the President, and later the *Führer*, had congratulated somebody to his or her one-hundredth birthday. Were we teenagers thinking about reaching old age? I doubt it, because this was simply beyond our capacity to contemplate. And nowadays one comes across centenarians in many places, and relatively quite often.

As early as 1933 the first samples of the *Volksempfänger*, the People's Radio, had been exhibited at the Berlin *Funkausstellung*, the Radio Exhibition (Ploetz). Not by coincidence was this basic radio promoted, and probably also subsidized, by Dr. Josef Goebbels, the Propaganda Minister (that was his official designation). This was obviously considered by him an efficient tool to disseminate the Nazi ideology and propaganda to the last humble abode anywhere in the country, and it worked even better than planned. I don't remember when exactly these sets went into production, but these basic radio receivers were later to be found in virtually every German household.

In 1934 a friend of my paternal grandfather had emigrated with his family to the USA. At the time I was not aware of it, but their name Gross suggests that they probably were Jewish. I do not recall what he did before, but there he owned or ran a Ford dealership in Miami Beach, Florida. I learned this from a postcard, which his son, who was about my age, had sent me shortly after they had left Germany. He wrote in German, of course, but the English word 'only' had already crept into his vocabulary. This I found remarkable at the time, myself having just started with English lessons at high school.

Also in 1934, a new 5 RM coin was issued in Germany. It showed the Potsdam *Gedächtniskirche*, the Remembrance Church, and commemorated the death of the *Reichspräsident* von Hindenburg and his burial in this church. Another friend of my grandfather showed me the new commemorative coin and asked me to look at the tiny figure of a man: "Is he entering or is he leaving the church?" I looked, but I could not see anyone. Because there was no one! He had successfully tricked me. I failed to find this funny!

At about the same time my father's parents sold their apartment building at Ammonstrasse 60 and bought another one, number 72 (but maybe I have juxtaposed the numbers?) in the same inner-city street. It was very similar, except a decade younger. Because the rooms were as high as in the previous building, my grandfather had lower ceilings fitted in his apartment, to achieve a cozier atmosphere and to save on the heating costs. However, this time their apartment was on the ground floor, and their ablution facilities were just for them. I don't know what the position was in this regard for the tenants in the upper four floors, since I never ventured up the stairs.

In his backyard my grandfather built, or more likely a contractor built for him, a large wooden shed, containing all his tools, ladders, push cart and his paint pots. He worked on his oil-paintings, however, in the living room, where he had an easel standing. I am not sure, whether this was only set up when he wanted to paint, but this seems a reasonable assumption.

After a few years our apartment in the suburb needed redeco-rating, which was done by my grandfather, wearing his hat as the house painter. In the morning he pushed his two-wheel cart, loaded with the paint pots and his tools, the seven kilometers from his workshop in the inner-city of Dresden to our apartment in Reick, and in the evening he went home by tram. The next day early in the morning he came back the same way, finished his work by late afternoon, and in the evening, he pushed his cart back to the city. This all happened in summer, so the days were long enough to enable him to finish the apartment in just two days.

When in 1937 I eventually had acquired the status of a teenager, I was now sleeping, obviously in a proper bed by then, in the so-called *Kleine Zimmer*, the Small Bedroom. I remember strongly the feeling of freedom and independence this room seemed to convey to me. In this room also stood a beautiful glass-fronted book-cupboard. I use here the word 'beautiful' because at the time it appeared like that to me. Even so it was in reality just a normal modern piece of furniture.

And later there was in this room also my upright piano. As usual for a teenager, I immediately could see the catch in this new acquisition. My room now became the torture chamber, where I not only had to practice the lessons on this 'wonderful' music instru-ment. Also, my swatting the numerous Latin and English and

Spanish irregular verbs was not exactly considered fun by me, but slightly less tortuous.

A much more pleasant and positive memory about this room was the magnificent chestnut tree on the other side of our street, the scene of our earlier glorious marble games adventures. In spring it was covered in bright white and pink candle-like blooms. When in winter this tree was occasionally covered in snow, the view was something so special for me that I can still vividly recall this picture even today.

This room's window was also the one where my parents flew the black-white-and-red flag of their party of choice, whenever there was an election before the Nazi take-over. Later, when this national symbol and all other political party flags had been outlawed, they had to use the obligatory swastika flag. And this was rather often, whenever there was a so-called election or referendum, which now every time ended with an over 90% approval result! And on any of the many political commemorative days of the Party.

An important aspect of a teenager's life was the weekly pocket money. In my case this consisted of thirty Pfennig, which substantial amount was spent like this: ten Pfennig on stamps, another ten Pfennig on a double scoop of ice cream, and the remaining ten Pfennig went into the money box. The complicating factor in this reminiscence is the fact that I cannot remember what I did with the ice-cream money during the long winter months. Already as early as that there were problems with the capital deployment, and all of this without the benefit of the bank investment advisor.

This was also the time when I started to pluck the hairs between my eyebrows, and when I tried to press some water waves into my chives-like straight hair. The first of these operations was successful to the present day, the second one a failure. I also had, for a few years, a variety of pimples in my face. This acne caused me substantial chagrin. Various cures were tried, all without success. But eventually this problem sorted itself out the natural way. Life as a teenager was really not that easy!

My father had kept contact with some of his war time comrades. One of these had a small itinerant business selling household textiles, clothing and footwear to farming communities and to residents of small towns without proper textile, clothing or shoe shops. This necessitated for him the possession of a car. He took my parents during the summer of 1938 on an outing to the *Riesengebirge* in Silesia, the mountain forming there the natural boundary between Germany and Czechoslovakia.

He also had a daughter, who was slightly younger than me. We did not decide to marry once we would be a few years older, because I hated her. She had made fun of a pimple on my nose. Very un-lady-like! But I got my own back, when our families were walking in some woods somewhere, and she had to go, you know, behind some bushes, and we all became aware of this embarrassing situation of hers. Vengeance was so sweet!

Another former army chap was apparently quite wealthy and lived in a substantial villa in Kötschenbroda, just outside Dresden. I do not remember what his game was, but I recall that his son had an electric rail set. His railway station building had red transparent windows, and the interior of the building was illuminated. Marvelous!

I have already mentioned the compiler of railway timetables. He had served with my father in the trenches, as an Army nurse. He later moved with his family from their inner-city apartment in Dresden to one in our street, but thereafter our contact with them sort of moved into hibernation. His son attended one of the prestigious Dresden *Gymnasiums*. Did they now, because of this, believe that they had achieved a higher social level?

Our apartment neighbor, a senior police officer, lent me one day his service handbook 'bible', after I had bothered him with a number of questions regarding the German police service. This book detailed all of the legal requirements a police officer had to be familiar with. It also described the organizational structure, including the *SIPO* (Security Police) and the *Gestapo* (Secret Police).

It was fun for me to quickly more or less memorize this material and to let him afterwards examine my recollection and understanding of the subject. As it happened, Organization and Methods as well as Law became after the war my fields of special interest, which eventually led to my occupation as a management consultant. It is funny, how minor events sometimes lead from one thing to something else.

These neighbors had taken out a subscription for a *Lesezirkel*. This was a system, where the subscribers received on a weekly basis a slightly larger than A4-sized stiff black cardboard folder with about six to eight different magazines, each bound in a green-mottled thin cardboard cover. We shared the subscription costs with the neighbors and received the packet of magazines after they had finished reading them.

The main titles were the *Berliner Illustrierte* and the *Münchner Illustrierte*, both of them black-and white magazines. But there was also the *Koralle*, a rather more modern (colored?) version. A puzzle magazine, a satirical and, finally, a fashion one completed the assortment. I don't know why this latter one almost slipped my mind, since as a boy I must surely have been very much interested in the subject. In the later Nazi period, I am almost sure we also received the *Völkischer Beobachter*, the Party propaganda magazine.

Once I had survived my basic piano training by my uncle Hans (the one remunerated by a small pack of cigarettes) and had advanced to more than Beethoven's *Für Elise*, I was further taught by Miss Leinert, a middle-aged lady. It was obvious that she had suffered the same rachitic chest problems as I had. With her I progressed to Brahms, Liszt and Chopin, and she managed to advance me to some modest public performances, but then the army demanded my participation in the war effort, and that was that. Please do not get me wrong here, I would never have become a half-way decent pianist.

A family with a son of my age had moved at this time into our block. I had finally found a close friend. Sometimes my friend and I went with our bicycles on longish trips into the different nearby suburbs, including to Striesen, where my friend's family had lived before moving into our suburb. This area was situated next to the River Elbe, and we often sat on the rocks of the riverbank and watched the ships.

Some of the larger barges had 1 000t, others 600t or 800t carrying capacities, and we were quite familiar with these details. The tugboats, even though they were small, pulled the big and fully loaded barges at a reasonable speed, even up-stream. We also watched the famous passenger steamers of the *White Fleet* and the odd pleasure motor or paddle boats. It was a low-level entertainment by today's standards. Life was definitely quite different then.

But this was only part of our observations. We also found some peculiar rubber contraptions lying in the sand and gravel, which were called *Gummi Fuffziger* (a distortion by our local dialect), Rubber Fifties, referring to the price of 50 Pfennig for a condom packet. We had a vague notion of the general purpose of these things, but they were without much interest to us boys and not worthy of our curiosity. Only much later were we informed, by the older brother of my friend, about the sordid purpose of these items.

The events of the 1936 *Winter Olympiade* in Garmisch-Partenkirchen in the Bavarian Alps were eagerly followed by the people, in the newspapers and on the radio. Germany had collected an impressive array of gold medals, probably helped because we were the host country. Female ski competitors were allowed to take part for the first time (Wikipedia), and Christel Crantz won a gold medal. Sonja Henie competed in ice skating and won her gold medal, as usual.

But I do not remember many other details, because winter sports did not interest me much. Only the bob-sleigh team of Herr Ostler still remained in my memory, probably because one of the three German commemorative postage stamps for the Winter Olympiad commemorated his team's gold medal. Oh yes, Germany had also won the ski jump competition.

These German successes were repeated at the Summer Olympiad of the same year. They were not just a sporting triumph for Hitler and the Nazis, but they also uplifted the German psyche. They were additionally a trump card in Germany's relations with the outside world. Many prominent foreigners were deeply impressed by these events and they admired the 'New Germany', particularly the exemplary organization of these games.

I clearly remember the sailing events near Kiel, the rowing competitions at the lake near the suburb of Berlin-Grünau, and the main athletic events in the newly opened *Olympiastadium* in Berlin. The outstanding star at the athletic events was Jesse Owens of the USA. I remember that he collected four gold medals: for the 100m and 200m sprints, the 4x100m (or 4x200m?) sprint relay as well as for the long jump. We later learned about the rumor circulating in Germany that this success by an American Negro had caused Hitler's profound consternation and displeasure. Victory of a 'substandard' Negro over the top-of-the range Arians was a personal insult to him!

The 1935 Italian invasion of Ethiopia/Abyssinia resulted in supply problems for Italy, caused by the international punitive sanctions. Germany had ignored these and had supplied coal and steel (and probably weapons and ammunition as well), in order to save the fascist regime of Benito Mussolini from collapsing.

1936 saw the establishment of the famous, or rather infamous, *Achse* (Axis) of Germany – Italy, which later in this year was, by the joining of Japan, enlarged to the *Anti-Komintern-Pakt*, the anti-international-communist pact. This partially established the basis for Hitler's future political strategy, as was shown three years later.

Another well remembered story in 1936 was the abdication of King Edward VIII of England, because of his close relation to a divorced American lady. This event was seen by Germans as a setback, because the king had been presented to us as a Nazi sympathizer and an admirer of Hitler. His 'demotion' to the title of Duke of Windsor was also astounding to us. Eventually, he found himself in the Government House of the Bahamas, well out of the way! We had never seen anything like that before in conjunction with any European monarchy. At the accession to the throne by Edward VIII a set of definitive stamps showing his likeness had just been issued by the Postmaster of Great Britain, and now a new set was required for the new King George VI.

In 1936 Hitler also announced the first (and I seem to remember, the only one) German *Vierjahresplan*, the Four-Year-Plan, to be implemented under the leadership of Göring. This kind of thinking was in line with the cherished socialist planning practice, as observed for decades in the Soviet Union. This master plan was the blueprint, not just for the envisaged economic development of the country, but also for the re-militarization of Germany and the re-armament of the *Wehrmacht*, the German Armed Forces.

Hitler's speech on this occasion was even longer than usual, because he was quoting reams of statistics. I remember the tremendously increased production of aluminum (probably to build airplanes) and the proud report on the completion of the first *Auto-bahn* kilometers.

At the end of 1936 the first 1 000km of *Autobahns* were completed, and in 1937 the first 2 000km were opened (Ploetz). In celebration of these achievements, Opel unveiled in the same year their newest car model, creatively named '*Autobahn*'. They stipulated that this family sedan could travel at a speed of 100km/h, maintained for extended periods. In those days, this was a fantastic claim, but I do not remember, if the facts lived up to this boast.

No mention was made of fuel consumption, however. To start with, the surface of the *Autobahns* consisted of rough concrete, but tire wear was not a great problem at this speed. These concrete roads had later to be covered with bitumen, when speeds and tire wear had increased.

Before the war, the *Autobahns* were constructed by placing large concrete slabs head to toe, but without being connected or tied together. After the war it became apparent that this construction method had been faulty and had created problems in later years. These slabs had over time settled unevenly, causing a bumpy ride, after steps had developed between the adjoining concrete slabs. After the war speeds of more than 80km/h were almost impossible to maintain on these freeways under these conditions.

In 1936 one of the first *Autobahn* sectors, from Darmstadt to Frankfurt/Main, was completed. 1938 this 30km stretch saw a terrible accident, when Bernd Rosemayer was killed during a test drive. He was the star performer amongst the racing drivers of the *Autounion*, one of the two German firms then active in motor racing.

The *Autounion* consisted of *DKW* (with its subsidiary *Audi*), *Horch* and *Wanderer*. Later the *NSU* firm was added, I seem to remember. The results of the 1929/1931 depression had forced these companies, mostly working in Saxony, to fuse in order to ramp up a satisfactory size. Horch was the division competing in motor racing. By the way, the *Autounion's* post-war successor in Western Germany was *Audi*, the luxury car builder now belonging to *Volkswagen AG*.

The other German motor racing firm was *Mercedes-Benz*. They had been building the famous *Silberpfeile*, the Silver Arrows racing cars. Their aces were Rudolf Caracciola and von Brauchitsch.

Both these companies competed against Maserati, Alfa Romeo and other European racing car firms.

At about this time my father bought a 35mm small-film, fully automatic camera. I seem to remember the make as *Korelle*. It looked a bit like a miniature of the famous *Leica* camera. Now taking photos took off properly for him. The pictures were black-and white, of course. Color photos were still a long way off in Germany. Photo albums were quickly filled, and two of them have survived (I don't remember how or by whom this was accomplished). Before that he had owned a Zeiss-Ikon camera, which used glass plates instead of film, and he had to develop and print his photos himself.

One of our neighbors, and a friend of the family, was a factory manager in Dresden, who was also a member of the Nazi para-military organization of the *SA*, the *Sturmabteilung*. In 1937 he marched with his *SA Standarte* (the size of a regiment) to Nuremberg to take part in the *Reichsparteitag*, the annual Nazi Party rally. He mailed me a special postal stationary postcard, which was very much appreciated for my stamp collection.

After the war he was arrested by the Russians, or more exactly by their German acolytes, the functionaries of the communist party of the Soviet Zone of Occupation and placed in a concentration camp. Yes, they instituted such camps after May 1945 for members of the Party. He was never seen again.

In 1937 German *Prinz Bernhard zu Lippe-Biesterfeld* married the Crown Princess of the Netherlands. This event I remember not only because of his beautiful first name, but also because I was happy to realize that a member of the *SS* and of the Party could with ease marry into a European royal house. Such Party member-ships and even those of the *SS* were not at all uncommon among the German aristocracy. Quite a few members of the many former ruling aristocratic families were members of the Party, usually of the equestrian and the sporting affiliates of the *SS*.

During the early and mid '30s we often read and heard about purges in the Soviet Union, particularly in the military, and every time with thousands of executions. We were wondering about these massacres, without quite understanding what went on. Only after the war against the USSR had started did we comprehend the consequences, because of Stalin's paranoia, of eliminating many of the competent Field Marshals and Generals and other high-ranking officers.

I especially remember the 1937 execution of Marshal Tuchatschewski, because he had co-operated with the German *Reichswehr* in clandestinely training our pilots and tank commanders, which was forbidden by the Versailles Treaty, and working together in other military matters with the German General Staff. He was described by our generals as highly competent. During these purges numerous field marshals and generals were removed: 3 of 5 field marshals

- 13 of 15 army generals,
- 8 of 9 admirals,
- 50 of 75 corps generals,
- 154 of 186 division generals.

Many of these were executed, but a third of them returned to the military during the war. These purges by Stalin probably help to explain the early costly setbacks for the Soviet armies in the coming war.

One Saturday morning the Dresdner Bank had something like an 'Open Door' event. My father took me there to show me his place of work. His desk, and the elderly spinster working as his secretary, were of limited interest to me, but the room with the Hollerith machines was a different story. These huge tabulators made one hell of a noise. What exactly their assigned work was I did not know or have forgotten, but when I worked for the US Army after the war in Frankfurt/Main, I was reunited with this type of machines.

Somehow, my life, or my reminiscences, seems to have been fixed around food. One day we went by train from the railway station in our suburb for a short ride of just one stop in the direction of Dresden and exited at the intermittent station of Strehlen (why?). On our way to the exit we passed a *Kiosk*, selling the most wonderful round *Makronen* and *Amerikaner*. The first was a crunchy pastry made with coconut flakes, the second a round soft pastry with a sugar icing on one side. Yummy.

On one of my shopping trips early in the war I was told to buy a white bread, which looked similar to a French *baguette*, but was much broader. By the time I arrived home, a good part of this tasty bread had mysteriously disappeared. And this at a time of ration cards during the war. The lady of the house was not pleased!

Both sets of my grandparents were decidedly anti-clerically inclined. It was therefore not surprising, that my parents were also not church-going people, and I was brought up in the same tradition. Now, something peculiar happened in 1938. My parents enrolled me, out of the blue, to attend confirmation lessons at the Lutheran Protestant church in Strehlen, the suburb which I crossed every morning on my bike riding to school. I can only speculate that they wanted to take out some political insurance, on the basis of "you just never know". Certainly not insurance in the spiritual way! And it was also definitely no "Street to Damascus". But something must have happened and got in the way, and my confirmation never took place.

Since I was reckless enough to promise to speak the truth, and since I do not intend to become a politician at my advanced age, I am willing and able to make the otherwise suicidal statement that I have never believed in any man-made religion. Today even less than ever before. No 'finding of religion' for me, while I am on the waiting list. If one studies my earlier book *"Parallel Developments"*, published on Amazon, the reasons become very clear and convincing, at least for myself.

The story and history of evolution is based on two different premises:

- science has proven beyond a reasonable doubt that the evolution of all forms of life is driven by mutations of the genetic material, sometimes in very small steps, and occasionally resulting in major sudden changes.
- most scientists now think that these mutations happen in agreement with the 'Chaos Theory', and therefore in a random manner.

The first of these points can nowadays safely be considered as proven. Even the pen-ultimate catholic pope (the German one, who resigned) has publicly acknowledged that evolution is a scientific fact (is this why he resigned?). The second point, however, will probably never be proven or dis-proven.

Whether these changes really happen at random, or whether a natural power, which I would simply call 'Nature', decides and/or influences these mutations, will be left forever to be decided by each individual. Such power would be way beyond my comprehension and imagination, and beyond anybody else's as well, I would think. However, I am not trying to convince any-body of my own believes, or rather disbelieves. After all, religion is for many people very important and helpful.

Why do people, and teenagers in particular, change their taste in music as they get older? As teenagers we used to crave jazz and swing, music somewhat similar to jitterbug, even though this was already dated by then. Before the war and up to 1940 we eagerly listened to Radio Luxembourg, the Mecca for teenager-taste music. The Party did, of course, not allow our radio stations to air such 'un-German trash'.

After Luxembourg had mutated to Luxemburg, in pursuance of the 1940 occupation by the *Wehrmacht*, and this 'decadent' music had stopped, we had a big problem. The London BBC was out of bounds for us because of the real probability of get-ting caught, and prison was the most generous assumption as the result of listening to an enemy radio station.

Already in 1919, when the Austrian/Hungarian double-monarchy had succumbed and had lost 80% of their land, the Austrian government wanted to unite their rump country, now exclusively populated by German-speakers, with the German Republic. The Austrian Postmaster had already overprinted their current postage stamps with *"Deutsch-Österreich"*. But the WWI Allies refused their permission for this earlier attempt of an *Anschluss* (Joining) attempt.

Early in 1938 the Austrian Nazis, which had grown in numbers parallel to developments in Germany, had staged a pseudo-revolution, in order to force a renewed attempt for an *Anschluss*, since the government of chancellor Dollfuss had refused this. Seyss-Inquart, the Austrian Interior Minister and an avowed Nazi, called on Hitler to unite Austria with Germany. He did not require any persuasion. After all, he was a born Austrian himself. The *Wehrmacht* marched in, to the general approval of the Austrians, and not a single shot was fired. This reunification was seen in both countries as a further stroke of Hitler's genius.

A referendum was held in April in the now renamed *Ostmark*, and a vast majority of the population voted for the *Anschluss*. This referendum, as far as we in Germany could make out, represented the genuine results. The tens of thousands of people filmed in the weekly newsreels showed genuine, spontaneous enthusiasm, which could not have been faked at such short notice. Not even by the devil's own propagandist Dr. Josef Goebbels!

This whole story is nowadays a bit of a sore point with our Austrian blood brothers, and they prefer to forget or to deny these events. During the war years, there had always been a perceived ambiguity among the soldiers about the former Austrians, similar to that towards our Italian allies. After 1945 the Austrian governments repressed any knowledge of their *Anschluss* ambitions in 1919 and again in 1938, in their desire to distance themselves from Nazi Germany, particularly after the hardships of the lost war became apparent in Germany.

Late in 1938 the *Sudetenland*, the area of Czechoslovakia bordering Germany and mostly populated by Germans, was under brutal pressure ceded to Germany. Needless to say, this was again seen as another bloodless victory by the 'invincible' *Fuehrer*. The main players of this particularly heavy political and military arm-wrestling tournament were the British Prime Minister Neville Chamberlain, his Foreign Minister Anthony Eden, the French Prime Minister Daladier, the Czechoslovakian Prime minister Benes and, of course, Hitler and the German Foreign Minister Joachim von Ribbentrop.

I remember all of their names well, because at the time (I was fourteen then) I was at a sanatorium for children on the North Sea island of Föhr. We not only listened to the radio and read the papers, but we also had the time to digest what was going on and to discuss this with the staff, most of them dyed-in-the-wool Nazis.

Boycotts of Jewish shops and book burnings had already occasionally happened from 1933 onwards. Everything started to change, however, with the so-called *Reichskristallnacht* on November

9 of 1938. The Jewish activist Grynszpan had assassinated the German diplomat vom Rath in Paris. This became the official reason, or the pretext, for these atrocities. During this night *SA* troops, or rather *SA* hooligans, 'spontaneously', but clearly directed from above, looted and demolished Jewish shops and smashed the shop plate-glass display windows, hence the reference to 'crystal' in that term. Afterwards they picketed the entrances, which made it suicidal for would-be customers to try to enter these shops.

This date of November 9 also had two different symbolic meanings for the German people. It reminded them of the end and the defeat of World War I, but for the Nazis it was also the commemorative day of Hitler's abortive 1923 *coup d'état* at the *Feldherrnhalle* in Munich. The latter association was presumably the main reason for staging this event on this particular date.

One of the consequences following these events was a new law, requiring all Jews to wear a David star on their outer clothing. I still remember seeing, some day on my way home from high school, an elderly Jewish gentleman slowly trudging from the Kreuzkirche on to the Altmarkt in Dresden with this discriminating symbol on his overcoat. I also seem to remember another legal provision of this law, that all Jews had to use the names of Abraham and Sarah, respectively, but my memory is not sure about this point.

Now the anti-Jewish discrimination had mutated to an all-encompassing Jewish persecution. Not surprisingly, this acted as the trigger for accelerated Jewish emigration (was this possibly the idea behind it?).

I believe this was also the approximate time when the first serious anti-Nazi resistance groups formed in the German upper-class establishment, including some academics and some of the aristocracy, the middle classes and members of religious bodies, but not yet from the military establishment. However, this observation is made with the benefit of hindsight.

The German people began now to slowly and dimly realize that the political climate in the country had changed for the worse, and that things were getting serious and out of hand. Even though nobody could imagine at this stage what would happen later on in the extermination camps, but an un-well feeling was spreading. People were subdued, insecure and started for the first time to doubt Hitler and the Nazis and all they stood for. They were definitely not anymore as happy and care-free as they had been up to this point. Naturally, no doubts or criticism were expressed publicly, because you never knew whether somebody would report you to the *Gestapo*.

The attitudes of foreigners towards Nazi Germany also began to change now. The honeymoon was over! Already in 1936 Wilhelm Gustloff, the leader of the Nazis in Switzerland, (yes, they also had a Nazi off-shoot) had been assassinated by a Jewish activist, who was in Germany of course called a terrorist! The foreign and mostly Jewish intelligentsia really started from now on to expose and fight Nazi Germany. The propaganda war was in full swing, and Goebbels emerged, for the first time, as the loser.

Germany was by now in the throes of extremely serious economic difficulties. On the one hand the country had, on Hitler's orders, very quickly to equip the huge Armed Forces. Simultaneously, the country was largely cut off from certain critical overseas supplies. This created problems also in areas not directly related to the war effort.

The shortage of butter was a case in point. Goebbels asked the German people in one of his radio and news-reel speeches (propaganda performances would be the better term) the (rhetorical) question: "Do you want butter or cannons?" It is proof of his demagogic capabilities, that the overwhelming, but probably staged, reply was: "We want cannons". The results were shortages of butter and fresh cream, amongst other things, long before the war had started. I have to admit that to the present day I have not figured out, why specifically these milk products were the subject of such shortages.

The most prominent victim of these negative developments was the *VW Beetle*, the *Volkswagen*, which had not even seen the light of day yet. Developed since about 1935 by Ferdinand Porsche, a completely new factory had to be built for this car on some remote farmland near Fallersleben, because the German car factories were unable to build the car with a selling price of 990 *Reichsmark*, as demanded by Hitler. When the new factory was ready in 1939 and if the car would have been built then, the real selling price would have been above RM2 000 (Wikipedia).

Because of the war, only military vehicles left the factory: the famous *Kübelwagen*, the four-wheel-drive and all-terrain version of the *Volkswagen*, and the *Schwimmwagen* with a hermetically sealed bottom, which even had a screw to operate in deep water. Around the new factory more and more houses, shops and public buildings appeared, and especially new factories and workshops for dozens of subcontractors and suppliers. This was the start of the new city of Wolfsburg, now the fifth largest of the German *Land* of Niedersachsen (Wikipedia).

In the summer of 1939, we all followed with bated breath the newspaper and radio news about the horse-trading taking place in Moscow. Germany as well as the Western Allies tried desperately to ally themselves with the Soviet Union. If it was not Lord Halifax, who visited Stalin and the Soviet Foreign Minister Litvinov-Finkelstein, then it was our Foreign Minister Joachim von Ribbentrop, a former commercial traveler in champagne. There were also some other names (Cripps?) bandied around at that time, but they have slipped my mind. The outcome, as we all know, was the renewed division and military occupation of poor Poland between Russia and Germany. And, of course, the start of World War II.

10

TRAVELS

1933 TO 1942

Memorable was a visit by the family, probably early in the 1930s, to a *Wellenbad* (wave swimming pool) at Kötschenbroda or Radebeul, just outside of Dresden. The name of a naturalist connected to this enterprise comes to mind (Bilz?). Some impressive machinery created strong waves in a rather large concrete basin, and swimming against these was for us a new experience, imitating ocean conditions. We had some snacks or sweets there, but this is about all my reminiscences were able to offer. No, I just remembered, in addition we also managed some sunbathing.

Probably in 1935 my paternal grandfather travelled with me by train to Waldheim to visit his sister. Tante Thekla lived in a very small and rather old little cottage on the slope overlooking the River Zschopau. On a Sunday morning the sun was shining so brightly onto a lightly colored factory wall on the opposite side of the narrow river, that I can still clearly visualize this impression today.

The other thing I remember in connection with this visit was the steepness of the ground all around their property. No, there was something else. We had *Mettwurst Brötchen* for the train journey. Unfortunately, I do not know how to translate this, so you are missing out on partaking of this German delicacy from Saxony.

However, there was another reminiscence about this visit: our walk along the river to *Burg Kriebstein*. This fortress belonged in the

Middle Ages to the family of some *Ritter*, a mounted Knight. It covered the complete surface area of a steep hill and was thus virtually unassailable. Most of these aristocratic guys made their living by waylaying the merchants on their way to and from the markets, when they robbed them of their money and merchandise. Any resemblance with modern tax assessors is purely coincidental. The descendants of such knights belong nowadays, of course, to the honorable German aristocracy.

For myself a remarkable feature of this tall building was the ablution facility, in the approximate form of a cubic box, which like an after-thought appeared to be glued high up to the outside wall. With the bottom of this construction opening about sixty meters above the river, it could be called a forerunner of the water closet. Practical people, these venerable knights.

The nearby village of Ehrenberg was the ancestral home of my paternal grandfather's family. As a youngster he was first apprenticed to Walter Kolbe, who later became a famous sculptor, before he studied painting at the famous Dresden Art Academy. This, presumably, did not work out and eventually he became a housepainter by profession, a proper qualified and rather successful one.

Beginning in 1936, Italy and Germany started to support General Franco in Spain. Coming from his command position in Spanish-Morocco, he had invaded the homeland and had won some territory, mostly in the north of the country. Italy had sent some army troops (infantry and armored units), and Germany had dispatched the *Legion Condor* of probably voluntary air force personnel, with their planes, anti-aircraft artillery etc., to help him overthrow the constitutional socialist-communist Republican government in Madrid.

It must have been the *Dresdner Bank* which had sent my father with his family to Northern Spain. We lived for about three months in hotels in Bilbao, San Sebastian and Santander. What exactly my father did there I don't know. Things like that were never talked about in our family. All I know is that he was involved with the Headquarters of the *Legion*.

One day two German air force officers visited us there and I over-heard mention of a new *Flugabwehrkanone* or *Flak*, an anti-aircraft cannon. According to the description, it probably was the later famous 8,8(cm gun). This whole military exercise was also simultaneously intended as the proving ground for new weapons and equipment, and to provide combat experience for the *Luftwaffe* soldiers.

During these months I picked up a useful lot of Spanish, which came in handy in later years at high school, but not enough to successfully chat up any of the Spanish girls. In any case, I was too shy to imitate Don Juan. What a bunch of missed opportunities! In the 1990's we were in this neighborhood, but I had only an extremely vague recollection of these places, maybe because so much had changed, but the historical parts of the towns were of no particular interest to me then. What a pity.

Before that, the family was in Southeast England for two months or so. Here again, I was unaware of the purpose of my father's work there. This sojourn helped very nicely with my English at high school. On my return my English teacher was quite surprised and pleased how things had improved. It was amazing, how quickly one could improve a language when so young. When we were in the area in 2010, the same dis-appointment as before in Spain: I did not really recognize any localities, towns or buildings.

In the summer of 1936 I found myself in a kind of children's sanatorium at Südstrand, a suburb of Wyk on the North-Sea island of Föhr, part of the German section of the North-Frisian Islands. This stay was financed by our *Krankenkasse*, the medical aid organization. I am not sure whether it was the state entity or a private one. The doctors sent me there because of my diagnosed weak constitution. In retrospective, I think that had at the time not really been necessary.

In later years I noticed a tendency amongst German people, including family and friends, to grab as much as possible of the goodies the medical aid had to dole out. Often all sorts of people, apparently healthy enough, went on a *Kur* at a *Kurhaus*. This was an establishment to undergo medical treatment or to improve the patient's general health. Afterwards they often went to a *Sanatorium*, to relax from the strenuous experience of the *Kur*, I suppose.

However, I enjoyed myself and was not complaining. Life on the beach and games was superb. We were about thirty boys and a similar number of girls, all between about eight and fourteen years of age. One day I got sick and had to stay in bed. *Tante* (Auntie) Gerda sat on my bed, talked to me and stroked my hair. I was moved by so much care and kindness shown, something I was simply not used to. I guess I was in love, sort of.

A memorable experience was gathered there. No, girls were of little or no interest just then. But I smoked there my first cigarette. The make was 'North Star', as I recall. I did not exactly lose my lunch, but I felt like being ready to die. This perceived initiation into an elevated age group took place in the restroom of a restaurant. For some reason us boys were forced to exit the cubicles by climbing over the transom. Sliding down on the outside of the door, I managed to rip some deep gash into the skin of my thigh just above my knee. The faint scar is still there. After all, this could have been rather serious, if you know what I mean.

In this establishment we boys conducted one evening a highly sophisticated experiment. One boy of the group was instructed to lower his pants and underpants, to turn around and to bend forward. Another 'scientist' had a box of matches at the ready. Thus, the parameters of a scientific test were in place. After the lights were doused, we were now able to demonstrate how ignited methane gas can illuminate a limited space. But this is maybe not considered suitable as a reading lamp for the sitting room.

From about 1936 onwards my parents occasionally took me to visit the sister of my father in Berlin. These trips were undertaken by express train, straight from Dresden main station to Berlin Anhalter Bahnhof. She had married a self-employed *Dekorations-malermeister*, a master housepainter. They lived in a semi-detached cottage in the suburb of Schmöckwitz, next to the small town of Eichwalde just across the Berlin municipal boundary, where they also did most of their shopping. In their basement they had a small shop selling paints, wallpaper, soaps, detergents, cleaning materials, etc. as an additional source of income. They had a reasonably large property, with many fruit trees and bushes of many sorts of berries, as well as a small asparagus field.

Between the back of this and the rails of the Berlin City Railways meandered the '*Tannenweg*', the Fir Close. My father could not suppress to mention the exclusively present pine trees along this passage. By the way: in Germany firs were considered upper class, whereas pine trees were seen as pedestrian, hence probably the fake name.

At about this time I first read about the Flettner Rotor ship. This novelty had three or four upright hollow cylinders as high as the masts of a sailing ship. They turned in the wind and produced the (electric?) power for the screws. A truly revolutionary concept, in its way somewhat like the much later Wankel motor, but neither of these innovations turned into a lasting success.

When I later went to visit them on my own, my travels were a combination of rail and bicycle transport. In Dresden I would load my bicycle into the luggage wagon of the through-train. In Elsterwerda, a stop-over half-way to Berlin, I would collect it from the train conductor and I would pedal the remainder of the distance of about 60km to Schmöckwitz.

Once the war had started, one had to pack some extras: something to sustain the hungry cyclist, since food was not any more on sale without ration stamps, and a wad of toilet paper, because all public facilities in restaurants, service or at train stations had long been stripped of such a precious and scarce supply.

A day or two after my arrival my cousin would accompany me on his bicycle through the pine forest to *Grünauer See*, a beautiful large lake, where in 1936 the Boating Olympics took place. Or we would pedal to *Schmöckwitzer See* over the *Schmöckwitzer Brücke* (bridge), where during the Cold War the prisoner exchanges between the Western Allies and the Soviets would take place.

Once a week or so my cousin took me via the *S-Bahn* (city express train) to Görlitzer Bahnhof, the terminal of the local southeasterly railway line. Nearby was the wholesaler supplying the small enterprise of my aunt. Lugging our purchases home was no great problem. The turnover of the shop must have been slightly below Wal-Mart's. Sometimes my cousin and I assisted my uncle in his redecorating work, by filling-in small holes in the walls with putty before he painted them, most likely against payment of some pocket money.

One of my more special Berlin reminiscences related to the typewriter, which my aunt used for the business correspondence and invoicing. It was an 'Underwood' machine, but without the usual typewriter keyboard. Instead, a pointer above a set of letters had to be placed over each letter one wanted to type and to be depressed, and – *hey presto* -, the letter appeared on the paper, - if one had not forgotten with all these goings-on to place a sheet into the machine, that is. I think I better stop complaining now about the idiosyncrasies of my laptop and its printer.

Another fond reminiscence referred to the local butcher shop. Whenever us boys were dispatched by my aunt to collect something from this institution, we always received a small *'Wurstzipfel'*, the cut-off ends of sausages, which had been truncated to improve their looks in the display cabinets of the butcher's. These benevolent Berliners knew how to uphold the standards of civilization. The nearby weekly *Wochenmarkt*, an open-air assembly of merchants from the surrounding suburbs, provided other delicacies, but unreasonably, these crafty people demanded payment for their goodies.

Once a year the *Hitlerjugend* went on safari, usually to a tent camp. Contrary to present parlance, a tent camp meant just that: each of the travelers brought with them their tarpaulins, from which the twelve to fifteen tents were assembled and erected, each housing about a dozen boys. Each tent required as many tarpaulins as boys were sleeping in it. A soak-pit was dug, an army field kitchen was established, and that was it. I think, 'rustic' is the word now used to describe such a basic situation. But we enjoyed every minute, as long as it was not raining. Unfortunately, no members of the *BDM*, the Nazi organization for girls, had been invited. Surely an oversight by our leadership.

In 1936 we went to a tiny village near Eckernförde on the coast of the Baltic Sea. There were only two things to report about this two-week adventure. The first was a visit to the Laboe *Unterseeboot Denkmal*, the memorial near Kiel, honoring the fallen submariners of World War I. We travelled there on board a tiny motorboat, and I almost got sea-sick, due to a gusty breeze blowing.

The other thing was the fact that it rained only once during our stay, namely permanently. The field, where we had pitched our tents, was converted into a mud bath. When I mentioned tents, these bore no semblance to the modern articles. To start with, they had no integrated groundsheet. As a matter of fact, we had no groundsheets at all, but had to dig a trench around the tent to prevent flooding, but that often did not work and turned out to be another one of the faulty theories of the grown-ups.

The following year saw us near the *'Grosser Arber'*, the highest mountain, outside a village close to Zwiesel in the *Bayrischer Wald*, the Bavarian Forest. For a change from the previous year, the weather was perfect, and the scenery around us was breath-taking. There I had my first close encounter with a *Kreuzotter*, a viper with a string of markings of crosses on its back. Highly poisonous and scary! Accelerated withdrawal was mandatory.

I remember practicing the throwing of my *Fahrtenmesser* at a tree, trying to make it stick. This implement was a large *Hitlerjugend* sidearm, emblazoned with the *HJ* lozenge, well sharpened and sheathed in a leather receptacle which was attached to the *Koppel*, our regulation leather belt. My efforts only led to mediocre results. The tree easily survived, and I had to realize that throwing knifes as a future profession was out of the question for me.

In the spring of 1938 I was sent to Breslau, for reasons I never fully understood. I stayed there with the family of a senior local functionary of the Party's district office. They lived in a recently constructed compound with very new and decent apartments. Apart from the nice and caring family, I only remember two things about this time: Das *Deutsche Turn-fest*, the German Athletics Festival at the Breslau *Jahrhunderthalle*, the Century Hall, and the best *Grobe Bratwurst* I have ever tasted in Germany, a coarse variety of a word which should not need translation.

In the summer I found myself again at the same sanatorium for children at Wyk on the North-Frisian isle of Föhr as in 1936. But instead of building sandcastles on the beach, there were now girls there. They had been there in 1936 as well, but the beach and playing games had been more important then. The change in perception had something to do with growing up, I supposed. Already during the long train ride, I had started with my first attempts at flirting. Probably an atrocious performance, but she played along.

Tante Gerda unfortunately had left. Her replacement was a she-devil and a witch! One day lunch consisted of a sweet-sour dish which, halfway through the sitting, fell out of my face. She forced me to finish eating this terrible stuff. What a cow! She could conceivably later have been employed as one of the concentration camp guards.

During our stay in this establishment, a local doctor came to examine all the children. An enterprising boy, about two years younger than me, tried to interest us older ones in a discovery he had made. The drapes on the window of the ground floor examination room did not quite close, and he claimed that one could observe the naked girls of all ages up to fourteen years during their examination. Surprisingly for him, we rejected this offer as immoral, and he got somewhat beaten up for his trouble. It must have been our *Hitlerjugend* upbringing, which made us forsake a surely very educational afternoon.

This is not meant to imply that this Nazi organization consisted solely of choir boys, but the official line was that sex, smut, alcohol, nicotine and all the other worthwhile things in life were definitely out-of-bounds for us, and this line was also strictly upheld in practice as well. With some exceptions, I am sad to admit.

11

RELAXATIONS

1933 TO 1942

My father owned a chess set in a small lockable decorated wooden box, which he had used in the trenches of the first war during any lull in the fighting. He taught me the chess moves and rules and we often played with this set, which he gave me as a teenager and which I still have and use today. This game I played in many locations, from Dresden to Italy, from Frankfurt to South Africa, but I never progressed much above that of an average club player.

He must have had his bicycle from the time we moved to the suburbs, because in any weather he pedaled daily to the bank, as I remember. This reminds me of the milk delivery man with his horse-drawn carriage. Every morning, as soon as my father appeared with his bicycle at the front door of our apartment building, the horse would approach him to collect the customary lump of sugar it was entitled to. Naturally, in the process it was pulling the cart halfway across the street, effectively blocking it off. No big deal, however, since there was practically no vehicular traffic to block off, even though this was a minor thoroughfare.

My mother also had her bicycle already early on. I received my first one, a boy's bicycle, probably around 1932. Our family's main entertainment was to go on Saturday afternoons or Sundays on bicycle tours in the surrounding neighborhoods. We usually cycled for three or four hours, but occasionally also for seven or eight hours. In summer it was light long enough, until ten o'clock or so.

My father had to work half days on Saturday, as was then usual, and I was on duty with the *Jungvolk* at this time, which entitled me to play truant at school on Saturday mornings. A welcome fringe benefit, this!

On one of our bicycle tours we went along the banks of the River Elbe, in the direction of the town and the fortress of Königstein. Next to the bicycle path we saw a sign, advising the existence of a viewing point over the river valley. We drove down this sidetrack, which was steeply descending and, being the adventurous (and stupid) teenager, I pedaled too fast and did not see in time a large tree root traversing the path.

My somersault over the handlebars was described by my parents as spectacular when they had collected me out of the dust. Miraculously, no damage was done to the bicycle, which would otherwise have landed me in some financial trouble. I must have survived this without serious damage, except to my dignity, and apart from a nosebleed and some bloody scratches on knees and elbows, which surely was par for the course for any teenager, anyway.

Bicycle tours to the *Erzgebirge*, the Ore Mountain, and the *Sächsische Schweiz*, by educated Germans now called the *Elb-sandsteingebirge*, the River Elbe Sandstone Mountain, gave us a chance to see maybe a deer or hares, which more likely were probably bunnies. Often, we went collecting mushrooms, at which I was reasonably successful, particularly with the popular *Birkenpilze* and *Maronen*, varieties of firm and tasty edible fungi with an underside of tubes.

Our family were naturists, and sometimes we cycled to the Moritzburg lakes, about twenty-five kilometers from our suburb, to sunbathe and swim. We usually met there a dozen or two likeminded people and swam, played ball, or just sat there and talked. Barbecue had not been invented yet, or at least was not yet known in Germany. Naturism was tolerated, sometimes grudgingly, in Saxony and generally in Northern Germany. The southern and western, mostly catholic, provinces suppressed this movement, however, with religious zeal, but without much success.

Sometimes we went to a *Buhne* of the Elbe, a pier built into the river to control the flow of the water in order to prevent damage to the riverbanks. This created a sort of lagoon behind this artificial obstacle. On one such occasion I got into trouble, when I unsuspectedly landed in deep water. When I had lost contact with the bottom, I started desperately thrashing the water to keep afloat. I don't remember, whether I knew to swim then, or whether I just panicked. My parents enjoyed the performance for a while, until they realized that there was a national tragedy in the making.

In walking distance from our apartment operated a privately owned public swimming pool. On the way there, through the fields, we skirted a small creek with old willow-trees. They were small and largely hollowed out. Not only were they ideal for hide and seek purposes, but their interior wood was so rotten that it was easy to set it alight with our magnifying glasses. It is interesting to contemplate that for us teenagers they were not called 'magnifying' but 'burning' glasses.

This establishment consisted of two connected concreted swimming pools, one for swimmers and the other one for kiddies. There were also wooden communal change rooms and individual lockable cabins. Because the wood used for these constructions was pine, knot holes developed over time and allowed some intriguing views of the female anatomy in the next cabin, as I was told by my friends. I myself would know nothing about such things, of course.

Starting from an early age I suffered from weak ankle joints. This has been a major problem for me. Walking longer distances had always been very painful for me, until I finally had acquired some orthopedic support inlay soles, individually manufactured for my feet. This happened as early as 2008. Why it took so long to overcome this obvious problem, I don't know. It just never occurred to me to do anything about it. And my parents, obviously, did not realize what the solution was, either. But these types of personalized supports did probably not even exist at their time. I wondered, whether these sore ankles had anything in common with my already mentioned sore shoulders?

Just now I fantasized what would likely have happened if the army doctors at my draft examination in 1942 would have known about such supports. Surely, I would have been drafted into a different military unit, the war would certainly have taken a different course and, of course, Germany would have won the war. But then I remembered just in time, that in this case I would probably have eventually landed up as a District Commissioner somewhere in Siberia. Thus, we better forget about such speculations!

Ice skating was always problematic for me, because of my weak ankles. Instead of standing straight on my skates, to alleviate the pain in my ankles, I collapsed my feet so that the edges of the skates rested on the surface of the ice. We often had long periods of strong easterly winds straight from Siberia, which allowed the freezing-over of ponds, and level areas could be converted to ice skating rinks, if they had been carefully watered. In winter there was sometimes an occasion to do some ice skating in the yard of our primary school.

Our skates could not be compared to the present combinations of boots and skates. With the help of a little key we screwed our skates onto our standard ankle boots. In order not to lose this important implement, it was attached to a string hanging around our necks. As soon as we started running, and this was our normal mode of locomotion, this key would jump up and down in front of our faces, and one day it knocked a corner off one of my front teeth. Not to worry, this tooth, together with all the others, went AWOL years ago.

In some particularly cold winters, the temperatures were low enough, and lasted long enough, to freeze-over the Carola Lake in the *Grosser Garten* park in Dresden. In the early years of our stay in the suburb my mother took me there by tram and we skated together for a few hours on this large expanse of ice. In between and afterwards we partook of a glass or two of *Glühwein*. This was, or was supposed to be, a diluted heated red wine, and was a high point for us kids. Later I went there on my own, but never made a success of ice skating. By then the *Glühwein* was in any case only half the fun.

From an early time as a teenager I possessed a pair of skis. Originally kid's size, but later I acquired the adult version. They also were no comparison with today's articles. The *Bindung*, the contraption which attached the ski to the boot (I don't know the English term) was primitive and often came undone. But it was very difficult to undo, if this became necessary after a fall. Nevertheless, we somehow managed. In some winters there had been enough snow cover for me to be able to go on longish ski tours. But here again my knuckles created problems for me.

In one winter, I skied all the way to my grandparent's house in Quohren. Clever me, I decided not to follow the roads which we used when we were going by bicycle, but instead I decided to take a short-cut and ski across country, because the snow on the roads was already less than suitable for skiers. Not surprisingly, I got lost in the snow-covered landscape where all familiar contours had been camouflaged, and it took me at least double the time to get to my grandparents' place that it would have taken me if I had followed the well-known roads.

After school I sometimes went with a friend to what I now know to have been a very small extinct volcano, or rather, the mouth of a volcanic pipe. Its flat and round bottom measured only about twenty meters across. The walls, still standing around three quarters of the mouth, were in places about six to eight meters high. We exercised our climbing skills there, surprisingly without any major mishap.

On Sunday afternoons from spring to autumn our family often undertook a walk in the near neighborhood, sometimes with friends which my parents had made by then in our suburb. These walks usually culminated in the visit of one of the many garden restaurants. Coffee and cake were the usual well appreciated treat.

The extension of our street led to Nickern, the next suburb after Prohlis. There, very nice detached and semi-detached single-family houses had been built from about 1934 on. All three of us often walked there, just window-shopping, because they were financially out of reach for us. Still, people are allowed to dream, sometimes.

One pleasant surprise was the occasional boat trip on the River Elbe. I recall only two such happenings, however. The white paddle steamers were quite large and were rather fast, even against the current, which could be very strong, particularly in spring and autumn. The boats went downstream to at least the borders of Saxony, near Riesa. Upstream, the voyages went all the way to Aussig, about fifty kilometers inside Czechoslovakia, via the *Elbsandsteingebirge*, the huge sandstone mountain on the border between this country and Saxony.

In the autumn of 1934 the *Reichswehr*, the stripped-down version of the German military of World War I, conducted some publicity display at the training grounds near Hellerau, north of Dresden. My father and I witnessed the march-by of an infantry battalion with their weapons: the water-cooled machine-guns 08/15 of the previous war and the 5cm mortars. When I referred to the marching soldiers in a popular derogatory term, I received a proper dressing-down from my father, the former proud infantry soldier. I was ashamed and felt cut-down-to-size.

They were also displaying some light artillery pieces and the poorly done mock-up of an armored car. Under the peace treaty of Versailles ending WW1, the *Reichswehr* was not allowed to have armored cars and neither war planes nor heavy artillery. Also, its total strength was limited to only 100 000 men, with a mandatory service of twelve years.

This was decreed to prevent the trick which the Prussians had played on the French forces of Napoleon I in 1806, when they trained large numbers of recruits for only a short time, thus acquiring a substantial number of at least basically trained soldiers. The result of the twelve years of service was a highly competent force of professional soldiers, which later formed the backbone of the *Wehrmacht*.

At about the same time my father took me to the Dresden airport near Klotsche, also to the north of Dresden. It was surely a Sunday morning, because on all other days he had to work. There was a grand total of one incoming-and-departing-again flight on the board. This was the international flight Prague/Dresden/Berlin, or the return one. I hate to think what a quiet day must have looked like at this pulsating international airport!

This brought up another reminiscence. One or two years later my father has taken me on a flight over Dresden with one of the famous JU 52 planes, the workhorses of the *Lufthansa* airline and the transport plane of the later *Luftwaffe*. Not much of this adventure is remembered, except that the plane was very noisy and that the view was rather foggy, but I could at least follow the course of the River Elbe and identify the crucial points of the city: the *Altmarkt*, city hall, *Großer Garten*, our apartment buildings and my school.

It must have been around 1934 that I started collecting stamps. Initially, I had the usual schoolboy collection, but very soon I started buying (cheap) stamps from a dealer in *Reitbahnstrasse*, on the way to my high school. Until I learned, that buying such material quickly filled the album pages, but did not create any value. With the result that the stamp album was worth more than its contents.

After having started my stamp collection I learned much about the times we lived in. When later becoming a serious philatelist, I not only had found an enjoyable hobby, but I had also built up some valuable knowledge about all aspects of philately. Furthermore, I had accumulated some worthwhile capital values. All of which, many years later, provided the basis for me to successfully starting my own stamp auction business.

This was also the approximate time when the local cinema offered the first 'talkies'. This establishment was not much more than a medium-sized barn, with seats, a screen and a projection cubicle installed. The 'talking' referred to a few minutes of speaking by the stars. With the help of a loudhailer, or more likely a microphone, the animator sitting in front of the screen explained the plot of the film and what was being said by the other actors of the cinematic opus. I cannot remember whether there was film music, or was there simply a record played behind the screen? Unimportant, the furious action of the films was all-absorbing for us kids.

The first ones I remember in this establishment were a number of *Zeichentrickfilme*, or cartoon strips. '*Micky Maus*', elsewhere known as 'Mighty Mouse', was a roaring success with us kids on many Sunday afternoons. Other unforgettable epic cinematic works included '*Dick und Doof*', literally translated as 'Fat and Stupid', the unfriendly version of the original title of 'Laurel & Hardy'. The 'Pat and *Patachon*' films were similar successes with us.

Eventually, the speaking parts grew longer, with the sad side effect of obviating the necessity for the animator's job. One of the first proper films I remember, the story of 'William Tell', introduced a further artistic addition: the first proper full-time film music.

But we also saw other demanding films, like '*Jugend*' ('Youth'), the story of a young girl who had been seduced or raped by a priest, or *'Reitet für Deutschland'*, an equestrian film with Willy Birgel. We also saw *'Die Feuerzangenbowle'*, a comedy with Heinz Rühmann, and many others. Westerns were still around by then, but they were considered by us to be for little boys, not for us 'almost' teenagers.

The films, by the way, came on two or three large reels into the projection booth. It was always a welcome source of mirth when the sequence of the reels was muddled-up by the butter-fingered hapless projectionist.

One of the outstanding differences between the films of this period and the modern productions was the fact that one could easily follow the dialog, because the background noises, also often jokingly called 'film music', did not interfere with the spoken word. Apparently, the actors were required to speak clearly, another one of these anachronisms.

And another one of the cherished modern artistic achievements, the cutting-up of the story line into dozens of different pieces, jumping backward and forward in time, had luckily not been invented yet. And most scenes were filmed by daylight, except if the storyline demanded otherwise. The filmmakers of the period expressed their artistic ambitions without interfering with the spectator's enjoyment.

But there was something else to be remembered: the weekly newsreels, which were shown before the feature film started. They were important, because they were the only way we could watch any illustrated happenings in the world. A compelling reason to visit the cinema almost every weekend. This allowed the always beavering Minister Goebbels to infiltrate our minds subliminally with his propaganda.

A further offering was the weekly *'Kulturfilm'*, which dealt usually with interesting worldwide cultural subjects. And I seem to remember that there were also advertisements, particularly for cigarettes. But it is possible that this only happened after the war.

During one of the high religious holidays, probably Christmas or Easter, we went in downtown Dresden to the *Frauenkirche*, the Church of Our Lady, to listen to some famous choir. Pöppelmann, the architect and builder of this reduced-size close copy of St. Peter Cathedral in Rome, had created a true masterpiece of a basilica. The acoustics were remarkable, even to my untrained ear.

Probably in the summer of 1938 I had a completely new experience. At about lunchtime I heard a deep, loud and pulsating noise in the sky. I went out into the street and could now see the reason: in a cloudless sky '*LZ 129 Graf Zeppelin*' was cruising majestically exactly above our street, our suburb and eastern Dresden.

While I was still watching this magnificent airship, the noise level suddenly increased again, and the crowd, which by now had assembled in the street, stood open-mouthed, so to speak, and watched '*LZ 130 Hindenburg*' to join this air show. Both zeppelins were flying so low that one could observe the windows of the large passenger cabins underneath the airship's bellies and we could easily read their identity markings. On their rear fins one could also not miss the black swastikas on their circular white background with the red surrounding.

After the *Sudetenland* had become part of the *Reich*, I went with my friend by bicycle to Aussig, a small town on the River Elbe, in what used to be Czechoslovakia. There we were able to buy *Schlagsahne*, whipped cream. A delicacy which was, due to the ongoing re-armament in preparation of the coming war, not to be found anymore in Germany. Our trip took us up to the summit of the *Erzgebirge* and the former border, and then along a steep concrete road down to the valley of the Elbe. It must have been about ten kilometers long, descending very steeply. We had a battle on our hands to brake our bicycles sufficiently to avoid a disaster. I believe this concrete road was at the time of its construction the first and only such road in Europe.

During these years this boy of my own age was my closest friend. Since most of the other boys in our apartment buildings where a year or so younger and the few older ones ignored us anyway, we had effectively a 'dominance duopoly' of power, after we had beaten the only other chap of our age into retreat. This happened without any violence, just the usual jousting of teenagers.

Any attempts to learn at this stage any details about the anatomy of the female gender remain subject to the censorship restrictions mentioned in the Introduction. Yes, that promise had been a bit over-hasty, maybe. On the other hand, such a subject was definitely not at the top of our agendas. That only developed quite a few years later.

In spite of the outbreak of the war in 1939, not everything was doom and gloom. The before-mentioned Sarrasani building in Dresden was sometimes used as a theater venue during the war. On some Sunday afternoon we went to see an operetta, which nowadays would probably be called a *Musical*. Our seats were right in front of the stage. Unfortunately, I remember neither the title, nor the story of this performance. But for some inexplicable reasons I vividly remember a dozen or so nubile ladies dancing on stage. Probably because of the scarcity of everything during the war, all the clothing they sported were some extremely thin and transparent gauze costumes. Shame! I felt very sorry for these young ladies, but we all had to suffer!

There were still some lighter moments in our lives. Sometime in 1941 we went to the Zirkus Sarrasani building again, to see the famous Spanish clown Charlie Rivel. His trademark was the cry: *Akrobat schôôôôn!* (acrobat be-au-ti-ful!). He was presented as a friend of Germany and an admirer of Hitler and the Nazis, possibly because of his sympathies for the Spanish Falange Party and its dictator General Franco. But irrespective of his political leanings, his act was tremendous.

We had just recently in biology class of our high school learned about the gingko tree and the distinctive form of its leaves. The teacher had explained that this once common family of trees was now reduced to a single species, and these trees were now very rare. During one of our visits to the '*Grosser Garten*' Park I discovered one of them. Much later I learned that millions of years ago this family of plants consisted of many species, but that there was now only a single surviving species left. In China, of all places! Our biology teacher did not know about the existence of this tree in this famous near-by Dresden park.

12

NIEDERFRAUENDORF AND QUOHREN

1930 TO 1942

I think that in the early '30s there existed generally no paid annual holidays for employees in Europe, because I seem to remember, that the socialist Blum government in France introduced this novelty only in about 1936. As a typical German middle-class family, we were, however, already much earlier able to afford a sort of summer holiday.

This took for us, as for most middle-class families in the same position, the form of a *Sommerfrische*, the summer break. This consisted of a stay of about one or two weeks at the home of a family member or at a *Pension* or a farmhouse someplace, where they took in paying guests to supplement their tight economy.

We went by bicycle to Niederfrauendorf, the home of the parents of my mother. These trips were quite an adventure for me, because we struggled uphill into the foothills of the *Erzgebirge*, the Ore Mountain for, I guess, about thirty to forty kilometers one way. It was quite a schlep, particularly in the summer evenings, when on our way home we had to traverse swarms of gnats dancing in the warm air above the sun-heated road surface. Some of these tiny chaps always found their way beneath my sunglasses into my eyes. But these trips gave me strong leg muscles, if nothing else.

All this cycling took place on gravel roads or on those covered with the famous 'Kid's Heads' square granite pavement stones with a vaulted surface, the size of a kid's head. Not a particularly tender expression, and no 'politically correct' concerns in the choosing of words in those days.

There were no tar roads then, except in towns and cities. All the highways had stone pavements, either the above-mentioned type, or what was called *Kleinpflaster*. This also consisted of square granite pavement stones, but they were only a quarter of the size and, thankfully, they had flat surfaces and were much easier to traverse and more bum-friendlier when riding our bicycles.

One of the many things I learned about from my maternal grandfather was how to remove, for a farmer or the village administration, the stump after a tree had been felled. Such a removal was obviously only occasionally required, particularly if the tree had been in the way of some development, or if it had been severely damaged by lighting or during a particularly heavy storm.

Grandfather used iron wedges, which he hammered with his sledgehammer into the stump until it split open like a pumpkin. This was heavy and tedious work and could last for an hour or more. He was smallish and looked rather puny, but how he swung that hammer was frightening!

Of the many contradictory or blurred memories of mine, one refers to Herr Stern, a Jewish businessman with whom my grandfather had dealings of an unknown purpose and character. He always was full of praise for this gentleman and for his fair attitude. Already at this time I wondered, how this agreed with his long-standing membership of the Nazi Party and the concomitant Anti-Semitism.

My grandfather had parted ways with the Party by 1934. He had written a scathing letter to Rudolf Hess, Hitler's deputy as Leader of the Party, detailing some examples of corruption in the local Party structures. The reply he received from Hess was unsatisfactory to him, and he returned his Party member-ship card. From there on, to the best of my knowledge, he abstained from any political activity, right up to the end of the Nazi rule.

Everything came for my grandparents to a premature end in 1934. The local farmers had constructed an earth dam above the village, and during a particularly heavy thunderstorm and cloud-burst this construction was swept away, creating tremendous flood waters. An avalanche of water, mud and stones was swept through the village. My grandfather just managed to avoid being swept away, by grabbing and hanging-on to two massive hooks in the wall on the lee side of his building, placed there to accommodate some long ladders. These hooks, and his quick thinking, saved his life.

Their cottage was inundated with mud several inches deep. The ground of the property was covered in a layer of rocks and loamy soil one meter deep. The circular concrete cover of their fresh water well in front of the house, which had a diameter of one and a half meter and must have weighed a ton, was carried away for a few hundred meters down to the next neighbor's cottage.

There lingered a peculiar reminiscence in connection with this catastrophe. As was usual in such cases, the leaders of both the mainline German churches, the Catholic as well as the Protestant ones, proclaimed their profound compassion with the victims. But there was additionally another voice: that of a *Reichsbischof* Müller, of some by me hitherto unheard-of church. However, as Wikipedia informs me now, at the instigation of Hitler, he had been elected back in 1933 as the leader of the Lutheran-Protestant Church of Germany. A telling illustration of how deep the party's influence reached already that early, and into which spheres.

Trying to translate his title made me realize, that the first part of this term cannot be translated properly. The term *"Reich"* turned up everywhere in Germany during the Nazi time, and even before. The literal translation would be "Imperial", but not having a *Kaiser* anymore, this made no sense. The term, as used by the Nazis, was meant to represent their *"Third Reich"* beginning 1933, after the first one, created in the Middle Ages and lasting until 1806, and the second one, lasting from 1871 to the end of WW1.

This flood had been quite a shock for my grandparents, and they decided to sell their property and to move to the village of Quohren, which was in walking distance (just three or four kilometers) to Kreischa. This was a typical German country town, with a few factories operating there. These were producing felt hats, mainly for ladies. My grandfather had already for many years been making the wooden *Hutformen*, the forms to press such hats, for these establishments.

Up to now he had to send them first by bus to Dresden, and then by tram to this small town. Things were now much more efficiently organized. My grandmother could load them onto her hand cart and deliver them directly to the factories, instead of the previous complicated (and costly!) method.

The property which they had bought consisted of an about eighty to one hundred years old double-story building on a parcel of land of about eight hundred square meters. It used to be a water mill, grinding the grain of the farmers of the surrounding villages. A creek had been dammed up, forming a pond, to provide the power to turn a two to three meters high wooden mill wheel fixed to the outside wall. Shortly after moving in the disposed of the dilapidated wheel, and they did the same with the equally dilapidated tenant living upstairs, but in a separate and different process.

My grandparents brought with them not only the wheelwright's and the hat-forms businesses, but also their menagerie of chickens and bees, but not the goats and sheep. Instead they now farmed carp and other fish in the pond formed by the mill creek. All these things were, of course, not hobbies, but supplementary forms for food or additional income.

I cannot remember whether the fishpond was drained every year or in some longer cycle. But I do remember the large bounty of fish from this modest pond. In order not to damage the fish us kids had to wade bare foot into the pond to collect the haul. Often, we had to dig them out of the mud covering the bottom of the pond. One of the fish species had long and strong spinal spikes, causing painful and festering wounds. But it was fun, or so we were told by our seniors!

Since my maternal grandparents were now living so much closer to Dresden, about twenty kilometers as opposed to about thirty to forty kilometers, we could visit them more often. By bicycle it took us, up-hill all the way, about two hours to get there, riding mostly through a beautiful valley.

On our frequent weekend visits grandma often dished up pickled rabbit as a Sunday Special. This had an unaccustomed and slightly sour taste, which was very pleasant. The meat had been marinated in a saltpeter lye. As dessert there often was pumpkin on the table. With its unusual sweet-sour taste, it was not exactly my glass of beer! But I suffered silently, since I was not given any choice.

The closer proximity to our apartment had some additional advantages. As mentioned already, my grandmother had a similar flock of chicken as she had had in Niederfrauendorf. From there we could not have taken home any eggs, because they would have perished on the terrible roads on our way back to Dresden. Now we could buy a dozen eggs every time we visited, for ten Pfennig a piece. This was particularly helpful, when during the war the monthly rations for eggs had again been reduced.

Don't be surprised about the ten Pfennig: sometimes grandmother was forced to buy eggs from her neighbors, and nobody gave away anything for nothing during the war years! Everybody was still very much aware, at least subconsciously, of the hard times not that long ago, when almost everybody had survived on a living standard one would nowadays almost consider as Third World.

As a young couple my grandparents, for instance, had to get up at three in the morning, to deliver newspapers in their Dresden suburb until five o'clock. Then my grandfather had to get ready for the trudge to his place of work, where he started at six, working until six in the evening. And that six days of the week. If he did not have his bicycle already, he had to march on foot, to save money. In any case, there probably was no public transport then in the suburbs.

I would guess that grandmother was also working in those days, possibly as a house maid, but I am not sure about that, because I know very little about her background, including her education and her working life.

A tram line, possibly a private one, was running from Niedersedlitz near Dresden via the suburb of Lockwitz to Kreischa. The rails of this line generally ran on one side of the road, and then, for unknown reasons, they appeared all of a sudden on the other side.

In those days we as cyclists barely noticed this, but when I visited Quohren in the 1960s with my wife and our son, driving my brother-in-law's big station wagon, I almost lost control over the car, when a tram appeared around the corner unexpectedly on the 'wrong' side of the road, squeezing us almost into the ditch.

This station wagon triggered another memory. On the gravel road from Kreischa to Quohren was a garden fence, which slightly intruded into the roadway, but the gap was nevertheless, in my memory, huuuuge. During our visit to Quohren in the 1960s the car just managed to clear this gap. This nicely illustrates, how a child's perception is preserved into old age, warts and all.

When cycling to Quohren, we had to pass through Lockwitz, down the steep street *Am Galgenberg* (On the Gallows' Hill). This small suburb must have been miniscule in the late Middle Ages and the early New Era times. It is frightening to think that such a tiny place needed gallows in those days. Even more frightening was the thought that on our way home we had to conquer this steep hill in the opposite direction.

13

MY HIGH SCHOOL YEARS

1934 TO 1942

In 1934, a for me momentous event took place: after an entrance examination I entered *Höhere Schule* (high school), namely the Ober-realschule Seevorstadt (named after a Dresden inner-city quarter) in the center of Dresden.

The monthly school fee for our school was RM30, representing 10% of my father's then salary. I recall that my father sold his beloved motorcycle at about this time, surely forced by economic circumstances, of which my entry into high school was probably the main factor.

This type of high school, as the German term implies, was more practice-orientated than the other main type, the *Gymnasium*. There the pupils were taught Latin and Greek from the beginning but, of course, also mathematics and all the other torture tools, with somewhat less weight on these latter subjects than in our type of school. In our *Oberrealschule*, on the other hand, we started with English in the first year and did not have to suffer Latin and Greek.

It turned out that I was the youngest in my class of thirty-four. I also found here a number of boys a year older than me, who had missed the transfer to the next form at the end of their first year. Later there were, naturally, many older boys in each of the classes, because every year the last two or three or so were not promoted to the next form. The modern mantra, that every single child must be pushed through the complete schooling system, right up into university, if possible at all, had not been developed yet, at least not in Germany.

These age differences led naturally to certain incidences of bullying, but nothing serious. Because I was able to assist some of my mates not only with their homework, but also in class by whispering the required answers to them, I survived the early years without any problems. Particularly, after I later became *Klassen Primus*, or 'First of Class'.

This was not the same as the prefect in the Anglo-American school systems, because this designation was entirely based on the achieved academic standards. But we also had the equivalent of the English prefect, who was appointed by the class teacher as the spokesman for the class. His main function was to keep the attendance record, and to report at the beginning of each lesson the class strength and any absenteeism.

The standard primary school *Abgangszeugnis*, the basic exit certificate, was issued at age fourteen to those pupils who had remained in primary school, which was the vast majority of all scholars. All of my references to age are based on the assumption that the pupil had been promoted each and every year to the next higher class.

In my time both types of our high schools were based on nine years of schooling.

- starting with the *Unterstufe*, the basic level: *Sexta* (sixth), *Quinta* (fifth), *Quarta* (fourth),
- followed by the *Mittelstufe*, the intermediate level: *Untertertia* (lower third), *Obertertia* (upper third), *Untersekunda* (lower second),
- and finally, the *Oberstufe*, the top level: *Obersekunda* (upper second), *Unterprima* (lower first) and *Oberprima* (upper first).

As one can see, these German educators did not only know their Latin, but they were properly organized as well. The critical reader has of course spotted immediately that somewhere in the past the system of the secondary schools consisted of only six forms, instead of the nine classes at my time.

This whole high school exercise covered normally nine years, from age ten to nineteen years. At age sixteen, at the end of *Untersekunda*, some pupils, sometimes with some nudging from the teachers, left with the *Mittlere Reife* (mid-level certificate), because they would not have survived the final three school years, which finally culminated in the *Abitur*, the university entrance certificate.

As far as I knew, all government schools in Germany in those days were either boys' or girls' schools, except those in the small villages. No such newfangled nonsense as co-ed establishments. The German education management was well routed in the ideas of the imperial pre-WW1 mindset. But I have the sneaky suspicion that because of that system, both boys and girls were deprived of some necessary life experiences in dealing with each other.

Already in 1934, when I joined my high school, I was given my adult-seized bicycle, because most times of the year I needed it to cycle to school in the inner-city of Dresden. This ride of seven kilometers one way was generally quite pleasant, but when the easterly winds were blowing, and they did this on most summer days, the ride home against a very strong headwind was a bit of a schlep. Only in winter, when there was snow and ice on the streets, would I use the tram or train.

In the summer months there was an additional aspect to report: if the outside temperature at ten in the morning read twenty-five degrees Celsius or more, we were spared the final hour of school and sent home, due to the excessive heat.

Here a funny incident during one of the winter months pops up in my memory: a few of us boys were standing in the tram, when a middle-aged lady joined us. She was wearing bright red lipstick. One of us asked *sotto voce*: "is it carnival already?" This clearly illustrates, how rare it was in those days for a woman to wear make-up, particularly lipstick, in public.

At the end of 1935, after having survived our first year at high school, the two lowest parallel classes were first amalgamated and then split again into a 5A and a 5B class for the next school year. Presumably this was done to balance out the academic levels of competence between the two classes.

But naturally nobody bothered to explain zilch to us boys. Communicating with the rising new generation was definitely not a priority in the authoritarian Nazi state. This dictatorial mindset had not been invented by them, but they further cultivated it for their own purposes. It had already existed in Germany under the *Kaiser*, and even well before. It was actually part of the national psyche.

Our high school building had probably been constructed in the 1880s or the 1890s. Everything was satisfactory in this imposing sandstone edifice, including the sanitary facilities. I suspect, these had been renovated, maybe in the 1920s. But not to over-do things: while we had a *Turnhalle*, a gymnasium, there were no showers anywhere to be found. As an aside, it was interesting to take note of the difference in the meaning of 'gymnasium' in German and in English.

In line with the vintage of the design of our high school building, the school yard was of Middle Age proportions. I remember that sprint events were only possible over sixty meters, and that at a push. The ground of this yard was covered by black cinders from the local *Gasanstalt*, the Household Gas Works, which used coke as their raw material. Any fall was not only painful, but usually required even more painful treatment with iodine.

Because of these restrictions, we had once a week sport lessons at *Ostragehege*, a wide grassy sports complex with a variety of soccer and other fields. On our way to these sports lessons we cycled past the Yenidze cigarette factory. This was one of Dresden's outstanding architectural sights. As an advertising gimmick, it was built like an oriental mosque. The chimney was disguised as the minaret, and the walls had oriental-looking mosaics (probably fake), and the whole large building looked decidedly outlandish.

Incidentally, this sports complex was also the home of the *Dresdner Sportclub* or *DSC*, which had between the wars very successful soccer teams, with German Championships, etc. I still remember their goal keeper's name, Willy Kress, and that of the central attacker, Helmut Schön, who after the war became the second national coach of the German national soccer teams, after Herberger, the first one, had left.

In 1934 or 1935 we had lost the only Jewish classmate I can remember. Why he left was, as usual, never explained to us. It was rumored that the school's director had suggested, or demanded, that this boy leave the high school. We never had another Jewish pupil in our class nor, as far as I know, in the school.

Two years after starting high school, another change took place. The *Annenschule*, one of the old-established gymnasia in Dresden, had to be closed down due to insufficient new student enrollments. This was one of the consequences of the diminishing number of the German population, as mentioned in the first part of this story.

To preserve the venerable name and traditions of this school, the education bureaucracy had decided to merge this failing school with our *Oberrealschule* (why not with another *Gymnasium instead?*). This combination of two distinctly different types of high schools received a new designation as an *Oberschule*, a neutral term without real meaning beyond that of a High School.

I remember very well that, as a sign of our opposition, we again dug out our distinct high school caps, which we previously had stopped wearing. Such a demonstration was rather atypical in the Nazi era! This new education regime caused one major change in our life, meaning in our curriculum: with the start of *Quarta* in the third year, we were now condemned to having to cope with Latin. I did not have any real problem with this innovation, but some of my mates battled constantly.

One of my lasting memories of the early high school years was, as usual, rather childish (but we were just kids!). After a new teacher had introduced himself to the class, he would ask us to state our names, and he would make notes about what he heard. If a name was unusual, he would ask the pupil to spell it.

Whenever it was the turn of one of our classmates, we would start to giggle in anticipation of what we knew would follow. To the consternation of the poor teacher, and to our merriment, Ryczynski would spell his name with the speed of a machine gun. I can still today repeat this as fast as he could.

Another memorable pupil was a German American. I think the father was American. This chap, very strong and built rather sturdily, often performed a feat which always amazed us. He would stand on the seat of one of our combined bench-and-table pieces of furniture, relax and simply let himself fall into these combinations, without ever injuring himself.

In 1942, shortly before we all went to the army, he suddenly had disappeared. Rumor had it that he had tried to cross the German-Swiss border and had been apprehended and executed as a deserter. Where did such rumors come from? Were they maybe lanced by the authorities, to discourage such behavior?

In about 1937 one of my classmates was transferred to the *NaPoLA*, the *National Politische Lehranstalt*, a special type of high school for the boys of the politically well connected. I did not know what his father's claim to fame was, but he had to have been high up in the Nazi hierarchy, or had to have some special attribute, to warrant such a privilege for his son. I regretted losing the boy as a friend, with whom I often had played chess.

Unfortunately for my teachers, I was rather an unruly and obnoxious troublemaker and rebel. In one of the higher classes, probably around 1940, I disrupted lessons so often that I collected thirteen *Strafstunden* (penalty hours), and the director of the school issued a *consilium abeoitum* (I hope to have remembered the correct spelling), the advice to leave the school in order to avoid expulsion. My father, who was still in the army, somehow must have managed to save me. He never mentioned this matter, ever, but the problem seemed to simply have evaporated.

Not only was I always a pain in the you know where for the unpopular teachers, we also played some nasty tricks on some of them. My pet hate was the history teacher, because I loved the subject and he managed to alienate me from enjoying the history lessons by his lack of knowledge and/or interest. When, for instance, I had asked him in class about the background to the recent appointment by the Japanese of the deposed Chinese emperor to the imperial throne of Manchukuo, his reply was: where is this place?

He had earlier made the mistake of boasting about his well-behaved daughter of our own age, as opposed to us hooligans. After school I went to a phone booth and wasted 10 Pfennig of my precious pocket money to phone a professional midwife and to send her to his home. She explained that she wanted to attend to the impending birth of twins for the young lady of the house. Surprisingly, and to our disappointment, he never mentioned this mishap, but in future he refrained from extolling the virtues of his daughter.

Another teacher, he was teaching German, was named Stein (Stone in English). He was so well fed that we called him the 'Rolling Stone', practicing our newly acquired sparse English knowledge. I cannot remember, whether we gave him this name, or whether the moniker was of older vintage, invented by previous classes. But now you know, from where a certain rock and roll band plagiarized their name!

A school friend of mine, whose parents ran a prosperous shop in the Strehlen suburb, possessed a complete collection of the in Germany famous *Karl May* adventure books, about sixty of them. He lent them to me, one after the other, and I read them all. Since time after school was too valuable to waste with reading, I was forced to read them under the bench during classes. I'm still amazed that I was never caught out. I suppose it helped, that I was occupying a bench in the last row of the classroom.

At this stage we were assigned a young no-nonsense teacher, who was not afraid to give an unruly pupil a deserved slap in the face. The first sinner who experienced this treatment was none other than my *Karl May* benefactor. This pupil was the only one I remember, who collected a thick ear in class, when this teacher had smacked him quite hard, after he had been insolent. This had no consequence for the teacher, because such reaction was deemed quite acceptable in those days in Germany.

He also classified one of our classmates as *DFFG: dumm, faul, frech und gefrässig* (stupid, lazy, insolent and gluttonous). No necessity then for any compliance with 'politically correct' standards, because this nonsense had not been invented yet. We found this reaction by him to be fair and reasonable, and we adored the man. Needless to say, that we lost him to the war effort immediately after the outbreak of hostilities.

One of my standing gripes at school was the, in my expert opinion, unfair weighing of subject notes. In our drawing lessons I excelled probably as the scholar on the bottom rung with my '6' note, the worst one. We also had so-called music lessons. But neither did that teacher know much about music, nor could he play a single instrument, as far as I knew.

Instead, during lesson time, he ordered us to read something or other in one of our textbooks, while he wrote critiques of theater and concert events for the local newspapers. Subsequently, we were tested in singing and similar efforts. And because I could easily clear a concert hall by my singing, I received another '6', which surely was not merited, since I could at least play the pianoforte. These bottom rankings were balanced against my '1' grades in history and German. Bloody nuisance!

In summer we always enjoyed our weekly visits to the *Arnoldbad*, a large (Olympic size?) open-air swimming pool, named after its donor to the city of Dresden. Unfortunately, he was Jewish, thus its name urgently had to be changed early in the Nazi years. But as happened in many similar cases, the old name remained in use by the locals.

There we learned to swim and dive properly, retrieving a brick from the deep end of the pool. We also obtained there our cherished *Fahrtenschwimmerschein*, certifying to have successfully performed forty-five minutes of uninterrupted swimming.

One of the highlights of the year was the stay at a *Schullandheim*, an establishment either belonging to the school, or which had been rented for the purpose. Occasionally we stayed at a *Jugendherberge*, a youth hostel, which before and during the Nazi era used to be a big thing in Germany. The whole class, including two or three teachers, would stay there for two weeks.

The accommodation was basic, but clean and quite pleasant. Our teachers would give lessons outside the normal curriculum, telling us about interesting facts and trying to interest us in some peripheral subjects. We also would go on excursions and would hike through nature. These stays would normally happen in summer, but I am not sure, whether during school days or the summer break.

During one of these stays we were roped in to go out and collect as many *Kartoffelkäfer* or potato beetles as possible. We were told that this North American pest had arrived only recently in

Europe. These beetles were claimed to be decimating the potato harvests. And when it came to potatoes, Germans got dead serious!

Another maligned pest was the *Gelbrandkäfer* or yellow-bordered beetle. They were also illegal immigrants and were accused of attacking our freshwater fish. They would therefore only be found next to rivers and creeks.

A further pest of similar seriousness was the *Woll-handkrabbe*, a large river crab, which was destroying the indigenous crab fauna, and affecting the fish populations as well. All these pests were considered 'enemies of the state' and were persecuted as fervently as the communists! We were entitled to fringe benefits for eliminating as many of them (the pests) as possible.

One such stay we experienced in winter in Seiffen, a small town in the *Erzgebirge*, the Ore Mountain. We went there with our skis and received lessons by a local ski instructor. I battled, as usual, because of my weak ankles and I just managed the snow-plough, but the slalom and similar more advanced activities were beyond my very limited skiing capabilities.

But we had a lot of fun with a large loose (our effort?) sheet-metal traffic sign, which was buckled in the middle and served as a very fast toboggan on the ice-covered snow. This contraption was rotating while shooting down a steep slope. Amazingly, nobody was hurt.

More sedately, I was able to buy a beautifully carved wild boar from a local wood-carving artisan, who finished the piece while I waited and watched him work. I wonder, where this artefact was lost to eternity.

Another year saw us at the castle of some former local lord near Rochlitz on the river Mulde. This area was the home of the famous Rochlitz Porphyry rock species. I still regret that I did not collect a specimen, which would have fitted very nicely into the rock collection I started some seventy years later. Instead, we had rescued a hedgehog out of the swollen river, but it had drowned, unfortunately. And it was ballooning already and could only be interred with the honors befitting such a distinctly prickly chap.

During one of these stays in these establishments we experienced something unsettling for us boys. One of our classmates climbed into bed with another boy. Today it is clear that these two were homosexuals. But at the time, we were still innocent enough to not really understand what went on, beyond the realization that something was very unusual with such behavior.

It has to be remembered that in Germany in those days the whole gay scene was shrouded in mystery and seclusion. Openly homosexual men did not exist, because such sexual inclination would have landed them in jail. Obviously, they did exist in secret, and occasionally rumors surfaced about certain well-known men. As far as the Nazis were concerned, such behavior could not possibly be happening in the Arian *Reich*.

In still another year the class found itself in such an institution at the *Königstein fortress*. This was a historical site, where many *VIPs* had been incarcerated over the centuries. Some had been competitors of the rulers for the favors of a court lady. Among the ruling monarchs it was particularly *August der Starke* (August the Strong), who made a name for himself in this regard.

During World War I some high-ranking Allied officers were incarcerated here, because the security was relatively easy to maintain, and at the same time the comfortable accommodation and ambiance was in line with the rank and status of the captives.

As has been honestly documented already, at our high school existed the usual unruly-teenager-syndrome. In addition, do I dare to mention a slowly awakening interest in the girls? Or in women, those unknown live forms, to plagiarize Oswald Kolle. By the way, the Nazi Party, and particularly the Hitler Youth, were very finicky about things like alcohol consumption or pre-marital sex. As all socialists, they were as prudish as the communists in the Soviet Union. But for us schoolboys this was probably just as well, I suppose.

The above does not mean to imply that there was no debauchery and hanky-panky during the Nazi time. Only that it was frowned upon and suppressed as far as possible, including any disclosure about such behavior. Fact is that there were some untoward goings on, in particular in the *SA*, and the rest of the *Hitlerjugend* was also not always as good as yours truly. Ahem!

It should be kept in mind that practically all our teachers during the war years were at or beyond retirement age, and most were well past this point. Because the younger ones were in the army, of course. This was not a big problem for the languages, history or mathematic lessons, but in the natural sciences, in biology, chemistry and physics, there existed for these subject teachers a huge knowledge deficiency.

They had gone to university or the Pedagogic Institutes, the specialized teacher training institutions, in the 1870s or 1880s, and their knowledge was generally frozen as of this period. Continuing to study, as is demanded from teachers today (at least in theory) was not usual then. The result was that they were simply not even close to being up to date in their disciplines.

They could neither explain an electron microscope, nor even some advanced electrical phenomena, nor why iron atoms could have different valences in their isotopes. I only found out much later from our son that fungi were not part of the flora kingdom, as we had been taught. But maybe I am unfair here: this change in taxonomy possibly happened only in later years.

The only teacher who kept himself up to date, as far as I could say, was our English teacher. He had worked for German military intelligence (G2 in US parlance) during WWI, and he was involved with listening to and deciphering enemy military signals traffic in France. Occasionally, he showed us a few tricks in connection with the use of English. If you members of the cellphone generation thought you have invented 'u for you' and 'r for are', I must disappoint you. The English army used these and other contractions already during WW1, and probably even before that time.

A peculiar thought has just hit me. Whenever we had to write an essay I sat in my bench and battled to fill two or three pages. No imagination, no fantasy! Now I write a whole book and whenever I go through what I have written, additional aspects and incidents just appear out of nowhere in my mind. But the comparison, as I very well know, is invalid: the essays required these attributes of fantasy and imagination, whereas this book is simply a string of reminiscences and facts, with some more or less original (?!) thoughts thrown in.

At the end of the 1940 school year, the two parallel classes of our age group in *Untersekunda* were reorganized again, similar to what had happened in 1935 in *Quinta*. This time the combined bunch of boys was separated in a mathematical/natural sciences stream and a history/language one. I opted, for obvious reasons, for the second choice. Both streams retained most of the studies as before, but in both were one or two additional disciplines added, and in many cases the importance of the remaining ones were now somewhat modified.

In my case, the additional language was Spanish. Despite the war, we also now had the opportunity to read and study newspapers from London, which came out of Gibraltar or Lisbon, probably via the *Legion Condor*. It was a bit embarrassing (but not too much) that in this new configuration I came again first in mathematics in my class.

But my poor results for chemistry and physics, which I blamed on the same teacher, confirmed the wisdom of my earlier choice. I always have had difficulties to learn by *rote* the things for which I could not see the logical connections, or for which I lacked the necessary interest. Worst were the formulas and free-standing terms like scientific names, whereas I had very little problems with history and the languages.

The winter of 1941/1942 was even colder in Germany than the infamous one of 1928/1929. At this stage during the winter months I was going to school by train. This meant a walk of about twenty minutes to our suburban railway station. One morning, before starting out, we checked the thermometer and were shocked to read a minus twenty-six degrees Celsius. Twice I had to find refuge on my way to the station in some building foyer because of the terrible cold, despite wearing mittens, earmuffs and all available winter clothing my mother could find.

Because of the by then terrifying auspices for the *Wehrmacht* the government decided that the military could not wait for us to finish our schooling, and that we would be needed immediately in the Armed Forces. Sometime in the spring of 1942 the remaining members of the two parallel classes of our school's *Unterprima* met after school. Some of the older boys, who had missed a promotion to the next form sometime in the past, had already been drafted earlier.

We had a drink or three of watery beer at one of the inner-city cafés. At this sad occasion, we took leave of our remaining class chums and also of our prematurely truncated school experience. I think we were all together less than a dozen or so from each of the two streams. I ask myself how many of us did survive the war? And are there still any around with me, I also wonder. These questions are justified, because of the 1924 vintage of Germans more than 38% did not survive, the third worst percentage (Wikipedia).

14

WARTIME TEENAGE YEARS

1939 TO 1942

After the war had started, we slowly but surely felt the consequences. Right from the start ration cards for food and many other things were introduced. The Government issued standard food ration cards, but also special ones for heavy-duty laborers and pregnant women, and also Traveling Food Ration Cards, which one could obtain by exchanging them for the standard ones.

In addition to the food rations, there were separate cards for clothing, shoes and later even for household goods. The latter were for the people who had lost all or most of their personal possessions in the Allied bombing raids. There was practically nothing, which was not rationed. Everything had been worked out in detail long before the war broke out and had been organized in the typical German fashion!

The issuing of all these cards was not done by state or municipal personnel, but by the *NSV*, the *National Sozialistische Volkswohlfahrt*, the social services organization attached to the Nazi Party. Until my draft in 1942 there never was, as far as I know, any corruption in these activities. Maybe because the consequences of getting caught would have been frightening, probably the death penalty. But I am also convinced that the strong social bonds within the population at this time contributed to the correct behavior of all participants.

From 1939 to 1942 the rations were slowly reduced as the war progressed and the economic situation of Germany deteriorated. More and more things either disappeared from the shops or were replaced by *Ersatz*. Already in WW1 the infamous *Ersatzkaffee*, coffee made from cereals, had appeared, but this was now joined by *Kunsthonig*, honey made from molasses and sugar, *Ersatzleder*, a leather substitute fabricated from some-thing or other, plus a few other substitutions.

One of the earliest reminiscences I have of the war years took place on Sylvester of 1939, at the end of the first year of the war. My friend and I were standing in the street and he said: "What a pity that the war will be over before we have a chance to join the army". This was the general attitude of the older teenagers. So much for our all-knowing teenager prophecies.

My father had been mobilized immediately before World War II had started in 1939 with the eighteen-day campaign against Poland. This time he was drafted as a corporal in the Quarter-master Corps, instead of as an infantryman as in WW1. Probably so because of his background of this first war and his internal audit experience at the *Dresdner Bank*. Possibly also because of his pre-war foreign assignments for the bank.

He soon found himself in Radom and later in Cracow in Poland. In the spring of 1940, shortly before the start of the campaign against France, Belgium, the Netherlands and Luxem-bourg, he was stationed near the Netherlands border. After the attack had started his unit was first deployed in Maastricht in the Netherlands, from where he dispatched home several tins of *Ritmeester* cigars for future consumption.

Shortly after Dunkirk he was able to send us a few times three vitally important things: several 1kg tins of lard and some tins of Scho-ka-kola, the famous caffeine and cola-laced dark chocolate for the German Special Forces, and finally many of the oval tins of 50 of the British 'Players' cigarettes, left behind by the retreating British.

From 1940 onwards, he found himself in a string of towns in France, including Paris, and finally Caen in the Normandy. One day in 1941 he sent us photos and a picture postcard of the abbey of Mont St. Michel. He must have been granted a short-term leave to visit this marvelous place. Sixty-five years later my wife and I went to visit the town as tourists, and I was able to see for myself what these photos had shown us then.

After the successful French campaign Hitler promoted twelve (Wikipedia) Colonel Generals and Generals to Field Marshals. This was out of all proportions to the size of the Armed Forces. Two or three such promotions would have been more appropriate. But excessive promotions happened thereafter regularly, right to the bitter end of the war, obviously to maintain the spirits of the officer corps.

In one of his later hours-long speeches over the radio, Hitler announced the promotion of Hermann Göring to the rank of *Reichsmarschall*, a title last used in the German Middle Ages. This made him the number two of the armed forces, after Hitler had appointed himself years earlier as Supreme Commander. Hitler also directed then that Göring would succeed him in all of his numerous other functions, if he should die or become incapacitated. Presumably this would have excluded the position of the Leader of the Party?

Early in 1941 German armies defeated and occupied in quick succession Yugoslavia, Albania and Greece, and Bulgaria and Romania subsequently became German vassals. This had rendered the complete Balkan peninsula a German-occupied territory. Having neutralized the imminent (?) Soviet military threat in 1939, and to have conquered Poland and France and to have defeated the British Expeditionary Force was seen almost as a miracle.

To have occupied the Netherlands and Belgium as well as Denmark and Norway additionally to the Balkan, Hitler appeared to win at whatever he attempted militarily. No wonder that the German people, including more and more of the lower- and middle-ranked officer corps, overwhelmingly considered Hitler an infallible military genius.

Even more importantly, the majority of the German generals seemed to think so, too. Combined with their pre-WW1 almost religious attitude towards their Supreme Commander, the *Kaiser* and his perceived successor, the *Fuehrer*, this partially explains why they could not manage to get rid of Hitler as soon as they had realized that Germany would lose the war, namely in June of 1941, when he started the sudden attack against the Soviet Union.

It was a new experience for us in Dresden when periodically the air raid sirens would make their infernal noise. Until February of 1945 Dresden was spared the air raids which had devastated most other German cities and towns by then, but we had to be prepared, nevertheless. This meant, all windows had to be blacked-out with blankets, paper or Venetian blinds. Motor vehicles and even bicycles had to have some cover over their lamps, which allowed only a small sliver of light to illuminate the traffic lanes. All streetlights remained switched off permanently.

Whenever the sirens went off and started their banshee howling, we quickly had to rush down into our basement, with a small leather satchel containing the vital documents of the family, including the all-important ration cards, the savings books and personal and ID documents. Also taken were some blankets and warm clothing. There was generally good companionship amongst the tenants, even sometimes with singing, to pass the time until eventually the sirens announced the end of the air raid alarm.

We also had to be prepared against incendiary bombs being dropped. We had to clear out our attics, removing as far as possible all combustible stuff to reduce the dangers of fires starting in the wooden roof constructions and supports. This had the probably intended side-effect that much raw material was collected for re-cycling and helping the war effort.

We teenagers were able to earn some pocket money by collecting the more important materials, such as copper, lead and brass. As a consequence of these activities it is probable that quite a few things disappeared from the households without the adults' knowledge or consent.

Shortly after the start of the war the government had ordered that in all continuous city blocks a passage had to be broken at basement level into the firewalls separating the individual buildings. This was meant to provide an escape route, in case one of the apartment blocks had collapsed. It was a well-intentioned idea which had, however, catastrophic consequences, because this order produced an unfortunate and unintended side effect.

If one section of the row of buildings caught fire, this would now sweep through the whole block, since the apartment buildings were built wall to wall, and without any break other than the firewalls. Because of these breakthroughs these prescribed walls between the individual buildings failed under the fire-storm conditions. This was one of the reasons why the bombing raids were so devastating, because uninterrupted rows of apartment blocks constituted the majority of the buildings in the German inner cities.

During the war, the propaganda machine operated at high speed. In addition to their many other often nefarious activities the Nazis were producing films like on a production line at the Berlin-Babelsberg studios of the *UFA*, the *Universal Film Academy*. At this time, we did not even know the meaning of this abbreviation, which ironically was in English! Probably because it was under the bad influence of the "Jewish smut-factory" Hollywood.

The Tobias studios in Vienna also produced dozens of films. In both cases they were mostly entertaining ones, to divert the people's worries about the negative news regarding the war. Comedians like Hans Moser, Heinz Rühmann, Theo Lingen, and dancing stars like Marika Rökk, or singers like Zarah Leander (Sweden) and Johannes Heesters (Netherlands) were not only entertaining the homeland, but also the spread-out troops.

However, there were also many heroic and political (propaganda) films, like Veit Harlan's 'Jud Süss'. I have to admit that I liked most of them, including the latter one. Quite apart from the intention to create anti-Semitic reactions, this one was, in my opinion, an excellent and historically correct film, showing the corrupt attitudes and actions of the German ruling classes of the 18th and 19th centuries. As mentioned already, I always have had a special interest in history.

I remember very clearly, how we sat in the evening in front of our radio, listening to the news, and in particular to the *Wehrmachtsbericht*, the daily bulletin released by the *OKW*, the *Oberkommando der Wehrmacht*, the supreme command of the armed forces. It reported the events in the various theaters of the war, interspersed with some propaganda, wherever this was feasible.

These sessions in front of the radio included those occasions, when German victories were dominantly reported, often linked to named individuals. Outstanding amongst those was the feature of *Kapitänleutnant* Prien, who managed to enter the Royal Navy harbor of Scapa Flow with his *Unterseeboot U47* penetrating all their defenses, and to sink some British battle ships and cruisers.

This success was particularly satisfying for the German listeners, because this was the place, where in 1919 the remainder of the German High Seas fleet had to be handed over to the British, but where the German sailors succeeded in scuttling their ships. There was a distinct element of sweet revenge involved here for us.

After a successful battle in the Rio de la Plata off Montevideo, Uruguay, the pocket-battleship 'Admiral Graf Spee' had to be scuttled. And after sinking some enemy ships in the North Sea, the battleship 'Bismarck', the crown jewel of our navy, was also lost, together with many others in various encounters.

The German navy of the high-seas did not really have a chance in this war, because its strengthening, from a small basis enforced by the Versailles treaty at the end of WW1, which would have required at least a decade, but was only started a few years before the second world war started. The mostly unsuccessful battles of our High-Seas Navy were heroic, for sure, but also too tragic to create feelings beyond our tragic feelings for the lost lives. We also had difficulty to properly envisage these situations.

Another victory which I remember relates to General Dietl of the Mountain Infantry. These troops found themselves in the unaccustomed role of a marine infantry, who managed to snatch Narvik in Northern Norway from the advancing British forces. Occupying this strategic town secured the connection to Lulea in Sweden, the source of the high-grade iron ore for the blast furnaces in the *Ruhrgebiet*, the industrial heart of the heavy industry in Germany.

Just like in WW1, the air aces were again highly popular with the people. Major Mölders was the first one to become famous, then Graf, and later Gallant, who eventually became the general in charge of all the fighter planes and their pilots. Whenever one of these aces was shot down, the whole country was in mourning.

After the Italians had attacked Egypt from their colony of Libya, and had suffered a bloody nose for their trouble, Germany was more or less forced to assist our allies in North Africa from February 1941 to June 1943 (Wikipedia). This expeditionary Army Corps was quickly established and sent through Italy into Libya.

Generalfeldmarschall Rommel with his *Afrika Korps* was a

popular hero in Germany. He and his troops surely were admired, but this theater was just too far removed to create the same mental attachment to these war heroes as to the soldiers fighting closer to home. People simply could not visualize what was going on in the African desert, so far away.

To start with, Rommel drove the British Army back into Egypt, but the hoped-for German blockade of the Suez Canal did not materialize. In the victorious battle of Tobruk the Allies, and in particular the South Africans, suffered heavy losses and many prisoners of war were captured.

The Korps was eventually forced back into Tunisia, where it had to capitulate. The Corps reserves stationed in Sicily and some of the units, which had managed to withdraw from Tunisia, were the first to defend Italy against the Allies after they had later landed on the island.

On the Russian front Colonel Rudel became a famous war hero, for destroying 500 or so Russian tanks with his battle plane, despite being a leg amputee. He received, as the only German, the highest German war medal. After the war he regrettably was an unrepentant and outspoken Paleo-Nazi, if I may be allowed to create a new word combination. Because I cannot very well call him a Neo-Nazi, since he had been a fanatical Nazi practically all his life, which he confirmed unashamedly after the war.

There is something else, which immediately comes to mind in this regard: I cannot remember, whether we still had our old *Mende* radio receiver, or did we already have one of the newfangled *Volksempfänger?*

Another thing I do clearly remember about these years is the fact that during the war years up to 1942 there were never disruptions of the electric power or the water and household gas supply in my hometown. Not even when almost all of Dresden was burned down in 1945.

Closer to home, actually only fifty meters away from our apartment, something new had developed. A family, which owned the largest sawmill in the district, was living there in a proper nineteenth century villa. They somehow had acquired a stash of Swiss cheese, sorry, always food on my mind in those days, of Swiss postage stamps. They had found out that I was a stamp collector, and they asked me to sort these stamps for them, offering me the duplicates as an incentive. I naturally jumped at this opportunity to enlarge my collection.

In an outbuilding of their villa, presumably a former chauffeur's apartment, they housed a dozen or so French *Fremdarbeiter*, the Forced Laborers of the Nazi war, who were working in their sawmill. However, I nowadays have some doubts about this current 'forced' terminology: there was nobody guarding these men and they could move around freely. The wages, and more importantly, the food rations were much better in Germany than in occupied France. I suspect that they may have come voluntarily after the French defeat. But one must not raise any doubts about the well-established figments of the global imagination of what is PC (politically correct), and what is not.

All our wishful thinking about the war soon ending evaporated painfully in June 1941, when Germany attacked the Soviet Union. I think that the majority of Germans, including yours truly, realized then that this was the beginning of the end. Even died-in-the-wool Nazis had un-good feelings about this development, since Hitler had declared in his 'bible' *Mein Kampf* (My Struggle) that simultaneous fighting on the eastern and on the western fronts during World War I had been fatal for Germany.

Hitler's reasons for starting this campaign were difficult for me to understand. As far as I remember, there was no known imminent danger of a Russian attack. The early setbacks for the Soviet Army, and the apparent disorganization of their military efforts at that time, seemed to bear this out. But the justification given by the Nazi propaganda machine was that a Soviet surprise attack was imminent, and that Germany therefore had been forced to react preemptively.

From the beginning of the Russian campaign on 22 June 1941 my father was again on the move, always following closely behind the advancing troops. Because of his age he was, as mentioned earlier, a member of the Quartermaster Corps. His unit supported in Russia the 6th Army, which was eventually encircled and destroyed in Stalingrad.

He was sufficiently far behind the front lines to escape the terrible fate of these sacrificial troops, which had been forbidden by

Hitler to break out of the encircling forces and ordered to fight to the last man. Because he was in the rear support area, he was at the time of this catastrophe stationed at Stalino, from where he was evacuated by a JU 52.

This year also saw the unbelievable spectacle of the flight to Great Britain of Rudolf Hess, Hitler's deputy as Leader of the Nazi party. This was dramatic news, because absolutely nobody could imagine what was really going on. Goebbels announced, in typical damage control mode that Hess had commandeered, in temporary mental obfuscation, a Messerschmidt plane from the Augsburg (or was it Regensburg?) air base. His declared objective, to try to arrange a separate peace between Germany and Great Britain, was officially ridiculed. The people were completely confused. Something like that could simply not happen! I still wonder today what the real background to this mystery was.

Sometime during 1941 I attended the *Tanzstunde*, up to this time the almost obligatory dancing lessons for teenagers. This was, of course, a very welcome novelty, because even the Party could not organize this entertainment without the presence of young ladies. And there were about thirty of them. I got paired, of course in all innocence, with the daughter of a prominent Dresden Huguenot family of the pre-religious wars French lower aristocracy.

Their ancestors had arrived in Germany as religious refugees almost four hundred years ago. My family, at least the male branch, seemed to have a special affinity with the Huguenot people!

I will not bother you with the ungainly results of this cultural enterprise. Suffice to say, that nothing apart from our dancing enterprise had developed between us.

Another of the young ladies was less reserved and sent me a *billet d'amour* shortly before these enjoyable exercises ended. Despite the fact that she lived with her mother in the Dresden suburb of Stetsch, about fifteen kilometers away from our apartment, I tried to be with her as often as possible. I would take our tram to meet her in the city, usually under the large public clock on *Postplatz*, the central place in front of the main Dresden Post Office. After a visit to the cinema or some other exciting adventure, I naturally brought her home, this time by using her tram.

After saying a quick good-bye for about sixty minutes, the last tram had naturally long left and I trudged home on foot. My mother was not pleased, but I did not mind the long walk all that much. There were, after all, compensations attached, which are, however, of no interest to anybody else. Throughout my army days we wrote to each other at least once a week.

In the spring of 1942, a peculiar thing happened on the way to my growing up. The suspected first great love of my father turned up one day to visit my mother. That would not be worth recording, if she would not have brought her fourteen-or fifteen years old daughter. While the old people had their (Ersatz) coffee in the sitting room, we went to our large living-in kitchen to listen to the radio. Nice music was playing, and we started to dance, and I could show-off my imagined newly acquired dancing prowess.

Somehow my hand must have wandered, and all by itself, from her waist upwards, and to my embarrassment and surprise, I found my hand cupping her breast. She started shaking, as if under an electric current. I didn't know what was going on and quickly removed my hand, which resulted in her quieting down. No word was uttered by either of us. Funny people, these young girls. All this commotion for no reason, I reckoned.

Better to delete this last paragraph, as it is not suitable for young readers. Any older readers, please uninstall what you just read, and be ashamed of yourself! On the other hand, I don't want to give the impression that I did not know anything about any of the facts of life. After all, from my time during my many summer holidays in Niederfrauendorf, I knew that the rooster climbed onto the hens to produce our breakfast eggs, and that the neighbor's bull pumped up the cows to make them release the milk! After all, I was a teenager and up to date!

In April 1942 (Wikipedia) the French general Giraud had escaped from the before-mentioned fortress of Königstein near Dresden. We only heard about this in drips and drabs and without any details, and only by way of rumors. The authorities were here in a cleft stick. On the one hand, they would have loved to keep the whole embarrassing story a state secret. But on the other hand, they needed the help of the civilian population in the Dresden region. As far as I know, he was not recaptured in the short period I was still at home, before I joined the army a short while later.

In June of 1942 (Wikipedia) another setback happened. Reinhard Heydrich, a high-ranking *SS* general in charge of their Secret Police, who had recently been appointed deputy of the German governor of the rump-Czechia protectorate of *Böhmen und Mähren*, after the *Sudetenland* had been occupied by the *Reich* and Slovakia had obtained her 'independence'. He was assassinated by terrorists, or freedom fighters, take your pick!

This was memorable for me because a black commemorative stamp and a stamp block were issued by the German postmaster, the block, however, only to some well-connected individuals, which sadly did not include me. I only knew this stamp block from the catalogs.

My father was demobilized only in 1943, when I was already a soldier myself for many months. The *Dresdner Bank* had requisitioned him to head again the internal audit section. He had been spared any mishap during his second participation in a World War.

In June of 1942 just about the last thing, which happened before the end of my civilian life, was the *Musterung*, the military inspection of the future recruits. We were checked out by a mixed team of medical doctors and officers, and the doctors found that that I was 1,71m tall and that my feet were not up to military standards. The problems with my feet were already well known to me, and my height was duly noted in my memory for future use.

At this stage the officers were desperately looking for recruits for their infantry regiments, which meant marching duty. Because of my feet they found me wanting for their preferred branch of the army and they drafted me instead into the motorized infantry. An elegant solution to their problem, since the German army was already then short of vehicles and, above all, of fuel. As I soon was to find out.

But then things developed in an unforeseen direction from what the German High Command had planned for me.

PART III

REFLECTIONS ON NAZI
GERMANY

- HOW AND WHY? (1933 TO 1942)

15

PERCEPTIONS OF THE GERMAN PEOPLE

Obviously, regarding the Nazi time prior to my joining of the army, I can only talk about my own experiences and what I saw and heard from family, friends and acquaintances, including my school friends. A large part of my reminiscences of this period is based on what I read in the newspapers, heard on the radio and saw on the weekly newsreels, and I am well-aware of the fact that most of this had been doctored, if not outright manufactured, by the Propagandaminister. Clearly, by necessity I was a biased reporter, but I strove to be always as honest and unbiased as possible.

On January 30 of 1933 the Nazis took over the government of Germany. Contrary to what many people nowadays may assume, they did so not by a political or military *coup*, but in accordance with the German constitution. After having fairly won the parliamentary elections at the end of 1932, they had been invited by the President of Germany, Field Marshall von Hindenburg, to form the next government.

There can be no doubt that the extremely able Minister of Propaganda and Enlightenment of the People (that was his official title!) Dr. Joseph Goebbels, over the following years successfully brain-washed the German people and indoctrinated them very convincingly in the Nazi ideology. This was easy enough, by building on the pre-existing perceptions outlined in the first part of this narrative.

This brainwashing, naturally enough, was particularly successful with the youth. The rate of success was originally almost one hundred percent for the school kids, especially since there was no counter-reaction from the democratic-minded people, such as many teachers. They simply did not dare to speak out.

The acceptance of Hitler and the Party by the adult population was from the beginning very high. Especially in the police and amongst the public servants generally. If one adds the situation regarding the military officers and soldiers, the early approval ratings were a political dream situation for the Party.

These latter groups were looking up to Hitler, particularly from about 1936 onwards, as some political and military genius, who had restored German military honor and national pride. The fact that he had built up a huge military machine, which by necessity created plenty of prestigious ranks and titles, had probably also something to do with this admiration.

Contrary to what many people believe, there was never such a thing as any censorship in Nazi Germany. For the very simple reason, that every single newspaper, magazine, radio station, book publisher, film or theater company was headed by a Nazi editor or manager, who made sure, out of conviction, or in their own survival interest, that there was no upsetting the applecart. There was, of course, no TV at the time, apart from some experimental emissions during the 1936 Olympics, which were in any case organized by the Party.

The November 1933 referendum about Germany's membership of the League of Nations clearly showed the German people's disenchantment with the past. 95% of the voters (Ploetz) demanded that Germany leave this organization. This result was apparently not doctored, as has regularly happened with later referenda and election results.

The general acceptance of a totalitarian system can also be observed in the question of the labor unions. Up to 1933 there operated numerous unions in Germany: politically neutral ones, some bound to political parties, and also some religiously orientated ones.

In 1933 the Party created the *DAF,* the *Deutsche Arbeitsfront,* as the only labor confederation allowed to exist, which took over all the previous unions (and their assets!), without any serious dissent.

The *DAF* almost never became active in the interests of the workers, but in a totalitarian state this was not considered necessary. Ask any labor unionist in a communist country! Typically, there never was any strike action during the Nazi period, as far as I know. No labor union opposition to be found here as well, as explained above.

The *NSDAP*, the *National Sozialistische Deutsche Arbeiter Partei*, had its ideology and its actions based on two main pillars, as expressed by its name: Nationalism and Socialism. During the election campaigns up to 1933 these two anchors of their electoral strategy were very successful in catching votes, but when the time came to actually govern the country, it was then realized by the top brass of the Party, who had now become the government, that these two concepts were in some instances at odds with each other.

The government took both of these election promises equally serious. During the first years of Nazi rule the objective of national assertiveness was played down, probably because the necessary tools to stress the nationalistic game were just not yet available.

In particular, the government realized very well that to re-establish the German armed forces at some later stage, which was a major part of the Nationalism ideology, would require the whole-hearted support of the leaders of industry, and of the Establishment generally. Therefore, the Socialism ideology plank must be assured to not get out of control!

The same considerations also applied to the rejuvenation of the German economy, after the lost war, the ravages of the war reparations, hyper-inflation and the economic melt-down of 1929 and the following years. This re-activation of economic activity was vitally important to be able to reduce the unemployment rate, which had reached catastrophic proportions. This reduction was also one of the main election and policy positions of the Party.

Promoting the nationalism plank automatically had brought the capitalists, big industry and their bigwigs into the ambit of the Party, if they had not been found there already. This development did not sit very well with the socialist wing of the Party. This faction was mainly represented by a number of the leaders of the

SA, the Sturmabteilung of the Party. Hitler was the nominal Commander-in-Chief of this para-military organization, and his Chief of Staff was Ernst Rōhm, as the de-facto leader of this organization.

Apparently, Hitler believed, rightly or wrongly, that Rōhm and some of the generals of the *SA*, together with the pre-Nazi prime minister General Schleicher and a few other high-ranking Party members intended a *coup d'état* to re-enforce the socialist agenda of the Party.

During a meeting of the suspected "revolutionaries" on June 30, 1934 at Bad Tōlz near Munich, Rōhm, Schleicher, the Chief of Police of Berlin and a dozen or so *SA* Generals were on Hitler's orders arrested and executed the same day by the *SS*, the *Schutz-Staffel*, the Party's trouble shooters, strong-arm enforcers and political elite unit.

Hitler insisted to have the right to summarily sentence these men to die, because he held, in addition to be the *Reichskanzler,* the constitutional position of supreme head of the judiciary. Since these men were killed on the spot, nobody knows what their side of the story would have been, and we will never know. Goebbels, of course, immediately was ready to arrange to have all sorts of nasty stories and rumors appear in the newspapers, about homosexual orgies and similar juicy tidbits. I suspect, that not all of this was just invented.

The almost exclusively German-speaking *Saargebiet* had been claimed and occupied by France after WW1, as a League of Nations mandate. Their only justification, if one could call it that, was the claim that the area was rich in coal mining and heavy steel-based industries, and therefore would strengthen the military capabilities of Germany, if it was not removed from this country.

In January of 1935 the *Saargebiet*, this region wedged in between France and Germany and shuttled to and fro between these states, had returned to Germany (celebrated by another stamp issue!). The population had voted to return this area to Germany, with an almost ninety percent majority (Ploetz). Another feather in the cap for Hitler and for the Party.

With the military re-occupation by the *Reichswehr* of the hitherto demilitarized Rhineland in 1935 there were now all the military restrictions of the Versailles treaty officially and legally declared void by Germany.

In the same year Hitler also announced the creation of the *Wehrmacht*, the Armed Forces, as successors to the *Reichswehr*. However, the new forces were, after a year of planning and preparations, finally established in 1936. Now the nationalistic pillar of the Nazi ideology had come properly into play as well.

The *Reichswehr* had been restricted by the Versailles treaty to an army of only one hundred thousand volunteer soldiers and fifteen thousand navy personnel. It had therefore automatically become an elite unit, but without neither heavy artillery or armored units, nor a high-seas navy or an air force, whereas the neighboring states had millions of heavily armed soldiers stationed on Germany's borders.

The strength of the new conscription Army was set at 36 Infantry Divisions, organized in 12 Army Corps (Ploetz), and presumably into 4 armies. The navy still had a strength of fifteen thousand, and the Air Force had to be built-up from scratch.

An Army Corps consisted of more than just its three divisions of up to 18 000 men each. The strength of the Army alone, including the staff elements, at this stage was 580 000 (Wikipedia). The total envisioned strength of the new *Wehrmacht* must consequently have been more than 600 000 men.

At the beginning of the war in 1939 the German Army had increased to almost 900 000 men, organized into 6 Army Groups, 18 Army Corps and 47 Divisions, consisting of 34 Infantry Divisions, 4 Motorized Inf. Div., 3 Mountain Inf. Div., 2 Light Div. and 4 Armored Div. The Air Force at this stage had already a strength of 400 000, but that of the Navy had only increased marginally to about 25 000. The total strength, therefore, was about 1 325 000 (Wikipedia). An impressive figure, but dwarfed by the numbers of the Soviet forces, and only proportional to the French and British.

There is some ambiguity in the records of the German Wikipedia regarding the above mentioned 6 Army Groups. An Army Group during WW2 was commanded by a *Generaloberst* and consisted of two or more Armies, under the command of army generals, which in turn had two or more Army Corps attached. Accordingly, the above Army Groups appeared to be synonymous with conventional Armies. But on the other hand, in 1943 the number of German armies exceeded 20, which supports the number of 6 Army Groups.

The *Wehrpflicht*, the conscription, was the one element which was going to affect the populace most. But there were no objections heard, and not even doubts. And why should there have been any? All the important neighboring countries had large and well-equipped standing armies at all of Germany's borders.

Originally, the duration of the conscription service was set at one year, but shortly afterwards this was extended to two years. Simultaneously, conscription was also legislated for the *Reichsarbeitsdienst*, the compulsory Labor Service, for six months (Ploetz).

All of these German actions were accompanied by some threatening diplomatic protest notes of the Allies, but without any serious reactions or repercussions. This created in Germany the impression, that the Allies were either weak or they were not interested any more in Germany's military situation. But more importantly, the Party managed to convey the idea, that it was Hitler's genius, which enabled Germany to rise from the ashes. Or, as they formulated it, from the shackles of the shameful Versailles Treaty.

These political successes further increased the popularity of the Party substantially. This feeling became frantic, when Hitler succeeded, later in 1938, to "free" Austria and the *Sudetenland* without a shot being fired. Both were almost exclusively populated by German-speakers.

The nationalistic emotions were very strong in all of Central Europe, not only in Germany. The good spin-doctor Goebbels had heated up emotions well in advance of the actual 'liberation' actions, to convince the population that these developments were deserved by the people. They were claimed to correct past injustices inflicted on Germany by the Allies, through the 'shame' 1919 Treaty of Versailles, ending World War I.

The Party and Government also took the Socialist pillar of their program very seriously, despite the above-mentioned 1934 Röhm affair. I remember very clearly the 1933-1934 period, when we were told at elementary school to bring to class *Pfundspenden* (pound offerings) for distribution to poor families, particularly the unemployed. The sons of the better-off parents were expected to bring a pound of sugar or butter, or at least of margarine or something similar, whereas the sons of working-class parents were expected to bring things like a pound of potatoes, rice or beans, for instance.

A strong feeling of solidarity among the people had been created by the Nazis, probably based on the feeling of common disaster just overcome, namely the lost World War I, the hyper-inflation of 1923, the 1929 economic collapse and the calamitous *Weimar Zirkus*.

The Party also started the *Winterhilfswerk* (Winter Help Work), where practically all the people participated in one form or another. Even the poorest were able to assist, by manning tables offering the solidarity pins, and rattling the collection tins. They all worked together in collecting money to achieve its motto: *Keiner soll Hungern, keiner soll Frieren* (nobody ought to be hungry, nobody ought to be cold).

Corny as this sounds today, it motivated and united the people, and the solidarity felt then was repeated during the worst of the air bombardments towards the end of the war. I had the impression that this solidarity was absent in Germany after the second war.

Many other social activities were originated by the Party during this period, such as *KdF*, *Kraft durch Freude*, literary 'Strength through Fun'. How corny can you get! This was one of the very rare exceptions, where this labor federation did something for the workers. This Party affiliation provided sporting facilities, holiday accommodations and leisure activities for the workers, including a fleet of cruise ships plying the Baltic and North Seas.

It also officially spawned the *Volksempfänger* or People's Radio, but it is doubtful, whether this was a purely socialist idea. I suspect, that our ubiquitous Dr. Goebbels was involved here. After all, this was a perfect means to spread the Nazi propaganda to the most remote corners of the *Reich*! And the party made extensive use of this excellent propaganda instrument.

Another feather in the socialist cap of the Nazis, in the perception of the German people, was the 1934 creation of the *RAD*, the *ReichsArbeitsDienst* or Labor Service. This gave back thousands of unemployed mostly young men and women dignity and a purpose of life, took them off the streets, gave them some basic training and imbued some military-type discipline.

The male section of the organization drained swamp areas and built rural roads and other infrastructure. The female section deployed their members to help the mothers of families with many children and the women of the farmers in the farm households and in the fields.

Here again, the smart socialist attitude of the Nazis was at work. Helping these families was both, a social benefit and was also popular with the people. As a bonus it furthermore reduced the unemployment numbers. As I noticed later, this became paramilitary and additionally a pre-army training organization.

The farmers, a huge block of voters and citizens, were also helped financially, by getting them out of debt (particularly out of Jewish debt). Government also decreed that upon the passing-away of the farmer, the farms were not any longer allowed to be divided up amongst the heirs or to be sold to non-farmers. The state also ordered the consolidation of all the small and isolated parcels of farming land into larger, viable farms. This was not only sensible, but also popular, especially amongst the Nazi farmers, who often received those consolidated or enlarged farms under preferential conditions.

By the way, all land transaction fees were paid by the buyers. Unfortunately for the sellers, the valuations were done on the basis of the 1934 tax values, which were never adjusted during the Nazi time. They were traditionally ridiculously low in Germany, probably to protect the *Mittelstand*, the middle classes, including the farming clientele. As far as I know, this practice of artificially low land values persisted in Germany at least into the 1990s.

The 1934 start of the constructing of the *RAB*, the *ReichsAuto-Bahnen* (no translation provided) started the employment of millions of workers, including thousands of unemployed white-collar personnel. Because almost all the work was done manually, as opposed to the use of heavy earthmoving equipment, this huge undertaking very quickly broke the neck of the endemic unemployment situation of Germany.

As a side effect it also created a further proud national symbol, which additionally happened to come quite handy later-on, before and during the war, when huge numbers of military vehicles had to crisscross the country.

By the end of 1938, government had reduced unemployment from 6 million to 455 000 (Ploetz). The main driver of this improvement, however, was the natural pick-up of the German economy generally, after the slump of the 1929 to 1932 recession.

The Winter and Summer Olympic Games of 1936 were other fortuitous events, which created pride and feel-good in Germany and, despite misgivings from some sides, were perceived to have enhanced Germany's standing in the world, which reflected on the German psyche. The excellent organization of the games, the peaceful conduct and the unusually good results of the German sportsmen clearly had helped in this regard.

The Nazi ideology had now become more or less acceptable for most of the previous doubters in Germany. In modern parlance: it had become 'mainstream'. Outside the country these effects were also observed. Even some members of the British Royalty were impressed.

These games also saw a novelty, a torch relay run throughout Germany (Ploetz), maybe starting at Olympus in Greece? Thinking about the Olympic Games triggers another memory. In 1935 Leni Riefenstahl (she died only recently, aged 101) produced *Triumpf des Willens* (Triumph of the Will), a promotional film for the coming Olympic Summer Games. This film became an international success and made film history. It showed, probably as a side-line, some shapely young women exercising *au nature* on a *Rhönrad of* two meters diameter, a double-rim exercise wheel, reason-ably popular in Germany at the time.

Nudity, by the way, was tolerated by the Party, at least to a certain extent, particularly if it was part of some Party-sponsored activity. It was also displayed in some publications of the *SS*. In 1938 or 1939, the Munich Art Festival showed some members of the *BDM, Bund Deutscher Mädel*, the League of German Girls, naked on a float in the festivity procession. This latter display became even the subject of a commemorative postage stamp issue, eagerly sought after not only by the teenage stamp collectors.

In 1938 the *VW, VolksWagen* (no translation needed) appeared. It was unveiled at the *IAA*, the *Internationale Automobil Ausstellung* (Fair) in Berlin, which naturally created huge interest. All this was credited (with the subtle support of Dr. Goebbels) by the people to the Nazis and explains their rising acceptance and popularity during this period. This is not to be confused, please, with the voting 'victories' produced in later years by Goebbels, the spin doctor of all spin doctors, with ridiculous approval percentages in the high 90s! Surprisingly, he never managed more than hundred percent.

During the years after taking power Hitler gave a powerful and impressive speech at least once a year, usually at the *Reichsparteitag*, the annual Party Rally in Nuremberg. These speeches were eagerly listened to by most people, despite the fact that they were over-long and usually full of statistics. He was after all a proper people's tribune, a super demagogue and rabble-rouser and a forceful orator, who understood to employ all the emotions based on the prejudices, anxieties and feelings of hate by the people.

Interestingly, in his speeches he always quoted the "*Vorsehung*" (Providence), implying to refer to God without actually saying so, and he never mentioning God by name. This was a high-wire act for him, having to balance the still strong religious feelings of the majority of the German people against the equally strong anti-clerical attitudes of the numerous atheists, which probably included himself. He made it very clear that the "*Vorsehung*" was with him, protected and guided him. The continuation of the established traditions of the German and European monarchies!

It should be interesting to investigate, why all these terrible things could happen in Germany during the rule of the Nazis. Why did a minority of otherwise normal and mostly middle-class people commit these heinous crimes, or tolerated their commitment? And why did the majority not object to and resist these crimes? There can be no question of making obfuscations here or provide excuses. But it would help to look at the past, in order to understand why the majority of the German people behaved the way they did. Maybe these reflexions will help to understand why such unmentionable things happened.

We can see nowadays, that atrocities and mass-murders, committed by political, nationalistic, racist or religious fanatics in the past and at present show certain similarities to what happened then in Germany, both regarding the background and the way these events unfolded. And let us not forget that the gigantic scope of the Nazi crimes was even surpassed by what happened in the Soviet Union, more or less at the same time.

Listening to some of the present-day fanatics makes it likely that they would murder to the same extent, if they only would be able to. The background, and the way things are developing in certain countries, displays similar basics.

Reading about the socialistic tactics followed by the Islamic radicals in Syria and the Lebanon, intended to win support within the lower classes of the populations, reminds me very much of the tactics applied by the Nazis during the first few years of their rule. And these concepts worked then, and they still work admirably now. We all should learn from this bloody section of our history, if only the political will would be there.

To sum up: from 1933 to 1938 the vast majority of the German population was happy and content in the feeling that, nationalistically and socially, the Nazi Party had succeeded to eliminate:

- the aftermath of the lost war
- the shameful Versailles Treaty
- the chaos of the democratic *Weimar System*
- the ravages of the hyper-inflation of 1923
- the economic meltdown of 1929 to 1932
- the five million strong unemployment.

Conclusion: an authoritarian but benevolent form of government appears to be, theoretically, the best solution to advance the broad interests of a nation. Unfortunately, such a well-intentioned form of government inevitably turns into a bloody dictatorship. This almost seems to be a Law of Nature, as witnessed in numerous examples throughout past history. As a matter of fact, I am not aware of a single exception to this sad rule.

One of the obvious reasons for such a development is the fact that even in an ideal dictatorship environment there will always sooner or later develop some political opposition. And that is exactly what any authoritarian government finds intolerable. Thus, oppression of such opposition will be the order of the day for the people in charge.

To start with, there will be intimidation and harassment, followed by oppression and violence. This in turn will strengthen the opposition, which will answer violence with more violence. And so, the spiral of violence starts and will lead either to a bloody civil war or to an abject cauldron of suppression and abuse of human rights and human dignity. Either way, the democratic order has perished.

16

HOW ATTITUDES CHANGE

In my opinion, one of the most striking aspects of history has always been a general observation, not restricted to the rise of Nazism: the sometimes drastic and violent mutations in the attitudes and perceptions of populations of many countries, and over often relatively short periods of time. The following is, of course, no excuse for the Nazi crimes.

Observe, for instance, what happened in Great Britain in the nineteenth century regarding the slave trade, and how fast and drastically the British people's views regarding slavery have changed. Before William Wilberforce started his campaign to abolish slavery, this practice was in Great Britain and globally deemed to be acceptable. Except by the slaves, presumably.

Between the 1807 Slave Trade Act and the 1833 Slavery Abolition Act (Ploetz), he and his small band of followers were able to convince the majority of the people in Great Britain that this barbaric practice must be stopped. Even though this change meant economic losses and hardships for the participants in the slave trade, but also for the country's economy generally.

Similar changes in attitudes and perceptions regarding slavery in other countries took place later, for instance in the USA. Eventually, the practice was condemned all over the developed countries of the world. This mutation in perceptions was the most remarkable aspect of this development, but the fact that this inhuman trade was for centuries acceptable by all western populations until very recently (in a historical time frame) was the real shocker.

Further sad examples were the attitudes condoning genocides by people prior to the Nazi era. The violent suppression of the 1857/1858 Indian Mutiny, which was definitely not unreservedly condemned by the British people of the time, fell into this category. Also consider the way the 1915 extinction of one and a half million Armenians by the Ottoman Empire was overlooked and therefore generally condoned at the time by the Western public opinion and the ruling political classes. Sure, this happened during World War I, but Turkey denies this genocide and any wrongdoing even today.

Would the Nazis, apart from some block-headed acolytes, still want nowadays to kill millions of Jews? And would the British Air Marshal Harris nowadays still order the bombing and burning down of Dresden and all the other German cities and towns, killing hundreds of thousands of civilians, Nazis and Non-Nazis?

A related subject is the debate for and against the death penalty. Eighty years ago, there was no such debate, because the death penalty was generally accepted as normal retribution for serious criminal behavior. After all, the bible, and therefore the Christian churches, accepted it as God-given, and therefore it could not possibly have been wrong.

Another example would be the fast-changing attitude in our days towards, or rather against, smoking. Many other incidents of this nature could be quoted, such as the only recently discovered awareness for the ecology, and so on. Or one could look at the metamorphosis in the USA of the situation, within just a few decennia, of the vote-less and suppressed 'niggers' to sought after Afro-American voters.

One of the most striking examples of these accelerated changes can be seen in the roles that women played in our society in the past. To stay with our Nazi subject, at the time there was not a single female minister or high-ranking official or Party functionary in Germany. Correction: there was one exception. The Party Women's League was commanded by a Valkyrie. Even in those days it would have looked a bit peculiar to have a pot-bellied Party-hack in charge.

Nor existed a single uniformed female police officer or soldier. Any such idea would have been considered no more than science fiction. However, there was one (for me) memorable exception to this situation: the *Wehrmachtshelferinnen*, the Armed Forces Female Assistants. They were civilians in uniform, so-to-speak, but they were operating only during the war, and only in support functions, generally far from the front lines.

Several times I have already mentioned that during the Nazi period women were practically invisible in the German public domain. The glass ceiling, as the Americans later called it, was in perfect working order during this era, and before as well. Today, we have in Germany a female prime minister, several ministers and many high-ranking female officials, as well as a fair number of business executives in the economy. And the roof has not fallen in! But even now there is claimed to be still some discrimination against women around.

Soon after the outbreak of the war the propaganda machine of the state, not surprisingly, concentrated on the war effort. One aim was to maintain in place the high spirit of the early years. Another one was to suggest certain ideas into the subconscious. A typical example was the slogan minted for the State Railways: *"Räder müssen rollen für den Sieg"*, 'wheels must turn for victory'. About 1942 it became known (was rumored) that this catchy slogan had been created by a young woman. An amazing and rare exception!

Changed perceptions could also be registered in the field of sociology. Nowadays there can be observed a more or less genuine concern about the interests of employees and the protection of jobs. Today substantial efforts are being made to minimize the social effects of job losses, and to find the least hurtful solutions. In my time we never heard or read about anything like that.

Generally, it can be said that the pre-WW1 generations in Europe were psychologically much harder and less emotional than the present ones. And this did not change much in the years between the two World Wars. People could then not be roused like today about human rights and other emotional issues.

They were then more likely to display their roused feelings in conjunction with the fate of their soccer team than about some human atrocities somewhere. The only large-scale manifestation of high-strung emotions that I can remember from those days referred to nationalistic, or even chauvinistic, and especially political passions. Obviously, there were also some exceptions to these observations.

Today, thousands will join a protest rally against the death of a few people somewhere, or maybe even just a single person. Or to demonstrate against the maltreatment of a small group of people, or the thread to a species of animals or plants somewhere in the world.

The generations of my grandparents, of my parents and my own did not generally display their emotions. It was simply not done, a definite and socially unacceptable no – no in Germany.

In my high-school days a teacher was reading one morning in front of the assembled school in the *aula* a eulogy for a fellow teacher who had passed away. At one stage his voice broke and he appeared to have shed a few tears. We school kids found this to be remarkable and rather peculiar for a grown-up. Later that day I overheard another teacher commenting to someone about the "undignified display of emotions" by his colleague. By the way: nobody then would have used an artificial construction like "he passed away" for the simple and more direct: "he died".

Here I have to exercise a "fast forward" in the timeline. My parents never hugged me, at least not from the age when I started to remember things. This was par-for-the-course, such soppy emotional exhibitionism was not cool, the present generation would say. Please remember, that I am only talking about the situation in Germany. Italians or the French, for instance, probably behaved also then very differently.

After the body of my father had by his colleagues been dug out of the ruins of the Dresdner Bank building in February of 1945, and when I had told my mother what had happened, neither of us were able to shed a tear, and that despite the fact that we both loved my father dearly, as I know from letters exchanged between them during his military service in WW2.

One day, still talking about the distant future, when our son returned from his Kibbutz time in Israel, he unexpectedly hugged me. I was momentarily surprised, even shocked at this soggy emotional outburst. But then I was pleased and on an emotional high myself. Ever since I enjoy hugging and to be hugged by our son. I even hug somebody else I like, but only very occasionally. It is amazing, how one gets soft in old age, or more accurately, how attitudes are changing and improving with advancing years.

Today this lack of emotions, or more specifically, this lack of displaying emotions, is difficult to understand, but it is essential to recognize facts. It is an important and obvious explanation and catalyst of what happened to the behavior of the German people in those years. And not only for the Germans. There were many equally ruthless persons willingly helping, for instance, to root out Jews, and to have them deported to the extermination camps, in many European countries under German occupation.

One of the things, which I also only recognized in retrospection, is the fact that at that time neither my family, nor anybody else, paid the slightest attention to what we call now the environment. The term had not even been invented yet. I remember that even well-behaved people thought nothing of throwing their rubbish just anywhere and leave it on the beach or a picnic site, for instance. The only recycling ever done happened during the war, when raw materials were needed for the *'Endsieg'*, the 'Final Victory'. This however had obviously nothing to do with modern environmental thinking. Global Warming was a further hot subject of the future, not yet discovered either.

But changes in our experiences happen in all spheres of our activities. When I used to relax in the past and read a who-done-it, which is now more sophisticated called a suspense novel, it took me to read a 150-page Pocket Book of Earle Stanley Gardener or similar about two or three hours.

Now I need to go to the fitness studio (to be honest, I have never set foot into one of these establishments) to build up my stamina to pick up my 500 or 600-page A4-sized book from the library and I have to take a week's leave to read one of these 'telephone books' (due to the hundred or so participants), because after three days I have forgotten who did what to whom, and I have to go back to Start. And, yes, I just remembered that I still need to find a publisher for my own books.

But I do get really good value for my (extra) money: in great detail I am informed what every one of the persons in this narrative is wearing, what they are eating and, in particular, what they are drinking. Not to forget, which of the current pop musicians are their favorites and the names of dozens of pieces of their music and songs.

All of the above to subtly explain the detailed descriptions of their anxiety fits, their messy sex affairs and similar important personal tidbits, which are utterly irrelevant to the story.

The coverage of our sexuality has also undergone dramatic changes, in this case over a somewhat longer interval of time. The 1928 novel "Lady Chatterley's Lover" had to be published in Italy, because of the Anglo-American censorship laws, and was promptly prohibited in England and the States when it appeared. The poem "Annus Mirabilis" by Philip Larkin (Wikipedia) is illustrative of the epochal shift in the sexual perceptions of the public:

> Social intercourse began
> In nineteen sixty-three
> (which was rather late for me)
> Between the end of the "Chatterley" ban
> And the Beatle's first LP

The older ones amongst us remember very clearly, how in the early '60s the sexual floodgates opened. Not only 'risky' publications appeared now, but in Germany brothels shot out of the ground like mushrooms, after the relevant legislation had been 'modernized'.

Maybe the most striking example of our changed attitudes can be seen in regard to the homosexuals. Until quite recently, this sexual orientation of men was a criminal offense in almost all countries. and was very definitely considered as abnormal. The churches condemned it, society was against it, the military suppressed it. It was, if at all possible, swept under the carpet. It was a no - no subject.

The sufferers were forced to stay underground and to deny their sexual inclination. Considering the strong forces involved in sexuality generally, it is not surprising that large numbers of human tragedies were the result, blackmail and abuse, discrimination and contempt were the usual consequences. There is obviously still some opposition in place, but generally it is now accepted, or at least tolerated, in many parts of the world. And the world is still turning, as if nothing had changed! But let us not forget that even today, for instance in Africa, lesbian girls and women are regularly killed, whereas the same behavior amongst men is overlooked.

17

GERMAN ANTI-SEMITISM

To understand the background of what happened to the Jewish people in Germany and in the occupied and dependent countries in Europe in the Nazi period and during the war, we have to go back a long time in history. Anti-Semitism certainly was not invented by the Nazis, they just 'perfected' it, transforming it into, first, a political and electoral platform, and then into a legal construct.

Events in the Austrian-Hungarian double monarchy, and to a lesser extent in Germany, in the later part of the 19th and the early parts of the 20th century, sharpened the focus of the anti-Semitic activists, long before the Nazi ideology had been developed. It was no coincidence that Hitler came from Austria, because there he was subjected in his youth, by his peers and by the media, to vitriolic attacks on anything Jewish.

The European anti-Semitism developed already in Antiquity, and particularly in the Middle Ages, and was rooted in three main sources:

- religion
- commercial envy
- xenophobia.

Let us look first at religion, which in those days played a much bigger role than today in the lives of the peoples of Europe. Both Christian churches had for centuries indoctrinated the German people with the accusation that Christ had been murdered by the Jews, or at least that he had been betrayed by them. This very effective brainwashing of generation after generation had resulted in deep-rooted prejudices.

We have to keep in mind here that in the Middle Ages and the following centuries the churches in Germany were very much more listened-to and obeyed than what we experience today. The priests and pastors of the churches were therefore much more influential then. In today's more secular environment it is difficult to envisage how engrained these perceptions were amongst all social levels of the population.

The Catholic church was instrumental in instigating the creation of Jewish ghettoes in many medieval towns, not only in Germany, but throughout Europe. Psychologically, these ghettoes were possibly the forerunners of the Nazi concentration camps for the Jews, but not of the extermination ones, of course. The Orthodox Churches in Eastern Europe were often as guilty as the two dominant churches in Germany. During the war the Nazis revitalized the idea of huge Jewish ghettoes in occupied Poland.

Economic envy by the German middle and upper classes was a second contributing aspect to the anti-Semitism. It was obvious to all, that Jews were generally more successful than the locals, in the professions as well as in business. This was attributed by most of the Germans to unethical business practices and to the suspected Jewish cabals. One strong aspect of this perception was the (perceived) fact that Jewish business cliques had, by their war profiteering and Black-Market dealings, contributed to the loss of the first World War.

Another factor was the perceived international Jewish involvement in the unreasonable reparation demands by the Allies after WW1, which led to the 1923 hyper-inflation, which in turn effectively destroyed the German middle class. Further ammunition was provided by the imagined Jewish manipulations which led to the 1929/1932 economic meltdown and the subsequent deflation, which gave the death-knell to the German economy.

All these unjustified perceptions avoided to admit the real

reasons why Jewish professionals and businessmen were generally more successful than German ones: the higher average IQs of the Jewish people, combined with their high work ethos and, of course, their excellent networking. This latter point, ironically, was one of the famous 'unexpected consequence' of their forced separation from the German people over the centuries, which in turn reinforced their tendency to keep themselves separate from their host populations.

The latter point of this unfortunate chain-reaction was subsequently used by the people as another reason to mistrust them. Xenophobia, the final aspect of this evil trilogy and providing the 'cherry' on a very ugly and nasty cake, was a phenomenon found from time to time in virtually all populations worldwide.

The fact that the Jewish people tended to keep to themselves created one of the breeding grounds for this attitude. This was, of course, also a consequence of being looked upon as foreigners and strangers, and especially as having a non-Christian religion. Therefore, they were mistrusted and locked-out by the Germans. This, inevitably, worked both ways in a self-fulfilling spiral.

It is sobering to visualize what would have been possible, if the Jewish community would have been completely integrated into the German social fabric. Jews could have created many more successful firms in Germany and could have contributed even more to the scientific and cultural world than they achieved in the late eighteenth and early nineteenth centuries. Their success in the States, where they were still not fully accepted until very recently, indicates the dramatic possibilities.

An interesting aspect of xenophobia is the fact, that this sentiment increases exponentially with the percentage of foreigners in the population of any given country. If this percentage doubles, then xenophobia quadruples or increases even more.

I remember some stand-up comedian's comment in his radio show in the early 1960s in Germany. He praised Finland, because there were no negative feelings towards foreigners, like there were in Germany against the five million Turkish immigrants. Upon inquiring about their Turkish immigrants, he was told that this country only had three Turkish carpet dealers. Further scrutiny revealed that they were Persians, actually.

On the other hand, consider the situation in South Africa before the end of apartheid in 1994: the palpable anxiety of the five million Europeans in relation to the overwhelmingly large population of fifty million Africans. This could easily have led to a bloody civil war, if the country would not have had the unique statesman Nelson Mandela as president and leader of the black majority.

During the 19th century there was a tendency by a minority of the Jewish community to try to get assimilated into the German population. In those days the German officials routinely demanded from everybody the disclosure of their religion. These Jewish families converted from Judaism to become, say, Catholics, to camouflage their recent religious past.

After a while even the slow-moving through and through anti-Semitic German bureaucracy caught on to this clever subterfuge. The officials now additionally asked for any previous religion. So, these families again converted once more from, say, the catholic to the protestant denomination. I believe that I already mentioned somewhere the high average Jewish IQs.

With all these mental acrobatics I wondered whether these families really ever changed their believes at all? In any case the overwhelmingly large majority of German Jews maintained their millennia-old religious traditions.

Already in the 18th, and particularly in the 19th century, hundreds of thousands of Jews left Galicia. This province was originally a part of Poland, which came under Austrian occupation after the third partition of Poland by the European powers. These Jewish emigrants came to Austria and settled mainly in Vienna. The large scale of this immigration triggered anti-Jewish sentiments in this country, resulting in anti-Semitic publicity and demagogy.

This province of Galicia, interestingly, was the home of Yiddish, a German dialect spoken by the Jewish people of Eastern Europe. The language is still very much alive today, at least in the USA. Even a Yiddish newspaper and Yiddish books are published and read by many in the States, especially in New York.

Before World War I most European Jews had their homes in Czarist Russia, which then included most of Poland, Lithuania and the other Baltic States. They represented a reasonably large percentage of the population. They formed, particularly in Poland and Lithuania, a volatile minority. Killings and persecutions of Jews, the infamous pogroms, happened periodically all over the country, occasionally instigated by the Orthodox clergy. As far as I know, these priests, at the least, did not intervene to protect the persecuted Jews.

During the pre-WW1 decades many Jewish families emigrated from Czarist Russia to escape the repeated persecutions, often moving to far-flung countries and continents, like the USA, Canada, Australia and to South Africa.

The situation in Germany was rather similar to the Austrian one, particularly after World War I, when again hundreds of thousands of Jews left the newly created Republic of Poland to settle in Germany. Probably they were fearing the pogroms they experienced in Czarist times, when Poland was part of Russia.

But more likely because of their hoped-for better economic prospects in Germany. Many families also went to France, Belgium and the Netherlands. Little did they know what would happen in Germany in the 1923 hyper-inflation and the 1929 to 1932 meltdown. But by then they were settled there and did not have a reasonable chance to leave again.

It is a well-established historical fact, that a small percentage of newly arriving immigrants does not create many serious problems, as illustrated previously. But an immigration 'tsunami' causes resentment almost automatically, particularly if the newcomers are economically more successful than the locals, and if they take away jobs and business opportunities. This applies even if these feelings are merely a suspicion and are simply not true.

This strong immigration created in Germany the same negative sentiments as earlier in Austria, also because these new arrivals were often forced to take on any work they could get and at any wage rate available, thus undercutting the local labor. And this on top of an already ever-increasing unemployment crisis.

After the first world war, and occasionally already before, very limited racial mixing took place in Germany. This was restricted to the middle classes and particularly the professions and artists, but virtually unknown in the upper and working classes. Consequently, there were now a certain number of people, very much a minority, which the Nazis would later classify as Half-Jews. They were, by the way, generally as much persecuted as were the Jews themselves.

Ironically, *Generalfeldmarschall* Milch (a name clearly indicative of a Jewish family), belonged to this group. He was in charge of the 1936 re-equipment of the German air force with new planes, and later, during the war, he was one of Hitler's highly decorated key generals. He was an officer of such high caliber, that the Nazis conveniently overlooked his 'unfortunate' racial background. How cynical can one get?

The leading Nazi theoretical publicist Alfred Rosenberg (another Jewish-sounding name!) belonged possibly also to this group. His book "Der Mythos des Zwanzigsten Jahrhunderts" (Myth of the Twentieth Century) was required reading for anybody who wanted to achieve anything in Nazi Germany. It was almost as obligatory as Hitler's "Mein Kampf".

Another instance of blinkered vision was a street name in our suburb. Herschelstrasse was named after the famous astronomer William Herschel (or his son John?), who had worked a hundred years ago in the observatory on the baronial estate in the neighboring suburb.

The family originated from the German state of Hanover (Wikipedia), which at this time belonged to the British crown, because its (German) monarch had by marriage become the king of England. The surname clearly indicated Jewish ancestry, but because he had also worked in England for a while, his 'awkward' background could be overlooked, and he could be considered an Englishman, and was thus acceptable for racial and political purposes.

After WW1 the Jewish hawker, with his *Bauchladen*, a stomach tray filled with match boxes or packages of razor blade, could be met at any of the more profitable street corners in all the larger cities, but generally not in country towns and the villages. I clearly remember to have experienced some of them in the early 1930s in Wildruffer Strasse, one of the main inner-city arteries in Dresden, leading from the Altmarkt to the Postplatz.

One of the more peculiar manifestations of the Nazi anti-Semitism was the appearance of the *Ahnenforschung*, the ancestry research. Oodles of magazines and books were published on the subject. Most families dug out dusty documents to proof their "Arian" ancestry. At the time, I wondered why nothing like that was done in our family. Only very much later I found the possible reason. Maybe my father knew something we did not know and felt that it was best to let sleeping dogs lie.

In the 17th century, when the German Jews were still under severe professional and other restrictions, they were allowed to work only in specially authorized occupations, such as goldsmiths, money lenders, pawnbrokers and tailors. When later these restrictions had been lifted, some of the goldsmiths became jewelers, many money lenders and pawnbrokers turned to banking, and some of the tailors expanded into merchants in textiles and the clothing industry.

The father or the grandfather of my paternal grandfather had been a tailor in Ehrenberg, a small village outside of Waldheim in Saxony.

Working for the US Army in Germany after the war, I listened every morning on AFN, the Armed Forces Network, to an emission called 'Merely Music', and preferably to the music of the duo of 'Ferrante & Teicher', the latter being a then famous Jewish pianist.

When in the 1980s our son twice went to work in a kibbutz in Israel and had also visited Jerusalem, he commented to us on a peculiar affinity of his to Jerusalem and the country of Israel generally. A feeling as if he had been there before.

Later, when our son lived in Copenhagen, we found during one of our visits in the telephone book a Jewish lady named Teicher, wondering whether she was related to us (she apparently was not).

At about that same time our son had placed on the internet a manuscript I had written, which included my e-mail address. This has in the meantime been published by him on Amazon under the title *"Parallel Developments, from the Big Bang to 3 000 B.C."* A gentleman from Canada emailed me shortly after, inquiring whether our family originated from the Jewish section of the city of Cracow in Poland, where many families of the name Teicher lived. A question, which I was unfortunately unable to answer.

When I was working in South Africa in the 1970s, a Polish-

Jewish architect employed by our company insisted that I appeared to him to be Jewish. No explanation for this assertion was provided.

After my retirement, when I had started my stamp auction business, one of my suppliers was a Jewish stamp dealer. He told me more than once that he was considering visiting in future the Talmud School more often. Why did he tell me?

Probably all just coincidences?!

In 1935 the *Gesetz zum Schutze des Deutschen Blutes und der Deutschen Ehre* (Law for the Protection of the German Blood and the German Honor) was published (Ploetz). This mouthful of emotional legalese established the legal basis for all the subsequent anti-Semitic actions by the Nazis.

The most ridiculous thing about the myth of the 'pure Arian race' was for me the fact that, apart from Baldur von Schirach, the Commander-in-Chief 'of the *Hitlerjugend*, there was hardly anybody in the top ranks of the Party, who even remotely looked like the cherished Arian ideal.

Hitler himself reminded me later, when my Nazi fervor had already markedly cooled, of a Southern European shopkeeper, Goebbels looked to me like a lady's coiffeur, and Himmler could have been a carpet dealer from Palestine or Persia.

Goering, well, he actually used to look like a proper Germanic warrior, when he was a fighter pilot in WW1. But then he had turned into a fat middle-aged playboy. Nowadays he would have worn a three kilograms gold chain with his open shirt, while driving a Ferrari *coupé*.

Anti-Semitism in Europe was, of course, not restricted to Nazi Germany. It existed even in an enlightened country like France. Nostradamus, born in Saint-Rémy-de-Provence in the South of France of Jewish parents, who had converted to Catholicism to avoid persecution.

From 1894 through to 1906 (Ploetz) the *Dreyfus Affair*, a nasty smear campaign and discrimination plot against a Jewish army officer, polarized the people of France. This persecution was mainly caused by the press and public opinion, which had been incited by the papers. In other words, something similar to what happened 30 years later in Germany at the beginning of the Nazi era, but fortunately on a much smaller scale.

Up to very recent times, there was in England a definitive anti-Semitic undercurrent discernible, particularly amongst the upper and middle classes. They may have courted the rich Jewish banker or merchant but were looking down on them with disdain. Barring a Jew from one's club by black balling him was the norm and a popular sport. These feelings were even stronger in the upper echelons of the Army. Not to mention the Royal Navy!

The anti-Semitism in the American Armed Forces was proverbial right up to, and some years beyond, WW2. I still remember in the 1950s a Jewish Vice Admiral Rickover in charge of the US submarine forces, who was quoted as the great exception to the rule. A parallel to Field Marshal Milch in Germany? Even in the early 1960s, my immediate boss in the US Army at the time, a Jewish DA civilian, was told by a Lieutenant Colonel not to expect, with his religion, a career in the Army.

18

KNOWLEDGE ABOUT THE HOLOCAUST

The decision to eliminate the total Jewish population of Europe was taken only in 1942 at the *Wannsee Konferenz*, based on instructions, which Göring had issued in 1941 (Wikipedia). The top Nazi leadership, meaning especially Hitler himself, and some of the top officers of the *SS* were involved in this meeting. Some key personnel of the chemical industry and of the *Reichsbahn*, the state railways, were also present.

There are still some defenders of Hitler's 'innocence', who claim he did not know about this decision, or about any of the other Nazi crimes, but this is pathetically unrealistic. Any explanation, which is trying to exculpate Hitler, is non-sensical in a totalitarian state like Germany was at this time.

After 1945 one of the most heated discussions in Germany, and abroad as well, centered on the knowledge, or the lack of knowledge, by the German population about the Holocaust. Obviously, I can only talk about myself, my family, friends and relations in this respect. During the war these people generally did not know about what happened in the extermination camps. This is more easily understandable if one considers the tight grip the Nazi Party, and especially the *Gestapo*, had on all and any public information available, including the many political rumors.

In theory, details regarding these camps would probably have been available from the Allied radio stations. But there was, first of all, to consider the death penalty for listening to 'enemy propaganda' as a very powerful deterrent. Secondly, the German population was by then, to put it mildly, wary of propaganda of any sort, remembering also the way the Allies had used propaganda lies during the first war.

In a South African newspaper, we recently found a reportage about the passing away of a secretary of Dr. Goebbels at the age of 106. At the start of 1942 she was therefore in her early 30s and unlikely to have been the secretary of a key minister. More likely was she a typist in the ministerial typing-pool.

She claimed not to have known anything about the death camps. I think this is likely, since a typist would not have been privy to state secrets. And the holocaust was a very definite and high-level State Secret!

In 1941 or 1942, on the way to my high school, I remember having seen on a *Lithfaßsäule*, an advertisement pillar, a large red poster with a bold black frame. A name was printed in large black letters and the message read that this man has been sentenced to death or executed, because he had listened to enemy radio transmissions and had distributed their propaganda lies. This kind of deterrent was extremely powerful, as I can confirm from my own experience! It was therefore not surprising that people with (partial) knowledge of the facts kept quiet.

There obviously had to have been a large number of people, who knew about one or the other aspect of what was going on in regard to the extermination camps. For instance, about the transport of millions of victims into those camps. Or about the production and the transport of the poison gas used for these purposes.

But the point is that these people would never have talked about these things, because they knew that this would have been a death sentence for them, and probably their families as well.

This subduing of the people is the main reason why all knowledge of these crimes could so successfully be hidden from the general German population. Only the top echelons of the Party would have been aware of the complete picture, and they obviously would never have talked either. The Nazi leadership must have known very well that the Germans would not have accepted these atrocities, if they had known about them from the beginning.

The results of these facts:

- a small number of top-ranking Nazis, mostly *SS* officers and top ministerial officials, designed in 1942 at the Wannsee conference the system for the planned extermination of the European Jews. They were the only ones who knew the whole extent of the *Endlösung*, the 'Final Solution' of the Nazis for the murder of the Jewish people of Europe.
- a somewhat larger, but still smallish group of Germans were aware of certain aspects of what was going on, but kept their mouth shut to protect themselves and their families. The Nazis had adapted from the Soviets, who had perfected this system, the concept of *'Sippenhaftung'*: the whole family was deemed to be responsible for, and had to suffer the consequences of, any serious political crime by any member of the family.
- finally, the bulk of the population was kept in the dark about these goings-on, to prevent a possible violent reaction by the formerly ardent Nazi Germans. They only became aware of the extermination camps after the end of the war, when the Allies, particularly the Americans, released film footage and eyewitness reports about these atrocities.

Please note, that this chapter deals only with the knowledge about the extermination camps. The knowledge about the original concentration (holding) camps to isolate unwanted or dangerous political opponents, is dealt with in chapter 8 of Part 2.

PART IV

MILITARY SERVICE

THE GREAT ADVENTURE (1942 TO 1945)

19

ARBEITSDIENST

1942

In late spring or early summer of 1942, I was drafted into the *RAD*, the *ReichsArbeitsDienst*, the compulsory Labor Service, which was by then also simultaneously used as a pre-military training outfit. I do not remember how I travelled from Dresden to the camp I was ordered to report to. This was located outside a small farming village near Landsberg/Warthe. This latter was a typical small country town in the north-eastern part of Germany, as it was in the 1937 boundaries. In other words, the camp was within pre-war Germany, not in the newly 'acquired' areas of Poland, which had been added to the *Reich* after the 1939 war against this country, because these districts were predominantly inhabited by German people.

Our camp consisted of many wooden barracks, each for about ten to fifteen men (no females to be seen anywhere, of course, with these spoilsports). The camp also had an ablution block and a kitchen barrack, as well as an administration building. There were also small single-family houses for about six to eight instructors and their families. The camp had a few hundred inhabitants altogether. The whole complex was fenced-in, had a guard hut and an entrance boom. Not to forget the obligatory flagpole, so the Swastika flag could be hoisted every morning.

Of course, we were issued uniforms (ideally, everybody in the Nazi *Reich* should have worn one!) Instead of a rifle we were given two spades, a common one for earth works, and the other one, which had its chromium highly polished by us, for guard duty and parade drills. Most of the three months' duration of our stay was spent on drills, and to establish some semblance of discipline into our lot of teenagers. For hours we were square-bashing, and then we had to clean our gear. This was a bit awkward, because the parade ground consisted of a loamy soil, which our efforts had turned into fine dust, or into sticky mud after a heavy rain.

Out of an intake of about three hundred youngsters the Camp Commander picked about twenty or thirty for duty in the guard platoon. I also found myself in this unit, which turned out to be a typical curate's egg. On the one hand, our drill sessions were even more strenuous than those of the other platoons. On the other hand, guard duty was less exhausting than working in the fields harvesting potatoes. A back-breaking exercise for us city dwellers. I landed up with this latter job for only one or two days, probably before the selection mentioned above. Most of the chaps of this intake were slaving in the fields of the surrounding farms for weeks on end, helping to feed the nation.

One strong reminiscence from this period is a little trick I invented while on gate duty. Naturally in violation of the rules, which was for me by now par for the course. On guard duty we had to shoulder our parade spade like a rifle, and this created for me after a while the before-mentioned shoulder problem.

The guard hut was constructed of timber slats, and there were small gaps between these. I inserted the blade of my spade into a suitable one of these gaps above me, rammed it upwards, and the blade of the spade was reasonably firmly clamped between the slats. Gone was the pressure and the spade rested lightly on my long-suffering shoulder. Bliss!!

Until, that is, the Camp Commander approached the gate, in which case we had to present the spade, just as the military guards presented in such situation their rifle. You probably guessed it: the spade was stuck between the hut's woodwork, and I had a bit of a battle to extricate it, in order to do what I was required to do. This could have led to serious repercussions, but our commandant almost oppressed a grin and warned me to be more careful in future with such tricks. The next day I was promoted to group-leader of about a dozen guards. A coincidence, probably.

A less-than-pleasant memory relates to an unsavory fellow in our barrack. I'm not going to go into details (dis-appointed?), but all of us hated this chap. One night, when he was asleep, we placed his hand in a bowl of warm water. Result: we had an instant bed-pisser in our barrack! We left no doubt what we thought of such demeanor, and we had (almost) no further problems with him.

Guard duty had, as a by-product, the advantage of us being able to listen to the radio, when patrolling the compound in the evening. The commandant's cottage played the radio with opened windows until late into the night. It is amazing, what difference it made to us that we could indulge in this simple pleasure. Without realizing this properly, we must have been homesick quite a bit. After all, we were, for the first time in our young lives, for an extended period away from our families, and from the surroundings we were used to. One has to remember that transistor radios had not been invented yet, not to mention CDs, DVDs and MP3 players! And owning their own radios was not at all common for grown-ups, and almost unheard of for the average teenager.

This raises in my mind another point of interest, namely the changing mood and preferences for listening to music. At age sixteen or so, all I was interested in was jazz and similar modern music, despite the fact that I liked to play Liszt and Chopin on my piano. But at that time, I was not much interested in listening to their music.

One of the most popular pieces of music during the war was in Germany the song *'Heimat, deine Sterne'*, 'Homeland, your Stars', sung during the then popular *Wunschkonzerte*, the Preference Concerts, by Heinz Rühmann. He was the most loved comedian of the time, who was surprisingly also a Major in the air force reserve.

Only *'Lily Marlene'*, sung by Lale Anderson, could claim more popularity. The lyrics were probably quite soppy for present-day tastes, but that did no harm to the appeal of this piece of music. After all, millions of young and not so young men were separated from home and family, and they all, and their families back home, had basically the same sentimental longings.

Our recreation in camp consisted of writing letters to family and sweethearts, if applicable. I also managed to organize the odd chess game. But all of that only after cleaning our gear and repairing our gear, such as fixing big gaps the size of mouse holes in our woolen socks. Surprisingly, I did quite an acceptable job with this latter activity.

Polishing the blasted parade spade and our long boots was a hated 'entertainment'. Special treatment was to be accorded to the leather belt and the shiny belt buckle. Also, the uniform trousers had to be pressed, by inserting them between the mattress and the wooden bed boards, to obtain the required crease. It was much easier, and looked better, when our dear mother performed this job, but we had not been allowed to bring them.

Occasionally we were given leave to go to the nearby village. I remember, however, only one such excursion during those three months, when a group of us went to the local pub. I had eight large glasses of beer, even though I almost never drank beer before, because I did not particularly like the taste of it. But there was nothing else on offer, and the beer was mostly water, so I did not get drunk at all.

But this drinking spree strengthened my calve muscles appreciably, due to the running I had to do as a consequence of this gourmet partaking of liquids. The fact that even beer was in short supply in a country where it was the national beverage illustrates the stress the German war economy suffered.

One day a group of us found ourselves in unexplored territory in the world metropolis of Landsberg/Warthe. As explained before, this was a small country town without any industry I could see, just some shops, a hotel or three. And of course, the obligatory pubs and restaurants. Additionally, there were many small businesses catering to the surrounding farming communities. If I have short-changed the place with my faulty memory, I duly apologize.

In any case, not all was lost: there was a so-called 'night' club advertised on some billboard. As it was open on this late afternoon, it must have been a Saturday, or the late afternoon was classified by the local entertainment industry as Night. The reason for us visiting this educational establishment was the fact that we had seen advertised on this poster a *Schönheitstänzerin*. This literally translated to a Beauty Dancing Girl.

What this turned out to be was a middle-aged semi-naked lady dancing on a dais, covered or sometimes not covered, by some flimsy gauze. Please note, this was not a strip joint, because the decadent American striptease either had not been invented yet or had not yet reached the upstanding and god-fearing rural districts of Germany. In any case, we followed the artistic performance with great interest, because this is expected from a polite audience. Otherwise, we could have played some snooker during this time.

I have tried to figure out how we could possibly have been so far away from the camp, probably over a hundred kilometers. I suspect that we were actually on our way home, back to civilization, and not on leave.

The trip home to Dresden is lost in the mystic mists of my memory, just as the original journey from Dresden to the camp has slipped my mind. Most likely that I have been asleep during both occasions.

The legal provision for the compulsory service in the *Reichsarbeitsdienst* was six months, as mentioned earlier. The fact that we stayed there for only three months is surely explained by the *Wehrmacht* demanding urgently new recruits. This shortened service period, just as our premature and abrupt truncation of our high school tenure, both indicate this assumption.

20

GERMANY

1942 TO 1943

Before we proceed into my military adventures, I would like to make a statement here: I have never talked about this time to anybody but my wartime buddies, and even that only rarely, other than by way of necessary information exchanges. And this will not change in future. On the other hand, to suppress these years in this narrative would have been nonsensical.

Already from the *Labor Service* camp I had volunteered to join the elite troops of the *Waffen SS*, the para-military branch of the *SS*. Their divisions operated under the Supreme Command of the *Wehrmacht*, the German Armed Forces, but in some respect, they were independent of the Army, because they also reported to Heinrich Himmler, the *Reichsführer SS*, commander of the Part's elite. How this dualism was intended to work in practice I do not know.

The *Waffen SS* consisted at the beginning of the war of volunteers only, and they had available the best of weapons and equipment. But they also had the most fanatical officers and soldiers. It was a military elite formation in every sense of the word, which would have greatly appealed to a teenager like me. Their one shortcoming was the fact that most of their officers lacked proper military training, which had caused a number of unfortunate decisions.

I never received any reply to my application, however. Only later did I realize the reason for this. I had mailed it to my home address for forwarding to the correct address, and I suspect, that my mother committed a crime against the Postal Service by tearing-up my well-resourced letter. Yes, she definitely had more sense than me, but she also had the benefit of more experience than a half-baked teenaged adventurer.

After a few days at home, probably in early September of 1942, the *Stellungsbefehl* had arrived, the call-up papers for the Army. And so, I became a slightly hesitant member of the *Heer*, the German Army. My mother brought me to the somewhat decrepit-looking *Wettiner Bahnhof* in Dresden, and off I went to *Lutherstadt* Wittenberg, where this troublesome monk Martin Luther had nailed (tacks had not been invented yet) his inflammatory reformatory manifest to the church door on October 31st of 1517.

By the way, all travel to and from the *Arbeitsdienst* camp and the army barracks was conducted with free military rail passes. Which was just as well, since our emoluments consisted of a sort of pocket-money. This was not exactly a train smash, because there was precious little one could buy during the war. The army postal service was, of course, also free. Otherwise I could not have sustained my rather voluminous correspondences with numerous (two, at this stage) young ladies.

Probably in early autumn of 1942 I reported for duty at the barracks of *Infantry Regiment 53 (mot.)* in Wittenberg. The *(mot.)* stood for 'motorized', a by now slightly euphemistic term, in view of the paucity of vehicles and fuel. Before the war these barracks had housed in fact only the regimental staff and one battalion. They consisted of four main buildings, each housing a company of about one hundred-twenty soldiers, plus the battalion staff buildings.

The regiment, with their vehicles, was keeping itself now busy on the Eastern Front, of course, and in these barracks was now quartered the *Ersatzbattalion 53*, the reserve battalion of this regiment. All new recruits, as well as any recuperated wounded members of the regiment after release from the field hospitals and/or recuperation facilities, were housed in these barracks, until further deployment back to the Elysian Fields of Russia.

The whole establishment was very modern, and therefore in good repair. It was one of the many new barracks, which after 1936 had been built on Hitler's orders. We had central heating, and even a cinema room, I think. Even more important for ever-hungry teenagers, were the regular very reasonable meals.

The first thing for us was to get out of our civvies. We became the (cringing) users of second-hand uniforms, shabby and not properly fitting, with poorly repaired shrapnel or gunshot damage, and in a few cases, with still visible blood spots. Yes, they obviously had belonged to fallen or badly wounded soldiers of the regiment. This had rather a dampening effect on a bunch of otherwise boisterous teenagers.

After we had been assigned to the proper company, platoon and squad, and accordingly to the correct barracks, floor, room and bed, we found ourselves standing in closed ranks on the parade ground. The lecture given by a sergeant was short and to-the-point: "you follow any orders given, you don't argue and ask questions, and you don't think, because prior to the successful completion of your training you are too stupid for that".

This concluded our first day as defenders of the *Vaterland*. But we got soon over this experience as soon as the *Stabsfeldwebel* or *Spies*, the Sergeant Major of the company, raised his soft, melodious and gentle voice for the first time, when he almost blasted us out of our ill-fitting boots with his voice reminiscent of the fog horn of a cruise ship on the high seas. Anyway, we also got used to that inevitable aspect of military life, the shouting and screaming of orders and, usually, obscene comments.

As in the case of the *Arbeitsdienst*, where the same thing happened, I cannot recall what became of our belongings. If they were stored at these barracks, then the army had an interesting problem later-on, because most of us never returned to this place. But then, on the other hand, there was no German army left after 1945, anyway. Problem solved!

The next morning, almost in the middle of the night (at about 5 a.m. or so), we were rudely removed from our beds by our shouting, shrieking, gesticulating corporal. He kindly advised us to get a bloody move on and to clean our stinking bodies in double time, if we intended to partake the gourmet breakfast of the establishment. In fairness, the food was very reasonable, considering we were after all in the fourth year of the war.

When this was done, we assembled on the parade ground again

and got sorted according to height. As recorded in the previous part of this story, my height had been established as a whopping 1,71m (5'7"). This placed me into the third or fourth of about forty-abreast ranks of the marching company. In other words, I was among the taller specimen of the club, whereas today I would bring up the rear, as our son would confirm, looking down from his dizzying height.

Then we started our first drill session. This was the occasion, when I thankfully remembered similar ones at the *Arbeitsdienst* guard platoon, which had prepared me very well for this environment. Apparently, our corporal also thought that I was reasonably well prepared, and something like this is worth a lot for a raw recruit. But I still ended up with hurting calf muscles!

To my consternation I had found out that the 4th Company of an infantry battalion, to which I now belonged, was called the Heavy Company. This designation referred to the heavy machine guns and heavy mortars. 'Heavy' did not only refer to weight, but also to the standard machine guns resting on a carriage, which was hoisted along like a (very heavy) backpack, and to 8cm mortars instead of the standard 5cm ones.

This latter difference did not appear serious, but the ammunition cases were 50% heavier. And to have to lug-around the base plate was pure hell for me! At first sight, this looked like a poor constellation for a teenager with sore shoulders, who is not exactly a Hercules. But it transpired later that things worked out all right for this newly established defender of the *Vaterland*, and dare I say it, as usual.

For three months, we were relentlessly chased about, with parade ground drills, but also with weapons training. We were trained to dismantle and to re-assemble in record time, blindfolded, an *MG34*, a *MaschinenGewehr (19)34*. After a short while, I was assigned the Number 1 position in the team of four. The Number 1 was carrying the machine gun and was in charge of the team, the number 2 carried the carriage, and the other two members of the team were carrying two ammunition boxes each.

Keeping in mind the weight (or is it nowadays the mass?) of the machine gun carriage and of two full ammunition boxes, the

Number 1 got definitely the better end of the stick, even though the machine gun was also not exactly made of foam plastics.

A large military training ground was in walking distance, or rather, in marching and, most often, in running distance, as is usual in all boot camps of any army. Half hidden underground earth bunkers had been constructed there, just like the ones we could later expect to encounter in Russia. To blow them up was great fun, but it dawned on us, that in the field this would not be so easy, because the Russians, these spoilsports, would surely shoot back. We soon realized that this would no doubt complicate things somewhat.

Sometimes I looked out of the window of our squad room and contemplated, how lucky we were to stay in a dry and warm room, instead of a muddy and ice-cold fox hole or trench in Russia. But we generally gave in fact little thought to what would await us after training. Our minds were sort of numb with fatigue, probably so intended by higher command, and there definitely was no hip-hip-hurrah sentiment in the high-spirited expectation to soon be able to face the enemy.

Anyway, give me a few minutes, I have to go and find some chap, probably one of the older soldiers, to exchange my cigarette ration against some *Kommissbrot,* the army brown bread, because I am permanently hungry. I have also put-on quite a bit of weight at this time, but more blubber than muscle, as I remember.

In approximately the middle of this three-month period I had an unsettling experience. My aunt in Berlin had written that she had mailed me a parcel with a cake and some other valuable good-ies. When I did not receive any parcel at the daily mail distribution in the evening, I made some enquiries about this, and it was found, that another recruit had signed for and received my parcel. He was arrested by the *Feldjäger,* the MPs or Military Police of the German military. We later heard (probably on purpose, as a deterrent) that he had been court-martialed and had been sent to the fortress at Torgau, a nearby military prison.

Towards the end of our weapons-training, we marched to a machine gun shooting range at a larger training establishment. Here we fired live ammunition for the first time. A very special feeling for a teenager! I did very well with my heavy machine gun.

The cardboard-and-wood target was almost completely destroyed. This earned me for my effort a week-end pass to travel home to Dresden. As a matter of fact, I managed to earn quite a few of these, either weekend passes or local day-passes. The latter required me to be back at barracks by midnight.

Collecting the spent copper or brass shells from the training fields was another way of earning such passes. For me the best and easiest way, however, to get points towards passes was at rifle practice. Lying-down flat and supporting the rifle, we shot three rounds at a distance of 100m. Usually I managed to get 33 or 34 rings out of a possible 36, which was good enough for another pass.

The local day-passes were no big deal, but they got us out of the barracks, and to a semblance of civilian life. Food was scarce by then, but some pubs and restaurants were still open, and they offered a *Tagesgericht*, what is now called the *Plat du Jour* in civilized society. It usually was just a simple soup, but it was served without food ration stamps being required. As we were permanently hungry and did not have ration stamps, this was much appreciated and of great benefit to us.

Whenever I managed a weekend- or a 3-day-pass home, I spent also some time with my girlfriend, but details about that would surely not be of any interest to anybody, so I skip them for the sake of brevity. By now I was in correspondence not only with my parents and, occasionally, with assorted aunts and uncles (sometimes yielding a parcel or an envelope with a banknote). But mainly I kept in contact with my girlfriend, but also with my cousin of the Severin family in Dresden. You may remember her for her peculiar, confusing and unexplained shaking and shivering in our kitchen some years previously.

Our last maneuver in November of 1942 was a forced march of about 80km, naturally with all our weapons and equipment, to a testing ground of the army engineers at Rosslau near Dessau. It took us two nights and a full day, with simulated fighting while wearing our gas masks, and moving to and fro thrown in for fun. We practiced what we had learned: firing our machine guns and mortars, felling trees, blowing-up walls and using flame-throwers to 'sanitize' bunkers. All highly desirable actions for teenagers.

Let me digress for a moment from the vagaries of the life of a recruit, since we happen to find ourselves in Rosslau near Dessau. My future wife was born here in January of 1943, which means that I missed her by just a few weeks. Amazing, how coincidences sometimes play out.

I survived this little excursion quite well, to the extent that towards the end of the march I was able to carry some additional equipment for a friend of mine, since I had to shoulder 'only' my machine gun, while he was ready to collapse under the weight of the carriage. This was possibly observed by one of the officers and may have been a factor in the subsequent events.

In preparation for this leisurely exercise we had undertaken and endured three night-marches of fifteen kilometers each, which should equal about three hours of marching with combat-ready equipment and weaponry. They took, however, four to five hours each, because we were subjected by our training staff to being fed misdirections, having to find our correct way again, and being shot at (with blanks, they were feeling generous – kidding!), to add to the entertainment value of boot camp.

On one of these outings it was raining cats and dogs. Not having any protection against the downpour was unnerving and depressing. Surely, this was exactly the purpose of the exercise, in order to prepare us for what to expect on the front lines. Amazingly, I did not catch pneumonia or even a sniffle.

The other two excursions took place while the skies were clear. The Milky Way with its billions of stars in all their splendor was magnificent to see, even if it was a bit awkward to peer at it from under the low brim of the steel helmet. The general black-out during the war did help here, as the nights were now pitch-black, without interfering artificial light.

As usual, my mind was wandering and dealing with some of the more complex problems of astrophysics and the chaos theory, while I was contemplating the fact that this view would be practically identical to what we would see later in the Russian *Steppe*. But, to the best of my recollection, I did not for one moment reflect on the implications of what would await me later in Russia.

When our boot camp had come to an end, out of our company of about one hundred-twenty men, a few members were transferred, including my best friend, who were sent to an *Unteroffizier* or NCO (Non-Commissioned Officer) training course.

Remember my carping about an example of sloppy thinking about organizational terminology in the *Hitlerjugend?* We have here, in my un-humble opinion, another example of that same phenomenon. An '*Unteroffizier*' could either be a corporal or an NCO, which would be the correct translation, including the ranks of corporal as well as those of the various ranks of sergeants.

This buddy of mine had been my bed neighbor during these three months, and we got along very well. I was sad to see him go a different way, and, not surprisingly, never saw him again. Did he survive the war?

I was also transferred on this day, but to a reserve officer training course. This would take up another three months, in the same town, but in different barracks. It appeared to me then as if the army was working in three-months cycles everywhere, but this was nonsense, of course.

About a dozen of us, selected from all four companies of the battalion, found ourselves on this course. We were issued new uniforms to replace the shot-up and bloodied ones, and new weapons and equipment. Gone were the machine guns, mortars and ammunition boxes.

We also were given a completely new set of NCOs. The man in charge was a well-educated and highly decorated staff sergeant, and we all wondered, why such a man was not an officer himself. Maybe something had happened in his past. The army could be quite unforgiving.

Now we received intensive training in completely different areas of expertise. *Heeresdienstvorschriften or HDVs*, the Army Regulations, became from now on our daily bread. I still remember the gist of *HDV 300-1*, the basic regulation for infantry field officers, and some details such as: "all decisions depend on the enemy, the position and the terrain.

We studied the organizational charts of most of the different army units. Other aspects covered lines of communication, or how to advance an attacking division or some other unit (the opposite direction was somehow not mentioned). Other subjects were how to maintain discipline and how to do so under fire, recognition of enemy uniforms, tanks and planes, and many other subjects.

Our accommodation in these old barracks was not as nice as what we had experienced during boot camp. They dated back to the Imperial times before WW1. However, this barely registered with us. This whole period is rather blurred in my memory, even more so than most others, because of the intensity and immense pressure of the training, and the resulting stress, which obviously were created on purpose, to evaluate how we reacted.

In February of 1943 we were shocked to hear on the radio that Stalingrad had fallen. The bare facts were terrible enough, but the fact that the entire Sixth Army had been destroyed and the survivors had been taken prisoners was almost impossible to accept. Sad as the death of so many thousands of soldiers was, we were even more concerned about the fate of the prisoners, knowing about the situation on the Russian front, the terrible winter and the attitudes of the Russian soldiers, justified as they were, because of the way we had treated their prisoners. We know today that this was the turning point of the war in Russia, but even then, we had the vague thought that the war could possibly be lost.

One of our instructors, a rather vicious and nasty corporal, was a proper sadist. Even our staff sergeant had to call him to order occasionally, when he thought we would not listen. I don't recall his name, but I will always remember his perpetual sneer. If he would have been a member of the police, he would have been the ready-made candidate for IA, the Internal Affairs section. His repertoire of obscenities and foul language was as amazing as it was disgusting.

For some reason or other, he often zeroed-in on me, the most innocent of the whole army. Possibly because I sometimes contradicted him and corrected him when he made a mistake. Yes, the proverbial 'pain-in-the-ass', well developed in my high school years. It was not exactly surprising that the animosity worked both ways.

On a certain occasion towards the end of the training course, and I don't recall any details about this, I punched him in the face (he was smaller than me) and called him a nasty bastard. As this was observed and reported by another NCO, this was the end of

my abbreviated career as a trainee reserve officer. This was probably just as well, as it turned out later.

The whole training course was shipped to the Russian front
shortly after this incident, when the training wound up. I wonder
how many of them may have survived, and what would have been
my destiny, if I would have gone with them.

21

RUSSIA AND VIENNA

1943

A short time later I also was on my way to the Russian front. Before leaving, I remember we were issued a small travel guide, describing the country, its people and other necessities. Heavily loaded politically, of course. Attached was a seriously under-nourished bilingual dictionary. I still remember, probably wrongly, a few vital words, such as *dom* for house, *kalya* for street, *jaijsa* for eggs, *marushka* for girl or woman, and some other words, unsuitable to quote here, which we had learned from some convalescent wounded soldiers from the Eastern front.

The trip to Russia in the summer of 1943, by train, naturally, must have been uneventful, because I remember nothing about it. Within a few days of leaving Germany we had arrived in the vicinity of Kursk at the front lines in the 'land of milk and honey'. A bleak and desolate landscape, with plenty of shell holes and bomb craters instead of the flowery meadows of back home.

Our transport contingent did not reach the 53rd Infantry Regiment as planned, because we got involved in a German attempt to encircle some Soviet troops with a pincer movement. We advanced through and behind a line of semi-submerged earth bunkers, and I found myself on the roof of one of these clever constructions.

Now I recalled what we had been taught in our training and stuck a hand grenade into their gun slit. This took care of the enemies in this bunker, all right. But as I had anticipated already during our training, the inmates un-sportingly fired at that very moment, and the tip of my left-hand middle finger was gone. No big deal, one would think, as far as most of the horrible battle wounds go. But the pain was something else, with all the nerve endings located in that fingertip.

As soon as our attack had lost its momentum, the Russians started their counter-offensive. In the ensuing confusion and pandemonium of exploding shells, shouts, cries of the wounded and general mayhem, a group of about twenty of us were cut off. All of a sudden, we found ourselves prisoners of the Soviet Army. But, again, my luck partially held. Instead of shipping us off immediately to the salt mines of Northern Siberia, we were temporarily forced to dig trenches for our gaolers.

By then our forces had in turn begun a counterattack, and our transport back to the Russian hinterland had again to be postponed by the Russkies for the moment. This time, the confusion worked in our favor, and I made it back to our lines. I cannot say what became of the others and I could only hope that they also managed to return to our by now again retreating positions.

One of the more bizarre rumors on the Russian front, which purported to deal with this kind of situation, was a so-called *Führerbefehl*, a personal order by Hitler. This order was claimed to stipulate that any German soldier crossing over from the Russian lines, and any Russian soldiers voluntarily coming to our front positions, were immediately to be evacuated from the Eastern Front. It was claimed at the time that there were worries that brain-washed German prisoners or planted Russian 'sleepers' could be infiltrated into our front lines as 'Trojan Horses'.

Judging by what had happened in my case, I tended to believe, as an exception, that this rumor was true, but also because it made sense. There existed another indication regarding the correctness of this rumor: much later we learned about the divisions of ex-Soviet Army soldiers fighting in Italy on our side. Anyway, within hours I was on my way back into the *Heimat*, the homeland. I was thus deprived of the chance to single-handedly subdue the enemy.

Back in Germany, in late summer of 1943 I found myself, again, in another army unit. This one was stationed in Leisnig near Waldheim/Sachsen. Only the gods know (or some staff officer), why I was not returned to Wittenberg, to my boot camp infantry unit, but I did not complain.

This time I had landed-up with a company of *Panzergrenadiere*, the armored infantry, which was supposed to use the *Schützenpanzer Sd. Kfz.* 251 (Wikipedia), the half-track armored troop carriers. The top of these vehicles was open to the elements, so that the ten soldiers could dismount quickly. This unfortunately also meant that the enemy, if close enough, could quickly lob a mortar shell or a hand grenade inside.

If one harbors any thoughts about the unit's designation, let me explain that the company was the proud owner of one single armored troop carrier, the type of vehicle, which gave rise to this terminology. I suspected that this one was probably not functioning anymore. It was only logical that all operational armored vehicles would be at or near the battle fields. We once sat quietly in that thing for a while, probably to get used to the idea of seeing nothing and expecting a mortar shell or hand grenade sailing through the open roof at any moment. But quite a few times we trained getting lightning-fast in and out of this 'sardine tin'.

These barracks consisted of only one block of the company-sized barracks of modern standard design. Hitler had these built all over Germany from 1936 onwards, to house the newly formed units of the *Wehrmacht*. There was also a nice single-family house on the grounds for the Captain in charge of this company.

One of the oldest tricks in the book of the sergeant majors of all armies was the question to the assembled company: "Who can play the piano?" The usual follow-up is: "You three, the kitchen sergeant needs potatoes to be peeled". When one day another well-known trick question was asked: "Who can drive a motor vehicle?" I got reckless and answered in the affirmative, as the modern US Army terminology goes. I got lucky! This time it had not been a trick question.

Finally, after all the frustration on this count during the so-called *Motor Hitlerjugend* and the supposedly motorized infantry boot camp, here I met up with motorcycles and trucks. Together with another two aspirants for driver licenses I was handed over to the *Schirrmeister*, the sergeant in charge of vehicles, weapons and equipment of the company, for the dual driving tests for motorcycles and heavy trucks.

I was lucky to get a sympathetic *Gefreiter*, a lance corporal, to attend to my motorcycle driving examination. He seemed a decent young guy, and I admitted right away to him that my motor-cycle experience was limited to about twenty minutes on a 50cc light motorbike. He told me not to worry, and to get on the Zündapp machine of probably 250cc, with him sitting in the sidecar. With his occasional help I not only managed to start this heavy combination, but to actually driving it. A bit jerkily, of course, but apparently not too bad. No ambulance had to be called.

So far, so good. But now came the hammer: Next I was told to drive the 5ton army truck, in which the sergeant had resided, and which had been following us while he tested some other poor bugger. A catastrophe was in the making and I was ready to throw in the towel, since I never had even been sitting in a truck.

When I relayed the sad truth to my lance corporal that my only remote knowledge of how to drive a truck was what I had observed as a small boy in the bus going to my grandparents' village, how the driver had handled his beast. My lance corporal asked the sergeant to please re-test one of the motorcycle aspirants, because he was not sure whether to pass him or not.

Thus, my savior landed up in the truck with me and ordered me in a gruff voice, obviously for the benefit of the nearby sergeant, to get my bloody bum onto the driver's seat. Now followed the same procedure as before with the motorbike. With his help the driving took place on rural roads between Leisnig and nearby Döbeln, which were, because of the war, almost empty.

In Döbeln, a mid-sized industrial town, disaster struck! I was required to make a sharp turn, from one narrow street into another even narrower one, and the 5ton truck took off the corner of an old disused building. The vehicle did not show much damage, over and above all the scrapes and dents it already had. All I can say about the house is that it did not collapse. At the end I received, to my great surprise, my military driver's licenses, for motorbikes, cars and trucks; the works.

In Hartha, a small town between Leisnig and Waldheim, I knew about a branch of the Teicher family. The husband, about my father's age, must have been a son of one of my grandfather's brothers. Soon I decided to pay them a visit. Nobody having a telephone then, the procedure was to put-on one's boots and march there from our barracks. Anyway, the distance to Hartha was only five or six kilometers, so a brisk walk of an hour was no problem at all for somebody who used to walk almost three times that far in Dresden in the interest of keeping in touch, literally, with my girlfriend.

While stationed in Leisnig I visited the family several times. Usually I managed to scrounge a piece of cake and a cup of *Ersatz* coffee, or some supper. Hunger was one of the immovable constants of a war-time teenager. The fact that there was also a daughter of about sixteen in the house is purely coincidental and had nothing to do with my repeated visits. Just in the interest of family affiliation, this is anyway, what I claim! This led to another entry into my address book, and we kept up our correspondence right to the end of the war.

We remained in this post for maybe four weeks, enjoying ourselves with occasional square-bashing, maneuvers with our gas masks worn, night-time marches and similar military diversifications. But most of the time our NCO's spent their efforts on the organized killing of time. Soldiers have to be kept occupied at all times! In the meantime, my military career made huge advances: I was surprised to be promoted from Private to Private First Class. This in the German Army unusual grade had been known to me only vaguely.

But eventually our marching orders did come, and we were issued new so-called tropical uniforms. Now we were matched with some other companies and were designated a *Marschbattalion*, a Transit Battalion, and received a Lieutenant Colonel as commander. In Waldheim we were loaded, with all our possessions, meaning our weapons and equipment, onto a goods train, and sent on our way. To the Caucasus or the Crimea, it was rumored, because of our unusual uniforms. We were unloaded at a likely stage on the way to Southern Russia, namely in Vienna.

Our temporary quarters were a very large, but unfortunately empty, beer brewery. The name, and the name of the suburb is temporarily inaccessible in my memory, probably due to a virus or

Trojan Horse or some other bug in my brain. No, false alarm! The name of the suburb came back just now. The brewery was in Mödling, on the outskirts of Vienna. The name of the brewery is still not available, so I am prevented from some clandestine advertising for them.

We had, temporarily, a wonderful time there, even without the beer. Since there was nothing else to do for us but wait, which is often the usual army way all over the world to spend the soldier's time, we got permission to leave the place almost every day, and there was no unduly strict control over the time of our return to barracks in the evening, or rather in the middle of the night.

This allowed us to visit the *Prater* several times. This is the Vienna amusement park, which was open all year round, I guess. Officially, the prime attraction was one of the largest Ferry Wheels in the world. We duly enjoyed all this, but there was another, and more important, attraction: because of the war, and since most able-bodied young men were away in the army, there was a pleasing surplus of nubile maidens to be found there.

As fearless soldiers we were prepared and capable to face the dangers and hardships presented by this gender imbalance, and in the interest of national security, as one would lie nowadays, we went there in spite of all these perils. No, sorry, rather in the interest of national entertainment of the civilian population, another convincing white lie.

One day, a group of our chaps proceeded to the inner-city of Vienna. Unfortunately, I cannot report that they went to visit the historical buildings and sites, the *Hofburg* and *Schönbrunn*, for instance. Somebody had heard, or had somehow found out, about the claim that Vienna rivaled Paris as to having the most luxurious *bordellos* in all of Europe.

An exploratory visit was clearly justified on the basis, that teenagers have an obligation to broaden their cultural experience in all spheres of life. It was, however, a vicious distortion of the facts, when it was later claimed that I went upstairs with this slim girl in the transparent top, since I had not even been part of this educational expedition, due to my lack of interest in such things.

When I came to Vienna again in the 1990s with my wife, on a stop-over on our way from Johannesburg to Frankfurt, we visited

Schönbrunn, the famous Imperial summer residence of the Haps-
burgs, as well as the monuments of Joseph Strauss, the 'king of
waltz' composer, and of Maria Theresia, the Austrian Empress
who was forced to fight Fredric the Great of Prussia in three
terrible wars, after he had occupied her province of Silesia.

As we strolled along the *Ring* and some of the other inner-city
streets, I thought I recognized a certain imposing but infamous
building. But I must have been wrong, because the name on the
beautifully polished nameplate next to the entrance did not raise
any memories. Yes, a 'selective memory' is sometimes quite
beneficial.

All good things, inevitably, come to an end. Even in the military, and particularly in the military! Out of the blue, we were one
evening each issued a bottle of brandy, a bottle of red wine (plonk)
and two or three of the famous Scho-ka-Cola tins. These round
orange-colored containers held two or three slabs of a highly
concentrated dark chocolate. As the designation implies, the chocolate contained a helping of Kola extract.

As far as we knew, these tins were ordinarily issued only to the
flying personnel of the air force and to the submariners of the
navy. Being by now a reasonably seasoned soldier, I knew what was
coming. Right! Immediately after this generous and unusual gift
bonanza the commander of the battalion announced that we
would ship out in the morning (in the army this translates to something like four or five o'clock), destination undisclosed, as always in
the military. The shock had hit all of us in the you know where,
even though we had known very well all along that this was an
inevitable development.

Part of our gear was the *Kochgeschirr*, a metal container with a
lid, used to receive our hot meals from the *Feldküche*, the field
kitchen. The deep lid served as a further container for liquid or
other nourishments. My decades of military experience dictated
that such valuable and fragile items of sustenance had to be
consumed forthwith, since we would very soon be partaking of
bellicose adventures.

Consequently, I decided to open both bottles and to transfer
their contents first into the *Kochgeschirr* and its lid, and after mixing
the contents properly, into my belly. I admit, this was not quite the

done thing, but I was convinced that the contents would be save there. Surprisingly, this brilliant and reasonable expectation was proven wrong shortly afterwards. Subsequently, there was only darkness!

I was told later that two of our chaps made me sit on my horizontally held rifle, and that I was thus hand-carried to the train of boxcars, in which our *Marschbattalion,* the Transfer Battalion, left *Gay Paris,* sorry, left beautiful Vienna. Thus, my undignified exit from paradise took place.

As mentioned before, the army is the rumor mill *par excellence.* The latest versions floating about in our quarters were talking about the Crimea and/or the Caucasus as our destination. This appeared to be a reasonable assumption, in view of our tropical uniforms. Maybe, as an exception, the rumors had a sound base in this case.

In any case, when I finally more or less had woken up, a few facts established themselves:

a) the Battalion doctor diagnosed severe alcohol poisoning,
b) I had lost my breakfast, and all the valuable alcoholic intake (which, according to the doctor, probably saved my life),
c) thirty-six hours had mysteriously disappeared from my life,
d) my throat had developed a tremendous thirst, and
e) the sun was shining in unusual surroundings.

I had not realized before, that Southern Russia could look so pretty and civilized. In other words: we had finally arrived in the country of our destination.

It astounded me, how fast the German railroad engineers had managed to adjust the width of the deviant Russian rails to the inner-European standard. Yes, a few things I still remembered from the geography lessons.

One of the other things I noticed in my befuddled state of mind was the fact, that the train had stopped amidst extensive vineyards. These people of Southern Russia really knew how to live!

We quickly left our boxcar to relieve ourselves, because the chances were slim that the train would carry-on without us. I had a closer look at what held up the vines in these fields and I discovered that the trees serving as supports for the wires which were keeping the vines upright, carried thick black berries, which looked like our German blackberries. Naturally, we tasted them, but only a few, not knowing which sort of poison they might contain. One just did not know what to expect from these people!

Our precaution had been justified, as we realized shortly afterwards. There was no poison in those berries, of course, but they acted as the most potent laxative I have ever experienced. Eventually, the train slowly started moving again, to enable the debarked soldiers to climb back into their carriages again. Apparently, we were indispensable for the future war effort.

At the next stop we found ourselves at a large railway station, and two Russian planes dropped a few small bombs, to welcome us into the reality of war, where live ammunition, shells and bombs are the tools of the trade.

But when I saw two signs at the station: *'Acqua'* and *'Firence'*, then the Penny finally dropped. Even in my tortured brain it became clear to me, that the train driver must have made a monumental mistake, since he had landed us in Italy, instead of in Southern Russia, as ordered.

Eureka!!

Again, destiny had intervened in my life, but this time, I am sure, not in the form of my father. We had suddenly a very much improved future outlook over fighting the Russians. Now the Russian dictionary could be thrown away, the German blackberries had mutated to mulberries, *'acqua'* turned to 'water' and *Firenze* became now Florence, or rather Florenz for us.

22

ITALY

1943 TO JULY 1944

We had read already back in November of 1942 that General Eisenhower had landed with US troops in North Africa. Shortly before our epic train ride had started, we had also heard that Mussolini had been toppled, and that Italy had changed sides in this war as well, just as in WW1.

This was confirmed by the two-page flyer, which we had been shown by some Italians. This is my translation:

MUSSOLINI TOPPLED.

GERMAN SOLDIERS!

On 25 July at 22.45, radio Rome announced officially:
The Emperor and King has accepted the resignation of the Prime Minister,
Chancellor and Secretary of State, His Excellency Benito Mussolini.
The Emperor and King has nominated as new Prime Minister, Chancellor and
Secretary of State, His Excellency Marshall Lord Pietro Badoglio.

ITALY HAS ABANDONED THE WAR.

THE AXIS IS BROKEN.

GERMAN SOLDIERS!

The Italians seek a separate peace!
Your ally has mutated into your enemy!
HITLER CANNOT SEND YOU ANY HELP!
The way through Italy to your homeland is
irrevocably blocked.
Italy has become enemy territory.
Two choices are open to you:
Either die senselessly in Sicily or
cross our lines back to your homeland.
Time is of the essence!
The experienced soldier knows what he has to do
when the battle is lost.

YOU HAVE THE ENEMY AT YOUR BACK

Recently I was given an original of this flyer by the widow of an Allied soldier, who is living in our retirement village in South Africa. Her husband had first fought in North Africa against Field Marshal Rommel's *Afrikakorps*, and then with the British 8th Army all the way from Sicily up to North Italy. Another widow of a former Allied soldier from the Italian campaign is also living here. For all I know, I might even have been fighting one or the other (of the men) somewhere, sometime in Italy. I am glad to record, that both men and their wives had become our very good friends in our village.

It became obvious now to us that we had been sent here to reinforce the German divisions in Italy, originally the reserves of our Afrika Korps. We now had a clearer picture of what had happened in Italy shortly before we had arrived here. In early September of 1943 Mussolini had been deposed as Prime Minister by his own party's executive committee, arrested and incarcerated at a hotel at the Monte Gran Sasso, the highest part of the Apennine Mountains. Hitler gave orders to liberate him, and in mid-September of 1943 Colonel Skorzeny, an *SS* officer, led an airborne rescue party, like a modern SWAT team, to bring the *Duce* to Germany. Mussolini later re-created a Socialist-Fascist government in Northern Italy, fighting (sort of) on the German side until 1945.

The *OKW*, the *Oberkommando der Wehrmacht*, had not been completely surprised by the Italians changing sides. Under the cover-name of 'Alarich' (after Mussolini's fall the designation was changed to 'Fall Achse'), they had made their preparations for these developments. German troops had been strategically distributed over all of Italy, which enabled them to quickly disarm the Italian military when it became necessary (Wikipedia).

I better explain right at the beginning of this part of my story a peculiarity of this Italian campaign. The Allied navies were the masters of the surrounding seas and their air forces had absolute control of the air space over this theater. During all of these years the German armies were forced to slowly retreat, usually a few kilometers every three or four days, and their armies advanced in the same fashion.

Sometimes we were stuck in one place for several weeks, but this was the exception. At other times we had to retreat fast for ten or fifteen kilometers in one go. It could, therefore, be said that most of the time we were involved in jerky retreat. A side-effect of this was that we had intimately learned about the topography of the areas we had just vacated, which substantially facilitated the clandestine activities of the outfit I will mention later.

The most important practical aspects for the campaign in Italy were the absolute supremacy of the Allied air and naval forces. Without these, I am convinced, the German troops would have been able to stop the Allied advances in this mountainous country, at least for an extended period of time. But with the situation as it presented itself in 1943, there existed no realistic chance for the German forces to achieve more than an extended defensive withdrawal.

Maybe this is also the time to explain that my rather defeatist attitude towards the war and the military had substantially changed after our arrival in Italy. Fighting the Americans and British in a well-known country took on a very different perspective from the prospect of the war in Russia. Also, we soon found out that here a more or less civilized war was being fought.

Now the future did not look as forbidding as it did a few months ago, even though it still was a bloody war. And now the adventurous side of the fighting came for us more into the foreground. After all, we were teenagers. There was for us, however, no more any political aspect to the war. Most of us had by now shed our misguided Nazi past. We were now simply serving as patriots and soldiers.

The train with our *Marschbattalion* had travelled from Florence, bypassing Rome, to near the front lines at Cassino in central Italy. The incessant growl of the artillery was dominating the air. We were unloaded, probably at the end of September 1943. The colonel in charge, or maybe the Sergeant Major, asked who could speak Italian.

Since this looked suspiciously like one of the famous trick-questions of the army, nobody claimed this vital knowledge. Until I opened my big mouth and explained my limited background in Latin and Spanish. Because amongst the blind the one-eyed is king, I was appointed as the interpreter for the battalion. As an experienced warrior I speculated that some fringe benefits might be connected to such a position.

An Italian regiment stationed near Cassino had wisely decided to end the war and mostly had gone home. At this time, we took part in relieving them of their weapons and equipment. I used the occasion to exchange my carabine 98k for an Italian machine-pistol, intended for their parachute regiments.

This weapon had a wooden stock, and it used the standard 9mm ammunition for automatics and machine-pistols. What baffles me to the present day: how I got away with this unauthorized swop for all those war years. The rifle was in the German army considered the 'soldier's bride', never to be abandoned.

As it turned out, our Transfer Battalion was destined to replenish the 29th *Panzergrenadier Division*, which had suffered heavy losses in the retreat from Sicily to Cassino. On our arrival, the battalion had been allocated a few trucks, requisitioned from the nearby disarmed Italian regiment. Because of my military driver's license, I was given one of these vehicles to transfer to the battalion's temporary destination.

It was a small truck, rather decrepit, and with a slipping clutch.

To my own surprise, I remembered the essentials, and managed to start this beast and drove reasonably well. Even the slipping clutch problem was mastered, simply by pressing the accelerator only lightly and intermittently.

In tropical heat the battalion marched from Cassino via Pontecorvo to Esperia, luckily without their equipment, which had been loaded onto the trucks. I knew about the history of Pontecorvo, an important historical place, and during the Middle Ages part of the Roman State of the Popes. Nowadays, it looked more like a large village to me, at least the part we traversed on our way.

There were two remarkable sights there for us new arrivals in Italy. A number of old women, sorry, elderly ladies, were sitting in their open doorways, and smoking big twisted cigars, black as their dresses. The other surprising sight was one of the women, who was walking in the dusty street with a desk sewing machine on her head. A similar view I only encountered again, more than twenty years later, in South Africa.

After passing Pontecorvo there came first a hair needle curve and then quite a steep climb. To nobody's surprise I arrived as the last one with my chariot in Esperia, our destination. This was a small rural village on top of a hill, as is usual in these parts of the country. Some of us were billeted in the local primary school. Luckily for me, the previous occupiers had left behind an assortment of schoolbooks, and I was able to start my preliminary studies of the Italian language. Which turned out to be quite easy for me, because of my previous basic grounding in Latin and Spanish.

My studies were periodically disturbed by some unnatural, piercing cries, which made my toenails stand up. Later I found out that these infernal tortured cries had been made by the local population of donkeys, or mules (I can never remember the difference) when they wanted to engage in some conversation with their neighbors. Otherwise I do not remember much about the place, other than that we had a beautiful view of the Abbey of Monte Cassino in the distance, silhouetted against the high chain of the Apennine Mountains and the blue Mediterranean sky.

At this time the German Armies in Italy consisted of the 10th Army, under the command of General von Viettinghoff, operating along the west coast, and the 14th Army, commanded by General von Mackensen, on the east coast of Italy. There is some confusion, whether they had the rank of General, or already had been promoted to *Generaloberst*, Colonel General. These two Armies formed the Army Group C of Field Marshal Kesselring.

Included in these two armies were the *I. SS Panzerkorps* (armored) and the *II. Fallschirmjägerkorps* (airborne), which included the *'Division Herman Göring'* (Wikipedia). The airborne divisions were, however, not fighting in their intended capacity, but as infantry units. The strength of the German troops in Italy at this point was approximately 410 000, that of the German forces in total was about 6 500 000 at the same time (Wikipedia).

Because of the absolute domination of the skies by the Allies I do not remember having seen any of our planes in action. The previously established *Luftgau Süd* (an air force command corresponding to an Army) had ceased to exist by now, because there were practically no German airplanes anymore.

I have no idea what the position was regarding the naval formations, if any existed in the Med, bottled up at Gibraltar and the Suez Canal, but they would also have been part of Field Marshal Kesselring's command as the "Supreme Commander of the Mediterranean Theater". I can only say, that neither of these latter two forces were visible to us soldiers, except for the paratrooper divisions.

Further, there were several divisions of former Soviet soldiers, which had been captured in Russia and were now fighting on the other side, for obvious reasons not in Russia, but instead in Italy. Occasionally, we encountered soldiers of these units, but I do not remember any details, other than that most of them did not look like Europeans, because they appeared to look not Russians but Mongoloids or Turkmenian people.

The 10th Army consisted at this stage of the XIV Army Corps, which included the 29th *Panzergrenadier Division* and at least one other infantry division, plus the LXXVI Army Corps, which would also have had at least two infantry division. In addition to their respective staff complements there were further Army Corps and Army combat and support units.

The 29th *Panzergrenadier Division* consisted of the 15th and 71st

Infantry Regiments, the 29th Artillery Regiment and about eight free-standing specialized battalions, such as engineers, signals, tanks, anti-tank, anti-aircraft, a field hospital and some smaller units.

In the following years both German armies switched positions more than once between west and east of Italy depending on the strength of the local Allied attacks. For the same reasons, the Army Corps in turn were shifted between the Armies, and the divisions were moved from Corps to Corps as required, depending on "enemy, situation and lay of the land" (the reserve officers course in Wittenberg!). The divisions were the largest unit, whose composition did not mutate like this.

Most of the soldiers identified themselves only with their regiment or their free-standing battalion. Their division was, for most, the upper limit of their knowledge and interest in organizational matters. This to-and-fro was naturally confusing for the majority of our soldiers, who were not interested in such things, the way I took an interest.

The German forces were confronted by the Allied 15th Army Group, under the command of the British General Alexander. This consisted of the 5th US Army of General Clark and the 8th British Army of General Montgomery (Wikipedia). They each also had numerous additional army corps and divisions of their allies under their command.

Prior to a conference between our colonel and the local mayor, the former talked to me, obviously bored and with nothing to do but waiting for the Italian. Amongst other things, he asked for my background and I told him about my unsuccessful attempt to volunteer for the *Waffen SS* and the abortive reserve officer course.

He suggested that I speak to a friend of his, a Major from the *Division Brandenburg*, who was just then visiting a German priest at the Abbey of Monte Cassino. I was keen to do so, because I had previously heard of this Special Forces unit. With the help of our commander I borrowed a side-car motorcycle and I was off to Monte Cassino.

While the Major was still busy, a German monk from the Rhineland gave me a tour of the monastery and showed me, among other interesting things, the imposing fortified building from the Middle Ages, and some manuscripts dating back to the time when the order of the Benedictines and the abbey were established by St. Benedict in the 6th century, if I remember correctly.

When the Major eventually was free, he checked that I had the basics of English, Latin, Spanish and even a tiny bit of Italian. He said he was happy that I was showing an interest in things other than purely military. When I asked how I could volunteer for this unit, he presented me with some printed papers, the details of which I have conveniently forgotten, because they were stamped 'Secret' in blood-red. Which I signed there and then. I was informed, that he was my new commanding officer, and that I was now, this probably was in October of 1943, a member of the local detachment of *Division Brandenburg*, and that he would get busy with the relevant paperwork.

He warned me to keep my mouth shut about all and everything in connection with my new outfit. Every little thing relating to my new 'home' unit was to be considered 'top secret'. He read me the riot act in case I would flap my mouth.

And he explained that the designation of this 'ghost' unit had only in the autumn of 1942 been upgraded from a regiment to a division, but that it was really neither a regiment nor a division in the normal military sense, but simply a loose accumulation of Special Forces units, spread out over all of German-occupied Europe, and a few in the not-yet-occupied countries!

The *Division*, he further explained, was part of the *Abwehr*, the Armed Forces intelligence and counter-intelligence set-up, under the command of Admiral Canaris. The various detachments were affiliated to large army units as required. As far as appearances went, we presented the same picture as any army unit, same rank insignia, same uniforms. This organization could probably best be compared with some Special Forces of the US Army.

The Major took me, together with another two applicants, who had not been part of the *Marschbattalion*, to the detachment, where we were sworn-in and our simplified job-description was explained:

- collect behind the lines details about the enemy forces,
- sabotage the opposing forces whenever possible,
- identify Italian partisans and their lairs,

- infiltrate the suspected network of people, who assist shot-down Allied airmen to return to base in Southern Italy.

The first two tasks were executed often and successfully. The other two in our particular case were flops, probably because we lacked the necessary competences and experiences, since we had no detectives in our unit. Later we found out that the suspected network actually had existed and had been very active indeed, and very successful.

In the early years there never were partisans operating so close to the front lines where we did our work. In our initial area of operation, the west coast of central Italy, we never came across any partisan activities. These only became a problem towards the end of the war.

Other detachments of the *Division*, as we discovered after the war, had been very active in discovering groups of partisans, but they had only become serious threats for the German troops shortly before the end of the war. Prior to that, they had mainly been a nuisance factor.

We received uniforms of the II Army Corps of the so-called "Anders Army". This unit consisted of exiled Polish men and operated at this time near the Adriatic coast of Eastern Italy. This made it highly unlikely that we would encounter them in our work behind the front lines on the Mediterranean coast of Western Italy.

When we used them, only very occasionally, they were worn over our own battle dress. Mine had belonged to a 1st Lieutenant (I was actually too young for this rank!). So, after the unfinished reserve officers course, I had now become a 1st Lieutenant anyway. Ha!

In addition to the fact that I had been promoted to Pfc some months previously, I was now advanced to the next step, namely to lance corporal, on my unstoppable promotion ladder to become a Field Marshal.

The shadowy commander of all the *Brandenburg* detachments in Italy was stationed in Verona, the HQ of Field Marshal Kesselring. If I understood correctly at the time, there were two such detachments, one each in the operational areas of the two German armies in Italy. But possibly this should read: four, one in the areas of each army corps of the two German armies.

Some of this information we already knew about at the time, but most of it only surfaced after the end of the war, once we were in the PoW camps, when people started for the first time to talk freely about the things which up to this point had been classified secrets.

Why did we volunteer for this shadowy and high-risk *Brandenburg* outfit? Was it the recklessness of youth, or was it the adrenalin push, or the result of patriotism? I'm not sure, probably a bit of all of them. However, what did not come into the equation, was political fanaticism. This had by now more or less evaporated for most of us.

In spite of the high-risk character of our missions, ours was not a suicide commando. The Major made it quite clear that the *'Heldentod der Dummheit'*, the hero's death of stupidity or recklessness, was neither acceptable, nor desirable. I must admit that this clarification went down well with me, and as I gathered, with my fellow 'suicidals' as well.

It was also appreciated that he confirmed the discontinuance of the previous SOP, the Standing Operating Procedure, of issuing Prussic acid pills to the members of the *Division*. Previously, the members of the *Regiment Brandenburg* were issued these pills in cases, where they might be taken prisoner, to enable them to avoid forced interrogations.

It was further explained to us, that we would receive our rations, 'pocket money' (service pay), field-post letters and, above all, our 'tools of the trade', namely ammunition, mines, flamethrowers, explosives and detonator cable, wireless sets, etc. from or through the 29th *Engineering Battalion*, the engineering battalion of the 29th Division.

We were not to mention under any circumstances our true unit, but to act at all times as if we were members of this battalion. With the benefit of hindsight, I can only assume that at least the battalion commander, Major Holzapfel, and some of his staff must have been in the true picture.

After sitting around for two or three weeks in typical army tradition we were finally issued our first mission orders. We were to cross the front lines in the direction of Salerno, to blow up an important railroad bridge and to gather intelligence. Our bosses were interested in unit names and designation numbers, their approximate strength and where they were stationed. And to create as much mayhem as possible on the way, if possible.

Six soldiers were placed under my 'command', probably because of my English and (perceived) knowledge of Italian, and because the sergeant, who originally was scheduled to lead this action, had been wounded in an unrelated event. We collected our explosives and wireless sets and were on our way south.

Crossing the front lines at night was not too difficult. The land was extremely broken, hills and valleys, vineyards and occasional brush territory, and not to mention the steep mountains and cliffs. We traversed farmlands most of the time, and we had thought barking dogs were the only real danger. But the farmers showed no inclination to find out what went on outside their houses. And those farms which were housing Allied troops were easily avoided, because we could spot their sentries well in advance with our night goggles and the glowing tips of their cigarettes.

We had to cross the *Garigliano* River, but this was not a problem, to reach the bridge over this river near Minturno, which we had come to blow up. While we did not overly worry about the dangers we faced, it is undeniable that the adrenalin was flowing so strongly that it could easily have been bottled.

Our intention had been to mine two pillars, but we managed only the one, when we encountered enemy fire. But the one was sufficient. This enterprise was highly successful, because we were able to blow up the railway bridge, with a goods train full of supplies and troops on top as a bonus, also tumbling down into the riverbed.

Two of our chaps were slightly wounded, and we had to half-carry them back to our lines. The Major was very pleased by the successful completion of our first assignment, because we had avoided heavy losses. Did we have sleepless nights about the soldiers we had killed? No, we had just done our job, and the enemy would have done the same to us, given the opportunity. We also had by now sufficient front experience and were adequately 'toughened'.

None of us will ever forget the peculiar smell of the dust of a very recently bombed, or shelled, or blown-up residential building. But the all-pervading stench from such building two weeks later, with some corpses still buried under the rubble, has escaped my memory. Perhaps because I wanted to forget it.

Were we worried during these times about the fate of the innocent civilians, caught between the two fronts, suffering from bombing raids, artillery shells and, not to forget, from hunger and deprivations of all kinds? Again, the answer is no, even though some such vague thoughts sometimes crossed our minds. But a soldier walking through the rubble with an army bread under his arm, searching for a mother to offer her body to get some food for her starving children, this was definitely beyond the pale! Such callous behavior should have led to the stockade!

Front line soldiers cannot afford to dwell on such thoughts too much, or they will suffer a mental breakdown. An important point here was the fact that we were not aware of what was happening in the bombed cities of Germany. This was a sort of state secret. Our families were well aware of the dangers to write about it, and of the censorship of the field post.

As explained earlier, some of our supplies we received through, rather than from, Engineering Battalion 29. We had to collect our mines and explosives and similar toys directly from the depot of the *KoPiFü*, the *KorpsPionierFührer*, a colonel, who coordinated the engineering battalions of the divisions within the Army Corps.

Sometime in December of 1943, with just two or three men and the driver, we set off at night in a 5-ton truck to collect *Tellerminen*, the flat disk-like anti-tank mines. On our way the truck had a flat tire, caused by an intriguingly shaped small steel contraption, which was constructed in such a way that in any position a triangle-shaped sharpened piece of steel pointed upwards. They were placed on the main roads by partisans operating in the rear area, way behind the front lines.

On our return trip, with a few tons of mines in the back, we were spotted by a fighter-bomber plane, even so we had travelled without any lights, because the night was not too dark. These planes had their machine-canons placed in their wings. Because the pilot was too clever for his own good, he aimed so accurately on this straight part of the road, that both cannons fired just to the right and just to the left of our truck. The fireworks of the shells exploding on the road surface was memorable, but somehow less bothersome than the flat tire on the onward trip. It is amazing, how the human mind can adjust, by becoming blunt and dull and suppressing the most obvious danger signals, at least temporarily.

This phenomenon manifested itself often enough, when we mined a critical area behind Allied lines, for instance between soldiers' quarters and where they had parked their tanks or pieces of artillery. For this purpose, we preferred to use Italian wooden box-like anti-personnel mines, because they were difficult to detect by their engineers.

But these mines were also notoriously 'nervous' and could blow up at any time, and for no good reason. Therefore, it was a risky business, to put it politely. On the other hand, they were easy to hide in the mostly sandy soil of the valleys, in which both sides were generally forced to operate.

This space between quarters of our 'clients' and their parked equipment was crucial for us, when we had come 'visiting' to place explosives under tank turrets or into the 'mouths' of guns. If the guards spotted something suspicious, they advanced towards the parking grounds. After the first mine blew up, they usually diverted their attention to their own problems, leaving us time to detonate our 'Easter Eggs' and withdraw from the scene. Sometimes this meant carrying our wounded with us, if we had encountered 'unfriendly' fire.

On many occasions, we performed specific raids on enemy rear quarters, where the resistance was generally weak, to supplement our provisions. Particular aims were the C-Rations of the US Army (we once carried away a large consignment of them), but cigarettes and cigars, tobacco, coffee and Nescafé and many other precious items, which we did not have ourselves, also found their way into our backpacks.

Our Major was not exactly pleased with our 'acquisition raids', but when we often also brought with us enemy documents or small weapons we had not encountered before, he was mollified, especially when I presented him with an authentic-looking six-shooter silver-plated revolver. Some GI cowboy must have been very sorry, and very sore, about his loss.

This period was more or less comparable to what the US Army in Vietnam very much later called R&R, Rest and Recreation. With the stress on Recreation. Rest we could have after the war, or when we were dead. Now was the time for Recreation! We had as much of that as we could manage.

By now, I had acquired a simple radio, und could listen to *RAI*, the state radio service of Northern Italy, our so-called ally. They had an emission called '*Al di la del Garigliano*', beyond the (river) Garigliano, at this time the line between the Allies and us. This program provided news from the Allied occupied Southern Italy. This was of great interest to us, because it gave us sometimes details about local conditions there, which would not have been available to us otherwise. This came in handy, when we set out again on one of our 'excursions' down south.

One beautiful sunny day I went as a passenger in a BMW 350cc side-car combination in the direction of Subiaco. Why and under which circumstances, I have forgotten. But I do remember the clear blue sky on this day, and the breath-taking view of the snow-capped Apennine Mountains above Subiaco (from the Latin 'sub lacus' 'under the lake'). Apparently, my parents' school fees for me were not completely wasted.

This was a smallish country town below a large body of a natural mountain lake, which had served two thousand years ago to provide water for Rome by way of one of the famous many kilometers long viaducts. I also remember the sunburn on my lower legs, which happened when we were waiting (for what or for whom?) on the edge of some forest.

Already in October of 1943, the *OT*, the *Organisation Todt* had started to build the fortifications of the *Gustav Linie*, from the valleys of the Liri and the Garigliano rivers, past Cassino and extending to Ancona on the Adriatic coast.

This semi-military organization was always utilized, when the German Armed Forces needed construction work on a grand scale performed anywhere in occupied Europe, sometimes under enemy fire or bombardments. To mention just their two largest contracts: they had built the *Westwall* along the French-German borders, and later the *Atlantikwall*, from Northern Norway to the Spanish border. Even today one can still visit the bunkers, along the Danish Atlantic coast, for instance.

The Cassino battles started in December of 1943. In four major offensives the Allies tried to break through the Gustav Line. But they succeeded only in May of 1944, after heroic resistance, particularly by a division of *Fallschirmjäger*, the paratroopers. 'Carpet bombing' by the US Air Force seemed to have annihilated all life and resistance around the flattened Cassino railway station, but these elite soldiers just refused to yield and blocked the Allied advances again and again.

Eventually, Polish and French elite troops of men, who had been caught outside their countries by the outbreak of war, broke through the lines of the *Hoch- und Deutschmeister Division*, staffed by troops from the former Austria.

This was also the time, when the Abbey and the Monastery of Monte Cassino were bombed by the Allied air forces and this European cultural heritage was reduced to rubble. And this was caused by the faulty judgement of a local Allied commander, who had wrongly assumed that the elevated position of the Abbey had been used by our artillery observers to direct our fire (Wikipedia).

After the first Allied offensive our 10th Army started a counter-offensive down the Garigliano valley. Our divisions took some villages and small country towns near Ausonia, but our attack soon petered out. The pandemonium caused during an offensive and the following counter-offensive is impossible to describe.

Our detachment took the opportunity, created by the general confusion, to carry on at night a few kilometers further down the valley behind the lines. By now night had fallen, which further increased the general disorganization. This enabled us to success-fully place some of our explosive devises. On the way back to our lines we captured a wounded Colonel and brought him back with us. A deserved bonus!

During some of our escapades behind the lines we made an unpleasant discovery: the soil in the old-established olive planta-tions was hard as concrete. It was completely impossible to lie there on the ground and relax or sleep. Every little hump felt like a sharp pebble digging into our bodies.

At one occasion, our 29th Engineers, who were laying anti-tank mines next to the main road between Cassino and Rome, roped us in to prepare excavations to place explosives ready to blow up the road, bridges and culverts, which was one of our specialties. To make army life more interesting, the nearby Allied units blasted our field of activity with mortars, but luckily without much effect, as was the case so often with mortars.

The Allied air force had the engrained obsession to bomb this road out of existence by employing the 'carpet bombing' technique. This consisted of something like five or six dozen bombers, flying in very close formation and simultaneously releasing their 'presents' from above over a small area. I hated to think how many bombs they wasted for any one effective hit, and their costs!

It sounds crazy today, but we often survived their attention by crawling into the fortunately numerous culverts under the very road they were bombing, and most of the time it worked. But then there were the times when, for some of us, it did not.

Our detachment became involved in the 2nd or 3rd of the four distinct battles of Cassino, probably because of the hectic attacking activities of the Allies, which barred us from our intended operations. We were dug-in at a factory, which was either a cigarette or a tobacco manufactory. The place was already partially destroyed when we arrived there, but there were still some large bales of apparently locally produced tobacco laying around. This was highly welcome news, because virtually all soldiers had their pipes, since tobacco was generally more easily available than cigarettes, and cigars were unobtainable anyway (except for high ranking officers, maybe?).

I remember one day when I was walking all by myself along a country road in the area, minding my own business, probably re-organizing the German armies (something I still do regularly today, but for different objects), when it appeared that the guns of the Allied Navy off the nearby coast started to aim specifically for me.

This was a silly idea, of course, but the fields on both sides of the road were pock-marked by more and more of peculiar and similar-looking shell craters in the soft soil. They were about thirty centimeters deep, and always on the same side they had a narrow funnel, reaching down to the bottom of the craters. It took me a while to figure out that the reason for this was the fact that these shells had time-delayed fuses. Very handy, if one was shelling the wall of a building, and the grenade only exploded, and did its worst, once it was inside. But they were a complete waste on a soggy farm field.

The funnels provided the exact direction from where the shells had come. A classic example of useless information: the ships were out of reach for our artillery, because the reach of the naval guns exceeded that of our guns.

From late 1943 to the middle of 1944, two separate but connected Allied operations caused a lot of confusion, damage and losses on both sides. In order to help break through the Cassino front, the Allies had landed troops way behind our lines in January of 1944 at Anzio and Nettuno, two small towns at the edge of the Pontinian Marshes, just south of Rome. The double purpose of this amphibian landing was to divert troops from our Cassino front and to cut off the retreat of our 10th Army, as soon as their troops, bottled-up in the bridgehead, were able to break out and the Gustav Line had been breached.

Our detachment, together with any other available small groups of soldiers near the front lines, had been roped in to contain and try to push the landing party back into the sea. Our troops did not succeed with this, but we managed to contain the bridgehead for some weeks.

This area was a badlands, because of the malaria infestation of the swamps. Mussolini had earlier ordered the marshes to be drained, to make them accessible to farmers. The mosquitoes discovered that these channels were ideal breading grounds for them. To counteract this shifty reaction by these critters, he ordered to cover the water with diesel oil. The idea was that the larvae of the insects which carried the malaria would be unable to breathe and would perish.

A good theory, but apparently of limited practical value, because shortly after my arrival there I promptly caught a malaria infection, which stayed with me for well over fifteen years. But before I could remove myself to a field hospital with a memorable fever, I caught something more unusual.

The Allied navy was insistently shelling our positions with their heavy naval guns, but with only limited success. One day, sitting in my foxhole, one of their large shells burst near me, which sounded different from all the others. I felt a pain like a burn on my lower leg. It turned out, that it was a tracer grenade containing phosphorus, or so our doctor told me. Later there were rumors that the Allies had apologized for the mistake. True? I don't know, but they definitely did not apologize to me for the skin damage which I could have proudly exhibited, if anybody would have been interested.

In early December of 1943, after we had been withdrawn from Anzio/Nettuno for our necessary revitalization, we were now stationed east of Rome in the small town of Palombara Sabina, near Tivoli and Castel Gandolfo, the Papal Summer Palace. At night, we sometimes performed guard duty at the top of the town tower, but nobody ever came near the place. We had a clear view of Rome from our elevated position.

One day after lunch, three of us set off to walk to Monterotondo, which we could see from our place. I forgot what we wanted there, but maybe we were just bored. Since we did not know which road to take, because all directional traffic signs had been removed by our military, we went cross-country as the crow flies, through fields and vineyards.

Arriving there, we realized that we were the only German soldiers in this isolated small town of maybe two or three thousand inhabitants. We had our machine pistols with us, of course, but we could easily have become the most recent victims of the communist partisans sometimes operating in this area. We had two or five drinks at a *trattoria* and decided to return to base, while dusk protected us on our way home.

One morning I was shocked: clear symptoms of gonorrhea! This was, at least for the younger ones of the soldiers, almost par for the course. But in my case, there was a complication: for a longish time, I had been deprived of sexual delights. Thus, *Avanti!* to see the uncle doctor. Not surprisingly, he was not impressed by my pleadings of innocence.

He mentioned the substantial number of sex-workers in *Castel Gandolfo* as probable cause and jabbed me with a syringe, which was in my humble opinion double the required size for the job. It has always been the unshakeable belief in the German army that in the case of sexually transmitted diseases the medicine as well as the injections had intentionally been made painful and oversize.

Only after this procedure he took a blood sample, because I insisted on my innocence. After the result was available, he apologized half-heartedly. He explained now that the exposure of the male attributes to wind or cold could produce the identical symptoms of gonorrhea. After the ingestion of a formidable pill or three I was certified sound and was again ready to partake of the pleasures of a soldier's life.

When told of my sufferings, the Italian teenagers, with whom I often discussed all sorts of things, just shrugged their shoulders. They explained that the relatively large number of prostitutes in Castel Gandolfo was not surprising, since during summer half of the Vatican City was assembled there.

All right, most of these chaps were young communists, but I was shocked to meet so many atheists in a perceived catholic country. But maybe this accumulation of "Ladies of the Night" (and of the Day as well!) was simply the result of the war and its shortages, and that the prelates were just handing out loafs of bread?

By then we had, of course against all regulations, acquired civilian clothes, and we wanted to have at least a look at Rome, one of the most famous and glamorous cities in the world. This city was closed to German soldiers and had been designated an "Open City" by order of Field Marshal Kesselring.

But it was not much fun to go there. The people were starving and mistrusting all strangers. Interest in the antiquities was not strong with us teenagers and only developed much later in life. The ruins of the *Coliseum* and the *Forum Romanum* appeared to us not that much different from all the destruction and rubble around us.

In late December of 1943 we found ourselves maybe thirty kilometers further north at Fara-in-Sabina (Google Earth). A place which I had in my memory simply as Fara Sabina. On Christmas Eve we improvised a German Christmas, with the help of the local schoolteacher or priest. I had volunteered (why?) to play the out-of-tune piano to produce two or three Christmas hymns. But to be charitable, and for reasons of self-preservation, I abstained from taking part in the choral singing.

More memorable was early in January of 1944 the opportunity, for the first time during the war, to send something home to our families. The army had managed to obtain a large volume of olive oil and a corresponding large number of three-and five-liter tin canisters. This enabled us to send such treasures home, a rarity by now in Germany. A few weeks later my mother reported the safe arrival of this godsend.

For a little while we led an almost peace-time life at this little town. Temporarily there were no jobs for us, almost as if the existence of our detachment had been forgotten. Not at all an unheard-of occurrence in the military!

The Commanding General of the bridgehead at Anzio and Nettuno was Major General Lucas of VI Corps of the 8th US Army. Luckily for us, he had his own ideas how to conduct the war. Instead of blocking our retreat from Cassino as ordered, he decided to cover himself in glory by 'conquering' the 'Open City' (meaning un-defended city) of Rome. This almost unbelievable tale cost him his command, of course).

When the Allies eventually managed to break out of the bridge-head in May of 1944, and Rome was lost, our 10th Army was able to achieve a hasty but orderly retreat from the Cassino front to the area north of Rome, which saved the day for the German troops in Italy (Wikipedia).

I cannot remember where we were stationed later, but Velletri comes to mind. One day on our drive north we came across a depot of our quartermaster section, which was in the process of being abandoned, and we 'liberated' quite a few bottles of liquor and a roll of ten or so tins of Scho-ka-Kola, together with some other useful items. A decent supply of beer also landed in our truck. After all, one should not drink wine exclusively. This is supposed to be unhealthy.

By the way, the word 'liberated', or similar terms appear a few times in these pages. It refers to the fact that during war and as a prisoner of war everybody had to see how he could survive. This applied much more to our side of the front line, simply because we were much worse off in this regard than our 'competition'. It had absolutely nothing to do with what the soldiers had done before or after they were back home.

To clarify another point: the possessions of our comrades were as sacrosanct as those of the civilians. We only helped ourselves to what we could scrounge from the supplies of our own side and that of the enemy, and later from the British, our gaolers. The latter without any influence of animosity, but simply the aftermath of our military background.

The sight of hundreds of bombers flying in the direction of Germany had become by now commonplace. Occasionally, one or the other of them was shot down by our 8,8cm anti-aircraft guns, but this hardly had any effect on the huge numbers of planes involved.

I remember an occasion, when a Lancaster bomber was crippled, and the crew had to bail out and landed near our position. Since I was the nearest English-speaking soldier, I took them Prisoner of War, and the pilot, a Canadian, offered me his wristwatch. When I questioned the reason for this, he told me that this was the expected procedure when one became a prisoner. I had to tell him that, while we 'requisitioned' from enemy positions what we could carry, we did not take from prisoners or the fallen. When he thanked me, for the first time I heard French spoken, which he translated into English, noticing that I had not understood him.

This is an illustration of the way this campaign was generally conducted by both sides. The already mentioned episode with the phosphorous grenades points in the same direction. A drastic and revealing difference to the war in Russia! All of this, of course, despite bloody battles, where each side tried to kill as many of their opponents as possible. Wars are not only senseless and brutal, but also utterly idiotic!

At about this time, several new weapons were introduced to the war effort by our side. The first was a new machine gun, the MG42, replacing the MG34 of our boot-camp. This new one, developed for the mud and ice of the Russian front, was less finicky and fired much faster.

Next came the *Panzerfaust*, the 'armored fist'. It looked like a grenade on a stick and was intended for destroying tanks by the infantry. Finally came the *Ofenrohr*, the 'stove pipe', which it resembled. This was another rocket to destroy buildings, vehicles and assorted other hardware, preferably of the enemy. The weapon had been developed from *US Army Bazookas*, which had been captured on the Russian front. (Wikipedia).

Our few still surviving macho young officers had to try them all out, of course. Which went reasonably well, except with the 'blow-pipe' (another name for the *Ofenrohr*), which almost blew away the crown jewels of the poor Lieutenant chap, who was trying to impress us with his superior weapons handling competence.

From about May to June of 1944 occurred another one of the relative lulls in our otherwise unrelenting retreat. For several weeks the front lines had reasonably stabilized just north of Rome. Our detachment, now independent once again, had just been promised new signals equipment to arrive soon. The powers-that-be decided, that I needed re-training as a wireless operator, together with another twenty or so soldiers. We were dispatched to the signals refreshment course, which was conducted by the 14th Army at Bracciano at the *Lago Bracciano*, north of Rome and east of Civitavecchia.

The aim for the wireless operators was to achieve a Morse code receiving and recording speed of eighty characters per minute, but I only managed sixty. Still, not too bad. I forgot what the required speed was to send our coded messages.

As part of the course, we also went through the good old *Fünfer-gruppen*, the standard army coding of messages in groups of five symbols with the help of secret code sheets, which were changed daily. They were the basic tools of the communication work for front line troops and the immediate rear command centers. At the same time, we refreshed what we had earlier been taught about field telephony and the installation of the phone lines.

What I had learned there is anchored deeply in the recesses of my memory. I can still more or less translate a text into Morse code. With some mistakes, I am afraid, because a few letters are lost, and the bl. Q-groups, which I never could remember properly even then, are also gone. Another example of useless knowledge, since the Morse system has apparently now been abandoned world-wide.

One night, while on guard duty, a bomb came screaming down in my direction and I had to take evasive action by lying flat on the ground. While waiting for the expected explosion I realized that the 'bomb' was actually only the jettisoned spare fuel tank of an Allied plane. That was the only 'enemy action' I saw at that period.

During this course I befriended a group of Italian teenagers of my age, refugees from Civitavecchia. We had a lot of fun together. I provided food and cigarettes; they supplied the *vino*. This gave me the ideal chance to improve my still weak Italian. And I taught them a bit of English, for the time when the Allies would turn up at Bracciano.

The good news was, that we now had received for my team of four operators a proper signals truck. It was a small Italian vehicle, much like the one I had driven from Cassino to Esperia at the beginning of my Italian campaign. The truck had the newest wireless equipment installed. An experienced middle-aged driver, a farmer from near Aachen, was part of the package. This new truck was a clear indication for us that our previous type of actions behind the enemy lines was more or less over.

With this new fancy equipment, we could now also listen properly to the Italian *RAI*, the *Radio Italiana* stations, which brought us the modern music which had been outlawed for years in Germany. Additionally, we were now also able to clandestinely listen to *Soldatensender Belgrad*, which purported to be a German Army radio station, but was actually an Allied one, which broadcast enemy propaganda and news, with modern music as bait. This clever naming subterfuge was helpful in case a listener was caught, who could than claim ignorance. I suspect that this story would not have worked for members of our detachment, however.

Often, we learned from them what was happening a few kilometers from our positions, long before we were informed, if at all, by our side. We were now, for the first time, more or less up to date on developments in Italy, and the war and the world generally. Meaning that we were now quite sure that the war was lost for Germany and would be over rather soon.

Another huge advantage of having the truck was that we had now a proper place to keep our things, and that I could sleep on a bench in the truck. At one stage, we even had a mongrel watch dog, but I don't remember what became of him.

Our driver had installed a large box underneath the chassis, where he always kept a few live chickens. Every other day or so we had a wonderful rice-and-chicken soup. If you wonder, where he got the fowl from: no, he did not sit on the eggs! The reason is simply that overnight the chickens of the farmers rested on some low branches of the small mulberry trees holding up the vines, and thus were waiting to be 'harvested' by hungry soldiers. I suspect, that this was another breach of the military disciplinary rules, even though we always paid for them! Not doing so would have constituted plunder, and that was punishable in the German army by execution.

One day we were stationed, as so often, at a farmhouse, and there were two or three horses still in their stables. No, no soup! Our driver got me on to one of them. As there were no saddles, I was riding this monster bare-back, and he led the horse for about five hundred meters through the fields. This was for me the first and last time for the next thirty-five years on the back of a horse. The farmer's dog accompanied us, probably because he was worried that we would steal the horse. Moving, nut what a far-fetched idea!

After our defenses north of Rome had been broken in July of 1944, we experienced another one of those step by step retreats. We had every few days to install our overhead aerial at another new location, to keep in contact with the Signals Battalion and the Staff of the 29th Division. Most of the times these over-head aerials looked rather home-made because we did not have a proper mast.

On one of the almost daily drives a few kilometers north, always in stop-go mode, we noticed a Signals truck similar to ours, but a proper German one with an installed extendable aerial mast. Which was missing on our vehicle. The tactical insignia of this truck told us that it belonged to the *Hermann Göring Division* of the Airborne Corps.

The brackets of the aerial mast were fixed to the body of the truck by two extra-large wing screws. Quick thinking, and quicker action, 'liberated' this convenient piece of equipment from one division to another one. Everything thus stayed in the family! This acquisition saved us in the future the almost daily chore of having to rig an over-head aerial and to dismantle it again.

During the same period, we were one afternoon resting on a minor hill above a busy road during the almost daily retreat, when we observed three extremely low-flying Allied fighter-bombers, as they kept strafing our traffic with their board cannons. A 20mm anti-aircraft gun on an articulate mounting was left on this hill, the gunner having been killed, possibly by one of these three planes. I had not been trained on these guns, but I had been shown how to operate them.

Since these planes presented themselves so neatly from our slightly elevated position, I decided to take a few pot shots at one of them and, by luck more than by anything else, landed some hits in its cockpit, and down it went. Luckily, the other two pilots did not catch on what, and who, had been responsible for this mishap of theirs.

If an officer had been around as a witness, I would probably have acquired some nice silverware. But the only memento I acquired on this day was a shrapnel from one of our heavy anti-aircraft guns. It found its way into my thigh, just breaking the skin and embedding itself in the muscle (luckily not a few centimeters further north!). In the early 1950s it surfaced again. Too late for the German equivalent of the Purple Heart.

23

THE END OF THE WAR

AUGUST 1944 TO MAY 1945

At the end of July of 1944, the unsuccessful putsch attempt to remove and kill Hitler took place. The activists of the attempted *coup d'état* were not only aware of the fact that the war was by then lost for Germany, but they also knew that only the removal of Hitler would offer any chance that the Allies would be prepared to consider an armistice.

Urgency was of the essence. The death toll of the German Armed Forces after July of 1944 was higher than that of all the campaigns of this war from 1939 up to this point added together (Wikipedia).

We on the front lines received at the time only carefully sanitized news about this event. Only years later was I able to form an opinion as to what had happened. With the benefit of the ever-helpful hindsight I could now figure out a few of the things in connection with this epochal event:

Background:

- Practically all of the senior German officers had served during WW1 under the *Kaiser*
- their loyalties lay then primarily with *Kaiser* and *Gott*, and only then with the country

- In spite of their originally reserved attitude to the 'Lance Corporal', Hitler was to them the ideological successor of the monarch
- from about 1936 to at least 1940 their admiration for Hitler's successes had sky-rocketed
- Hitler had provided them with military honors and glory, as well as with wealth and recognition of their profession
- they knew that the vast majority of the German people, and therefore also of the soldiers, had felt like them

Basic Questions:

- why had these officers revolted? They wanted to end the lost war, and this was clearly impossible with Hitler still being around. They generally did not act as anti-Nazis, even though some of them were opposed to Nazism. As later disclosures revealed, even admired war heroes like Field Marshal Rommel was involved
- why had they waited so long? Logically they should have acted after the Stalingrad catastrophe, when it was becoming clear that the war, while not yet lost, could no longer be won. This dramatic set-back would also have created an acceptance by the German people and the soldiers for the inevitable
- what were the facts which became obvious during the putsch? In my opinion the main reason was the apparent half-hearted approach to the whole exercise. Nobody seemed to be quite sure, whether this insurrection would actually be successful. There was also a surprising lack of proper planning and execution of this undertaking, but it has to be kept in mind that it had been extremely dangerous to approach the various potential conspirators. There were still many die-hard Nazis around, and the *Gestapo* was everywhere
- which were the psychological brakes? Most importantly the subliminal considerations about any murder, and especially the murder of the Head of State and the

Supreme Commander of the military. But also, the
more general aversion regarding a revolt against the
(God-given) Authority (there was no such sentiment
discernible when some German officers had murdered
leftist politicians in 1918/22)

- why was the revolt unsuccessful? The brutal truth is
very simple: all involved officers took a big risk in
participating, but none of them was prepared to
sacrifice his life out-right for the cause. If one of them
had blown himself up while standing next to Hitler, the
assassination, and therefore the putsch, would have had
a chance to succeed. I suspect that I would waste my
time to apply for the German *Bundesverdienstkreuz* any
time soon.

Speculative Conclusions:
There are a few possibilities of what could have happened, if
Hitler had been killed.

- the revolt could have succeeded and one of the officers
could have taken over and could have tried to negotiate
an end of the war, similar to what Marshall Badoglio
had done in Italy. Unfortunately, not a very likely
prospect so late in the war, and after the crimes already
committed by Germany.
- the revolt could have failed nevertheless, and Göring
should have taken over as planned, and the outcome
would probably have been the same as in reality
- in the worst-case scenario Himmler would have stepped
in and the war would have continued to the bitter end,
because he and the *SS* could not have done anything
else, with their record of war crimes hanging over their
heads

A few things changed for us after the collapse of the revolt. The
universal military salute was replaced by the raised right arm of
the Nazi salute and *"Heil Hitler"*. One of the staff officers of each
battalion, usually a young First Lieutenant, was appointed as *Politis-*

cher Offizier, to ensure that the unit, and in particular the commander, followed the Party Line correctly. Very similar to the function
of the Political Commissars of the Red Army of the Soviet Union.

The Nazis knew very well why they had insisted, against the
resistance of the senior officers, to introduce these changes. After
all, it had been part of the top echelons of the army, who had
conspired to get rid of Hitler. Interestingly, not a single front line
unit commander had taken part, I think.

On a more subtle and psychological level, what had changed
most profoundly of all was the attitude of most of the soldiers
towards the remaining time until the soon-expected end of the war.
A still present minority had fought out of political conviction,
whereas the majority had acted up to now only with a national and
patriotic motivation. But many members, and probably the
majority of the military were from now on more interested in their
survival than in defending the fatherland, the Nazis, and fighting
against the Allied forces.

This survival mode required some luck and careful maneu-
vering to succeed. The formations of the *Waffen SS* were keen to
arrest and to execute deserters as a deterrent to the breakdown of
discipline and the collapse of the front line. But there were others
as well. After the war I read about a Navy military judge, who had,
a few days before the end of the war, sentenced a naval mate to be
executed for desertion.

We stayed for two or three days somewhere in the Toscana, in a
village or small town of artists, which I remember as Positano, but
my memory must be faulty, because the only place of this name in
Italy is apparently located near Salerno in Southern Italy (Google
Earth). Maybe the correct name will still pop up, as has happened
a few times already during the preparation of these notes. There I
met a local school teacher. I enjoyed my interesting conversations
with him, trying to keep up and improve my Italian.

On our way from south of Florence to the 'Gothic Line' in the
Apennine Mountains, one late evening we were driving along a
road following the rim of what one could call an amphitheater,
high above Firenzuola. The sky was of this diffuse light-blue color
so typical of late summer evenings in the Mediterranean countries,
and especially in the Toscana. Even today I can still visualize the

unreal appearance of this sky above the endless view to the distant mountain ranges. But enough of this soppy aside, let's get back to the very real, and most of the time very nasty war.

During all the fighting, the constant moving northwards along the length of the 'Italian boot', and the lateral movements between east and west coast areas, we always kept up our exchanges of field post letters with parents and assorted female correspondents. I must say that this service by the civilian German Postal Service was reliable and well organized, despite all the commotion and difficulties.

As a matter of fact, in retrospective it must be said that the logistic organization of the German forces, in spite of the incessant bombing raids by the Allies, and all the other problems, was outstandingly well organized and was always reliable.

In August of 1944 our forces were now dug-in at the 'Gothic Line', which stretched more or less along the crest of the Apennine Mountain range from near Pisa on the west coast to the neighborhood of Rimini on the east coast. Holding the high ground, our forces were able, for the last time, to block for several months the further advances of the Allies. This was helped by the June of 1944 withdrawal of several divisions of the Allied Forces from the Italian Theater, to prepare another invasion, this time at the coast of Southern France (Wikipedia).

We now most of the time lost contact with our *Division Brandenburg* and submerged ourselves more and more into our supporting 29th *Engineering Battalion*. They were busy mining bridges and roads and cutting down trees to provide open firing lines for the guns of our 29th Artillery Regiment. In both activities we assisted them. Sawing through thick tree trunks with a two-men manual tree saw was no fun for somebody not used to such physical work!

By now, our special missions behind the front lines had practically come to an end. Partially, because the Allied Forces were now much more careful and made it almost impossible to penetrate their lines. We had lately lost several good comrades in attempting to penetrate their positions. The fact, that we were now much less inclined than before to recklessly risk our lives must also have played an important part in this development.

However, I had one last lucky break in September or October

of 1944. After a localized rare German counter-attack we stayed behind the lines and we stumbled across an abandoned command post. We scooped up a small consignment of documents in a language, which I took at first glance to be Spanish.

Back 'home' I took a closer look and realized that the language, in addition to numerous documents in English, was Portuguese. It became clear to me that our 'find' could only refer to a Brazilian unit. The Allied *Soldatensender Belgrad* had informed as lately that Brazil had now also joined the Allied war machine, and that a Brazilian division had recently been landed in Italy. Did we have here a case of new arrivals panicking during their 'baptism of fire'?

To my surprise, I could translate the text reasonably easily, because of the similarity to Spanish, Italian and Latin. My meager knowledge of these languages helped, and because the documents dealt with military matters, the terms of which are often similar in many European languages. The documents and my translation were quickly forwarded to our *Division* HQ.

Sometime in October or November of 1944, after Florence had been lost, we found ourselves halfway between Florence in the south and Bologna in the north. We were staying in a small mountain village (name is forgotten) near Vergato and handled the wireless traffic of the 29th Engineering Battalion with their division HQ.

After lunch I used to post a translation of the daily German Armed Forces Bulletin for the locals, which included many 'displaced' Fascists from Florence. in the window of the house, we stayed in. This was the summer villa of a wealthy Florentine family of Fascists, who were very supportive, and who stayed in an outhouse on their property. I used the opportunity to polish-up on my Italian very nicely, even though they regrettably did not have a daughter of a suitable age.

Once a week I went with them to the nearest market village or town, some three or four kilometers away. My machine-pistol was an obvious trump card in this connection, because the *partigiani*, the partisans, of the district had become a bit of a nuisance by then. Apparently, they also had cottoned-on to the fact that the war would be over quite soon.

All of a sudden, we were moved in October 1944 from the

Porretta Terme area to the *Via Emilia*, the mostly straight-as-a-ruler highway between Bologna and Rimini on the eastern coast of Italy. The 29th Division was shunted, again, into a different *Armeekorps*, LXXVI Army Corps. This unit issued, once only, as far as I remember, a four-page newsletter, which they called a *Frontzeitung*, a front-line newspaper.

It was difficult to comprehend, why the German command, and especially the Propaganda Minister, did not bother with what is now called Public Relations, and did not attempt to address the soldiers directly. The Allies were much more forthcoming with their troops in this way. From our 'excursions' we often brought back examples of their information material for their front line. Our people could easily have issued information leaflets, similar to the Allied air-dropped ones, keeping us informed, at least when the front lines were more or less static.

This was probably a late manifestation of the old Prussian-German military attitude: "A soldier just obeys his orders, because he is not capable to think for himself". Personally, I did not have much of a problem with this lack of foresight, because most of the time I managed to get hold of the local Italian papers, or could talk to the locals, who always seemed to be well informed by the Allied propaganda.

On our new front sector near the *Via Emilia* we started out between Rimini on the Adriatic coast and San Marino, the medieval mountain fortress in an officially independent midget state. Here we finally encountered the II Polish Corps we had mimicked so often before on the other side of Italy. Our Polish uniforms had been discarded quite a while ago.

These Polish troops were subjected here to the devastating fire by one of our battalions of *Nebelwerfer*, the 'fog throwers'. This was a rocket system similar to the Russian *Stalin-orgel*, the Stalin Organ (no, the music instrument). These newly developed weapons, the famous rumor mill told us, used com-pressed-air shells, which upon explosion tore apart the lungs of the enemy soldiers. This partic- ular rumor seemed spot on, because their fallen soldiers showed blood clots in a corner of their mouths. Yes, even a reasonably civi- lized war was indescribably brutal and inhuman!

In the nearby village of Savignano I made a proper fool of

myself. A soldier from some other unit kept harassing a young girl in the farmhouse we were staying in. I, the knight in shining armor, told him to stop, and he challenged me to step outside. Why exactly I followed his invitation we leave open, but the result was a bloody nose, namely mine. But it was worth the wounding of not only my nose, but also of my pride, because the young lady attended lovingly (probably just wishful thinking on my part) to my wounds.

The way I recall it, we retreated step by step, via Forli, Faenza, Castel Bolognese and Imola, to the vicinity of Bologna. Heavy fighting around Bologna resulted, before the city fell to the Allies in October of 1944 (Wikipedia). My own memory dis-agrees with this date, placing it several months later, but who am I to question this source? Well, the only point in my favor is the fact that I was there. We all know, how memory mistakes can slip in anywhere. During this period of constantly moving postings, upheavals and confusion, it would not surprise me, if my memory was misleading me, again.

P.S. Another Wikipedia page, which I found later, mentions April of 1945, which agrees closely with my own recollection.

Our next reasonably stable posting was just south of Bologna, in the valley of the Reno. The commander of the 29th Division, Lieutenant General Fries, was almost daily driven to the front line in his four-wheel-drive staff car, right past our quarters. It was rumored that any soldier he found with his top uniform button undone, landed himself for two weeks in the stockade. Because he was known as a stern disciplinarian, he had acquired the nick-name of 'The Last Prussian'. He was a hard but always fair officer. For some unknown reason our uni-forms were always well buttoned-up during this period, as I recall.

One night, on guard outside our quarters, I was watching the clear star-studded sky and minding my own business, when a tank, somewhere above us in the foothills of the Apennine Mountains, landed a shell not more than a few meters away from me. The shrapnel flew away from where I stood, and not a scratch on me. This sort of thing we observed a few times in the mountains. Apparently, the angle of the incoming shell, and the angle of the rocks at the point of impact, decide the direction in which the shrapnel fly. No, I'm not an astrophysicist, but I kept my eyes open.

While we were stationed in the Reno Valley, it only rained occasionally, like for twenty-three out of twenty-four hours, seven days a week. The ground was not just muddy, but of a peculiar semiliquid substance, with only a few solids mixed in. Behind our quarters was a moderately steep hill. Climbing up there was absolutely impossible, even if our life had depended on managing the climb. Or even, if a nubile lady had been waiting for our attention up there, which is an even more convincing illustration.

In this same area we experienced one of the most bizarre events of the whole campaign. Behind our position, quite some distance away, stood a stately and impressive white villa of two or three stories, appropriately named *Casa Blanca* by the locals. It was said to belong to the owners of the restaurant in the Bologna main railway station.

A group of perhaps thirty or forty soldiers, led by two or three officers, went there. We smashed open the door and demolished several internal walls. Hidden behind them we found linen, such as tablecloths, serviettes, towels and similar goodies, and also many other things of value for a large restaurant.

On the face of it, this looked very much like plundering which, as in all armies, was strictly forbidden for us. If no officers had been present, one could have assumed that this was one of those isolated events, which can happen in any army during war. As usual with the army, no explanation was ever forthcoming for this peculiar situation. We could only speculate that an informant had possibly provided information that the owners had hidden weapons and ammunition there. But we each received some of the 'booty', and arrangements had been made for us to send these items back home to Germany.

In January or February of 1945, somewhere in the flatlands south of the River Po near Bologna, we were roped in to lay telephone cables for some command post or other. Normally a sought-after easy job, as long as this happened far from the front lines. But during this week we encountered a wet and clinging snow, which lay in places deep enough to find its way into the top of our boots. This was a truly unpleasant experience, and which should not be allowed to happen in 'Sunny Italy'! But Mussolini had by now obviously lost all control over what was happening in his (former) country.

One day our Major surprisingly turned up again once more. He suggested that maybe it was time to quietly bury the *Division Brandenburg*. The fact that he 'suggested', instead of 'ordered', illustrates best how circumstances were changing at this time. He explained he would be able to arrange that all evidence, that we had ever belonged to this unit, would be erased in the central archives of the Armed Forces back in Germany.

After all, considering our past activities, nobody knew, what the Allies would do with us, or to us, once the war was over. He pointed out, if we would agree with his suggestion, that he could not give an absolute guarantee that this would go through as planned, but he recommended to take this small risk. It did not take us long to agree with his proposal. When I applied for a copy of my army records twenty years later, there was no trace left of this Special Services unit.

This meeting also spelled the end of our clandestine operations. Our Major was never seen again after this, nor did we ever hear of a replacement for him. As a matter of fact, we never heard from or about the *Division* after this.

At the end of 1944 or early in 1945 the remnants of the *Division Brandenburg* were converted to a *Panzergrenadier Division* and *'verheizt'* (uselessly destroyed) on the Russian front (Wikipedia). The accumulated talents, knowledge and experiences of linguists, demolition experts, forgers, safe crackers, con-artists, etc. - they were all sacrificed for no good reason, because the war was clearly lost by then.

From now on, we finally and completely submerged into our Engineering Battalion. Up to now, we had been teenagers, and had behaved like them in an adventure, largely disregarding or suppressing the dangers to our lives. But from now on we tried to stay alive. Mind you, the saying then was: "enjoy the war, the peace-time will be awful". We enjoyed as much as we could manage, and the second part of this saying was later found to have been spot-on.

Sometime in February, we were informed of the introduction of a new field-post code, something like number 10 000, to which we were asked to mail any suggestions or proposals, how to improve the efficiency of the Armed Forces. How did you guess? Yes, the budding management consultant had to submit a report on how to improve the utilization of the vehicles allocated to the division by combining the travels by the staff officers.

This, naturally, was an exercise in futility, because the war would likely be over in any case within a few months. But this obvious fact was not acknowledged at all by higher command, being clearly under the whip of the Nazi party and Hitler's secret police. They were occasionally still using the term *Endsieg*, the final victory of the Nazi *Reich*.

It is pure speculation on my part that the battalion or the division opened the letters addressed to this field-post code, to suppress any possible negative facts coming to the attention of the higher echelons.

Fact is, in any case, that two or three days later I was sent back home to Germany, on my first and only *Fronturlaub*, the front-line leave, probably for four weeks. Another one of the many unexplained lucky coincidences of my life! It is surprising that I cannot recall a single incident when any member of the battalion was sent on leave during the Italian campaign. Another gap in my memory, surely? As far as I can remember, I was the only one of our battalion who drew this lucky ticket. And that at a time, when the front in Italy was ready to collapse at any moment!

Or was the real reason, maybe, to have me out of the way, if higher authorities had any ideas to follow up on my suggestions? A further line of my wishful thinking dealt with the possibility that the Brazilian documents I had 'liberated' were more valuable than I had assumed? The ways of higher command are inscrutable at the best of times.

I remember absolutely nothing about how or where I left my Signals truck, and how I got to Germany. I must have been in some sort of animated coma. My first recollection is, of having to change trains in Magdeburg and subsequently my arrival in the night of 13 to 14 February of 1945 at Leipzig train station, one hundred-and-twenty kilometers west of Dresden. The public address system reported "heavy air bombardments of Dresden". I was so much not-with-it that I barely reacted to this unexpected announcement, since Dresden, as far as I knew, had been spared bombardments up to now. But more likely, this was the result of my total exhaustion.

When I had arrived in Dresden the following morning, and as soon as I had left the main railway station, I was confronted with the devastating results of the previous night's bombings. All I could see were burnt-out ruins everywhere. Not a single building was undamaged. And the dust and smell, so well-known from bombed and destroyed Italian towns, was thick in the air. A few burnt corpses, lying in the streets in front of the station, created the right impression of what had happened, and what I had to expect.

The tram lines were out of commission, and I warily trudged the seven kilometers home. While on my way, there was a further bombing raid on Striessen, a suburb as badly affected as the inner city. Up to 25 000 people had perished in these bombardments of the previous night and the following day-time attacks (Wikipedia). An aggravating factor was that tens of thousands of refugees from Silesia and the Sudetenland as well as from Eastern Europe, fleeing from the advancing Russians, were then also in the city.

Only once I had reached our suburb, and after I had passed a number of damaged and destroyed buildings there, did I realize that my parents were completely unaware of my coming home, since there was no possibility to let them know of my arrival. With a heavy heart I approached the final corner, before our apartment block would come into view behind the semi-circular Post Office of Dresden A 36. This was when I first could see our building. No apparent damage!

But as soon as my mother had opened the door, I realized that something was terribly wrong. She told me that my father had been during the previous night on air-raid watch at the Dresdner Bank, and that he had not come home yet. At this point there existed no possibility to enquire what had happened, even if the telephone lines had still been working, because there simply was probably nobody to ask for information.

I walked back to town; all I could do. On the way I saw a few dozen carbonized corpses in the streets. Many had their clothing either burnt off, or it had been fused with their skin. A few of the victims of the thousands of incendiary bombs dropped on Dresden the previous night. When I got to the ruins of what used to be the bank, I saw that a few civilians were already busy to dig out the dead members of the air-raid watch.

My father was lying together with some others in the rubble, a trickle of blood solidified in one corner of his mouth. Immediately I was reminded of the fallen Polish soldiers near Rimini. He and all the others had suffocated in the basement of the bank, which had been serving as a bomb shelter. As we learned later, the fire storm caused by the burning city had absorbed virtually all the oxygen in the air, and the people just ran out of air to breath. Did they suffer, or did they die in their sleep, or maybe some sort of coma? I wondered and did not know.

The site of the bank was next to the *Altmarkt*, the central place of Dresden. Orderly five or six deep stacked up, there were there many hundreds of corpses, and soldiers with flame-throwers were busy to burn them, obviously un-identified and un-recorded. The stench was suffocating. The families would never be notified about what had happened to their loved ones.

Under the circumstances I only could return home and confirm for my mother what she already had been afraid of. The frightening thing was that neither of us was able to cry, even though both of us loved my father dearly. This was not an example of the 'stiff upper lip', so common and also so necessary in those days. We were just 'empty' and, of course, under shock.

I went to our neighbor, the previously introduced *SA Mann*, who was a close friend of the family. We got out our hand-cart, added a blanket, and we both walked back to Dresden. My father had by now been joined in the rubble by the rest of his colleagues, and one of the bank managers told us that there had been no survivors of the fire watch.

We collected my father's body and placed him as best we could in the handcart, which was naturally too short for this purpose, and we covered him with the blanket. Then we pulled the cart to Leub-nitz-Neuostra, a neighboring suburb with a cemetery, since we did not have one in ours.

There we were shown a place where we could dig a grave. The cemetery caretaker gave us two shovels, and we started to dig up the grave. I removed an amethyst ring from my father's finger, as a memento. *Rigor mortis* had come and gone by now. There was neither a coffin, nor a shroud. Just the two us, and a few other parties busy with the same grisly task. What a home-coming!

After this had been attended to, we were both still under shock, but life had to go on. In the beginning there was not much for me to do in Dresden. Surprisingly I cannot remember whether or not I visited my girlfriend, but I surely must have done so. Nowadays I ask myself, why I did not contact the bank management. This would have been the logical thing to do, but whether they would have been able to assist us is questionable. With the benefit of hindsight, we could at least have withdrawn my parent's cash balance, to avoid it being frozen a few months later at the end of the war.

There were still frequent air raid alarms. Of course, I participated in the air raid watches, which were kept every night at every apartment block. This should have provided opportunities for speculating about the immediate future. The Russians already had by then encircled Breslau in Silesia in the east, and the Americans or British had occupied Aachen in the west. But: dead silence, and nobody opened their mouth. And to what avail? Nobody was in a position to make any plans for the future, because nobody knew what was going to happen.

But we all knew by then, what to expect. Everybody was obviously frightened of the Russians coming soon, but nobody talked about it. The mood was akin to the unnatural quiet at the sick-bed of a loved one. And not to forget: there still was the Party, with quite a few fanatics around. Fear was palpably in the air, and the daily radio announcements of jailing and executions of 'traitors' enforced the oppressive atmosphere.

Since I did not have a permit to wear civilian clothes during my leave, I had to move around in my grubby front-line uniform. My mother told me, that a supply of household coal had been released, probably one or two hundredweights, which had to be collected. After I had 'appropriated' my father's 6,35mm automatic handgun in a leather holster, and had fixed this to my Army belt, I got hold of the hand-cart again and drudged to our suburban railway station to collect these valuables.

On my way back, I was stopped by a young 2nd lieutenant in a shiny, brand new uniform, questioning the handgun on my belt. It transpired that this was another violation of Army Regulations. I was dumbfounded. For many years we had dis-regarded such niceties as military regulations and conventions, and now this obvious *Etappenhengst*, a far-from-the-front busybody, was nitpicking on me, shortly before the end of the war. Luckily, I kept my cool. That minor incident could easily have turned nasty for me.

By the middle of March of 1945, I had started my return back to Italy. I forgot to mention previously that my travels to and from Dresden were documented by a two-page military leave pass. This had to be carefully stamped by the local military authority on arrival and departure, and by each military post encountered while in transit.

My first stop was the *Frontleitstelle* Vienna. These military offices behind the fronts directed personnel, which had become separated from their units, to meet up with them again. Because of the constant moving of units all over the show, this was very necessary and quite a job. And the constant movements of the fronts did also not exactly help in this regard.

A rather rotund Captain (we were not allowed to call an officer "corpulent" or "fat") had ordered me first to the *Frontleitstelle* Milano, but he corrected himself and changed this to the *Frontleit-stelle* Verona. He had, however, made the mistake of not recording this correction in my travel documents. It is possible that he was under shock, since the Russians were already closing in on Vienna. I decided there and then to go anywhere but to the office as ordered, nor to the one in Bologna, where I suspected that the 29th Division was still stationed.

I boarded a train scheduled to 'proceed' via Klagenfurt and Villach to Northern Italy. On the train I befriended two young ladies, who had boarded the train at Wiener-Neustadt. They wanted to travel to a village near Villach, to get out of the way of the advancing Russians. I seem to vaguely remember *Pörtschach am Wöhrter See*, but I am not sure about that. The slightly older of the two had just been crowned some sort of local Beauty Queen (peculiar priorities at this time, or Nazi psychological diversion tactics?), and she postured accordingly, but I fancied the younger one, who behaved more naturally. We played cards, talked and tried to sleep a bit.

Near Klagenfurt our train was attacked by a fighter-bomber

plane. The train had stopped, and we all ran into the adjoining fields. The pilot used the board cannons, but without doing much damage, because he had probably disposed of the bombs previously. We carried on to Villach, where my travel companions left the train. I wonder what has happened to them?

From there the train proceeded via Tolmezzo to Verona. This whole trip must have taken two or three days, with all the interruptions. In Verona I did not contact the *Frontleitstelle* as ordered, because by then I had formulated my plan, how to try and survive the dying days of this war. I had decided to live again dangerously from now on, but in a different way. Not by risking my life in action, as sometimes up to now, but by playing the army's games to my advantage, in order to try and survive the end of the war. This change finalized my metamorphosis from a committed soldier to an 'unwilling war participant'.

From Verona I now moved slowly but surely in the general direction of Milano. The idea was to gain time and to avoid meeting up with the 29th Division while the fighting was still going on, but at the same time to cover my back all the way. My survival, I figured, depended on the risk-free procedures to avoid being picked up and executed by the *Waffen SS*.

This dual purpose was achieved by proceeding from military post to military post at a speed, or lack thereof, which could always be justified as realistic, or at least could not be proven to be wrong. Of course, documented with the proper rubber stamps from each post. This became possible by relying on the well-established mania of the German military to want to rubber stamp everything in sight. By the way, these posts additionally also issued rations, and once even my monthly 'pocket money'.

Visiting these offices gave me for the first time some insight into how many military personnel were stationed far behind the front. As a matter of fact, much more than near the actual front line. There must have been valid reasons for this, but I now understood, why the High Command had ordered the introduction of the *Heldenklau*, the 'hero robbery', activities in those areas far from the battle fields, which was intended to find all available personnel which could be dispatched to the front.

I started out in the general direction of the *Lago di Garda*, arriving via Pesciera and Torbole at Riva, the two northern corners of the almost rectangular Lake Garda. Riva had a *Soldatenheim*, a military establishment similar to a youth hostel, providing the few comforts the army had to offer. What were also available were plenty of bedbugs. Next morning, the side of my face was swollen from their loving attention. This resulted in being sent to the local *Entlausungsanstalt*, the de-lousing unit. At least, they did a proper professional job!

Cleaned up and made presentable again to fellow humans, I moved on, via Castelnuovo (Google Earth) to Desenzano, the two southern corners of this lake. In the latter town I admired the historic ruins of the fort, famous from Napoleon's time and before, which I remembered from my history lessons. I would guess that not too many people have visited the four corners of this beautiful lake in one continuous circumnavigation.

By now, I better explain my mode of travel at this time. In addition to the precautions regarding my travel documents and their stamps, there were, of course, always the questions of transport, accommodation, and sustenance. Transport consisted sometimes of a short distance of rail travel to the next bombed and not yet repaired bridge or rail section.

Sometimes I scrounged a lift from a military lorry, but often I simply walked a few kilometers. All very much in line with my survival plan. Accommodation was sometimes provided by the military posts, sometimes I slept in a farm house or a barn. The rations issued by the posts were sufficient to keep me alive.

From Desenzano I followed the Via Emilia more or less. I passed through Brescia and Bergamo and finally arrived in Milano without any particular mishap. There I went to the *Front-leitstelle*, where I presented my travel documents, which by now had acquired one extra A6 (postcard size) double page full of closely spaced life-preserving rubber stamps.

Here also my *Soldbuch*, the army pay book, had to be presented. The Captain in charge carefully scrutinized my documentation and questioned my appearance in Milano, because he said that our division was stationed nowhere near that city. I explained that I had followed the instructions of the *Frontleitstelle* Vienna, which had sent me there.

You may remember, this was erroneously so recorded in my documents, and Vienna was by now in Russian hands. He probably did not believe a word of my fairy-tale, but he had not much choice and sent me on to the *Frontleitstelle* Bologna. I was relieved to see that my *Soldbuch*, doctored and sanitized by the people of my former *Division*, had passed muster without a hitch with this thorough and experienced controller of documents. Or did he possibly also consider the soon-to-be end of the war?

On my travels from Milano to Bologna I was accompanied by a most interesting fellow soldier, who was a few years older than myself. He was also a lance corporal, he was a sniper, wearing the appropriate insignia, namely a thick silver-braided cord. He had been awarded the probably largest-sized German military order, the *Deutsche Kreuz*. The soldiers called it the *Fried Egg*, because this is what it resembled. It sported, on a white background with a silvery or golden surround, a large and prominent black swastika in the center, and was awarded in silver or gold. This was the first time I had met a soldier wearing this spectacular order, which was on a higher level than the Iron Cross 1st Class.

His family lived in Eger in the *Sudetenland*, the districts of Czechoslovakia, populated predominately by Germans, which had been annexed by Germany in 1938. They must have been wealthy, because he used a platinum (he called it 'white gold') cigarette case with a golden lighter. He played exactly the same survival game with the military as me. We travelled together for at least two weeks. In company this exercise worked even better and was also more interesting.

On our way to Bologna, my travel documents acquired a further two A6 pages full of rubber stamps, so I guess it must have taken about two weeks to cover a distance you could manage today on the *Autostrada* in hours. The only reminiscence regarding this trip is an occasion, when we struggled to traverse on all-fours a badly damaged bridge between some villages. Well, some fun interlude was healthy.

It must have been the middle of April, when we had reached the vicinity of Bologna. We never were able to actually enter this city, because the Allies had occupied it on the twenty-first of April of 1945 (Wikipedia), shortly before we had arrived nearby. You may recall, that I referred to the fall of Bologna earlier on, where I had the nerve to question the date of the Allied occupation as recorded by a different Wikipedia page. Now I am satisfied, that this date was correct.

Sometime around this time I somehow lost my travel companion and was on my own again. It is surprising that I cannot recall any details about how this happened. But everything was so chaotic in these final days of the war! Prudence dictated that I changed direction again, from now on generally heading north towards the River Po, the Alps and the Fatherland. The previous leisurely mode of travel had to take on some urgency, with the impatient Allies hard on our heels.

On about the twentieth of April of 1945, (Hitler's Birthday, one of the highest Nazi holidays, which presumably nobody was celebrating by now), I was approaching the River Po. Our previously orderly retreat looked in some places more like a panicky stampede, with all sorts of army vehicles converging on the only bridge for quite a few kilometers up or down the river.

In addition to our own people, there were also some locals, who tried to approach the bridge with their beasts to get to the northern banks. It was a complete shambles and panic reigned all around. I had clung to the door of an army truck on its way to the bridge in Cento. The truck passed one of the beasts too closely, and the horn of a cow struck me on my hip. Rather painful, but I managed to keep my grip.

This town, Cento, was said to be the location of a famous *bordello* for the German air force. Everybody was talking about it, but I never met anybody who had been in there or had even seen it from the outside. Did it really exist, or was it just wishful thinking and a chimera? Or maybe the deep-seated envy regarding the privileged-deemed air force?

I intended to cross the river to move further north and to get out of harm's way. But the Allied Supreme Command must have somehow gotten wind of my innocent intentions, and they had the bridge bombed and badly damaged. Surprisingly, there were some boats available to ferry us over the river, without any vehicles, of course, accompanied by some half-hearted, so it seemed to me, cannon fire from a few airplanes in the vicinity. How did the farmers with their beasts manage, I wondered? Mind you, this is something I ask myself now. At the time I had other worries.

Once arrived on the northern bank, the crowd moved towards Verona, mostly by means of pedestrian locomotion, but sometimes we were able to catch a lift with vehicles which had managed to cross the Po. Otherwise, we would never have made it to escape the Allies, who now advanced faster and faster, since there was not any serious German resistance anymore.

When I mention 'we', I'm talking about an amorphous mass of individuals, instead of a disciplined army, which was streaming north in this section. I bypassed Verona and avoided this city, having decided to visit the Romeo and Juliet balcony at some more appropriate time. Because I had foreseen that there would most likely be some attempt there to arrest this uncontrolled retreat.

And, as often before, the seasoned soldier's instincts were spot on. Some ten or fifteen kilometers further north we met at night a road block, established by the *Waffen SS*. They were clearly looking particularly for dispersed members of our 29th, the *Falken Division*. A crudely painted falcon was blazoned on a wooden board, and a member of the *SS* pointed unmistakably with his machine pistol to a path off the road, leading to a farm house dimly seen in the distance.

We had no choice but to follow this friendly and polite invitation, but after a few steps a cloud covered the moon momentarily, which up to then had illuminated the road and the surrounding fields rather brilliantly. Two or three of us took the chance and dived into the adjacent vineyard and moved smartly away from the path. A few machine pistol salvoes were fired by the *SS*, which served to speed up our retreat. But by then we were far enough away to be invisible amongst the vines.

Round about the twenty-eighth of April we had reached South Tyrol, the relative safety of the foothills of the Alps. The name of the village, where we found ourselves after our accelerated retreat, has slipped my mind, but it was somewhere east of Bolzano.

A large number of members of the 29th Division had reached this refuge, and there must have been several dozens of members of the Engineering Battalion. I was billeted in the farm house of a South Tyrolean family. A brother and his sister, both school children, spent some time with me, enquiring about the war and where we came from and what they could expect from the near future. This I also would have liked to know! During our time together, I noticed something peculiar: they both spoke the local German/Austrian dialect fluently, but when they were counting, they did so in Italian.

It was here, that the battalion's *Politoffizier* announced on the 2nd of May 1945 Hitler's death in his bunker in Berlin. Remarkably, he used the word *'Führer'* instead of his name and saluted with his raised right arm, closing with the remark that this sad event did neither mean Germany's defeat, nor the end of the war. A true believer! Probably the only one by then. It is almost ridiculous, that this super-Nazi was the only one, of all the people I had met during the war, whom I ran into after the war.

The next day it was announced that the German Armed Forces in Italy had surrendered to the Allies. The rumor mill, being as active as usual, if not more so now, was announcing that General Wolff of the *Waffen SS* had gone to Switzerland to negotiate the surrender. This extremely unlikely appearing story seemed credible to us nevertheless, because without the agreement of this elite Nazi formation, or at least their toleration, this development surely would have been completely impossible.

This unusual development must be seen in connection with two future, even more puzzling events: we would not be Prisoners of War, as to be expected, but instead we would become Surrendered Enemy Personnel, as well as the fact that we would after the capitulation still have our vehicles and weapons, albite under Allied control. More details about this in the next Part.

Now that the war was over for us, this seems to be the appropriate time to explain my feelings and my attitude towards the Italians. Germans never thought much of the military qualities of the Italians. I suspect this had more to do with the fact that they had left Germany in the lurch and had changed sides in the middle of both world wars, than with their real military prowess. But of much more interest to me have always been the civilians. They had a tough life during the war, and I always got along well with them. And being able to speak their language reasonably well also helped.

Thereby ended an important chapter of my life, which saw my

metamorphosis from a boy, via a teenager to almost a man, and from a dyed-in-the-wool Nazi to an apolitical by-stander, disillusioned and bitter. For the sake of completeness and rendering a balanced account, it could not have been suppressed in this narrative. But also, for the reason that it obviously shaped my future development. In any case, I had to explain what I did from 1942 to 1945.

PART V

PRISONER OF WAR

HARDSHIPS AND THRILLS (1945 TO 1947)

24

RIMINI

To start with, I have occasionally and intentionally used in this part of the story some unsanitized versions of military and civilian jargon, save the blasphemies, in the way the soldiers used them at the time. If this should violate your sensitivities (what's that?), then I am not sorry. More PC (politically correct) versions are surely available from more sensitive authors.

For a few more days we stayed at the same place in South Tyrol in the foothills of the Alps, after the announcement of Hitler's death (I am sure his suicide was not mentioned), and the capitulation of the German Forces in Italy. The wars in Europe and East Asia, however, were not yet over.

We still had all our weapons and (some) vehicles, and we were wondering about this peculiar state of affairs for an army which had capitulated. Obviously, we were all rather apprehensive about what would happen to us. The *Brandenburger* had the special worry, whether our sanitized records would stand up to proper post-war scrutiny by experts.

Luckily, we were sitting in a German Quartermaster Depot, with enough food and drink to last us several months. Unfortunately, this was just a short reprieve, because after a few days a US Army Jeep, with a Captain and his driver, arrived in our little paradise. He confirmed that the war was now over for us, and that we were now SEP, Surrendered Enemy Personnel. It was clear to me that this unusual designation, instead of the expected Prisoner of War or PoW, had to have some special and peculiar reason.

His announcement, in English naturally, was probably fully understood only by myself, and I offered to translate. This was accepted without arguments, also by our officers. Thus, I had managed to re-establish myself as an interpreter. Such a position usually encompassed some fringe benefits and was therefore worth occupying.

We offered these two gentlemen something to drink, because in May it gets quite hot in the southern foothills of the Alps. When they saw what we had to offer, they opted for a *grappa*, a vile (in my personal opinion!) Italian brandy. The reason for such a negative view of this drink was the fact that I regularly felt bilious when I was just smelling the stuff. I suspected that the bottle of brandy we had received in Vienna before leaving for Russia/Italy had rather been a *grappa*, which had led to my alcohol poisoning. Being army, "a *grappa*" translated as a bottle of it. Result: two quite incapacitated warriors. But, what the heck, the war was over for us and for them.

I asked them where they were billeted and drove them in their Jeep back to their unit. An additional illustration of the previously said, regarding the relatively civilized way this campaign was conducted by both sides. Staying at their place overnight, the next morning I was returned to our refuge on board of a 'hundred-pack'. This was a tractor-trailer combination, supposed to be able to transport one hundred standing men. It was driven by a Negro (the Afro-American had not been invented yet), like most of the heavy US Army trucks.

We now proceeded, accompanied by a Jeep with four GIs, to our destination, a huge camp complex at Bellaria, just outside of Rimini, which had been prepared by the Allieds to accommodate the German surrendered troops. Obviously no question of any effective guards! The trip was long and exhausting, and sometimes interrupted by some stone-throwing, and by some Italian women on the roadside shrieking obscenities at the prisoners.

One of the interruptions of our 'guided tour', to allow us to relieve ourselves, was utilized by our chaperones to check for and relieve us of personal weapons. But these chaps either did not care what they were doing, or they were not exactly sharp, or the whole exercise was just a pretense. They made us stand in a single line on a sandy piece of ground. I still had my father's automatic on me, which I simply dropped, buried it with my foot in the sand and stood on top of it. On this occasion, while I was able to safe-guard my gun, I was robbed of my wrist watch. I had loved this watch, with its black face (like my soul), even so it was nothing expensive. But it was a present from my parents upon joining high school. Damn!!

On arrival in the Bellaria camp complex, among the first things ordered by the Americans: to dig out huge soak pits for disposal of human waste, to issue (German or American?) tarpaulins as make-shift covers against rain and sunshine, and to set-up a German camp administration. One of the waste pits, incidentally, became the grave of a German supply officer, who was accused by his people of having sold critical German supplies during the war on the Black Market, and who was pushed to his terrible death.

To organize all this took our jailers a few days to accomplish, and the first days after our arrival in Rimini were, not surprisingly, rather chaotic. I had then, and I still have now no idea how many prisoners were in this complex. Searching the internet to establish the approximate numbers was fruitless. But in 1943 we had more than 400 000 troops in Italy. How many had perished or been taken prisoners before the May of 1945?

It took some nifty Quartermaster work, to organize the necessary supplies and services for such a huge crowd, particularly since the US Army did not have advance warning of the German surrender. Probably, they knew what to expect, but could not know exactly when it would materialize.

The German camp administration took over the distribution of the daily rations and the preparation of a warm meal. Later they organized groups dealing with the arts or entertainment and educa-tion or training in various disciplines. The rationale for this was the old military maxim that soldiers, and particularly PoWs, had to be kept busy, to avoid unrest.

The establishment of such a command in a PoW camp complex was SOP, Standing Operating Procedure, in all armies. This one was billeted in a building, which looked suspiciously like the terminal and control tower of a small airfield. I was unable to ascertain, whether Bellaria did have one before the war, and neither Wikipedia nor Google Earth helped with this question. The nearest present one seems to be near Rimini or Cervia, but this latter one does not ring a bell at all in this connection.

In the beginning the camp housed our officers as well as the 'other ranks'. It was rumored in the early days that a German 4x4 staff car parked near the place, where some of us 'phantoms', together with some of the regular members of the 29th Engineers had settled down, belonged to General Fries of the 29th Division, our previous 'home from home'.

To have officers and soldiers in the same prisoner camp was unheard of. Historically, the officers were entitled to their separate camps. The reason for this exceptional situation here was that the surrendered German armies in Italy were kept in semi-readiness by the Allies. Our weapons and equipment were kept at the ready by them. As mentioned earlier, we were not Prisoners of War but Surrendered Enemy Personnel. The reason for these semantics became now clear.

At that time the Western Allies faced two distinct and realistic possibilities of an armed conflict with the Soviets: on the one hand there was the possibility that the Russians would not honor previous Allied agreements about the different future Zones of Occupation and would attempt to occupy territories not allocated to them. Remember that Churchill was still in charge in Great Britain, and he was a bit paranoid in regard to distrusting the Russians!

On the other hand, the Allies had the problem that the Soviets had demanded the handing over of all captured former Soviet Union soldiers, who had fought on our side in Italy.

Unfortunately for these poor chaps, this demand was acceded to. As far as I remember, all these soldiers were reportedly liquidated by Stalin. Only the II Polish Corps was able to protect the Ukrainians, who had fought on our side, by claiming that they were of Polish nationality.

In the event of an armed conflict with the Soviets, it was rumored that we would return to war. In other words, the Allies appeared (reluctantly) ready for the worst. We had been aware of these considerations at the time. After all, all our officers, including the generals, were still among us. And they, by necessity, had to be made aware of what was going on. It was, therefore, only natural that this information and thinking immediately filtered through to us soldiers. Also, I am sure that they ascertained the opinions and attitudes of our senior officers. But of course, nobody had asked our opinion, as usual. The tension was near breaking point. Any silly shooting incident could have led to an out-of-control explosion, and to the out-break of World War 3.

As I remember these days, it took about two weeks for the tension to slowly subside. Possibly, after the Allied governments had acceded to the Soviet demands. We knew the situation had calmed down, when our officers at the end of these two weeks, were transferred into their own proper officers' camp section. Slowly but surely, our status of Surrendered Enemy Personnel metamorphosed into the more usual Prisoner of War status. It should be obvious, that under these circumstances the rumor mills were working overtime, and we had no possibility to distinguish them from the facts.

The camp complex consisted now of a number of separate sections for the various categories of prisoners. The ones I remember, in addition to the one for the officers, were for army priests and one for female prisoners. The priests were rumored to receiving preferential supplies of cigarettes and specialty rations and toiletry articles.

Both these special camps were adjacent to our section. The female prisoners mentioned here were not soldiers, because the German Forces did not employ female combatants. They were the before-mentioned *Nachrichtenhelferinnen*, or Female Signals Assistants. They had almost exclusively worked at the Theater HQ in Verona. and they were 'civilians in uniform', if there was such a thing. These young ladies enjoyed the chance to obtain a nice tan under the Italian sun. And we enjoyed the view. Some of them I had met on a visit to our Headquarters in Verona and remembered particularly well Miss Gerda. No, not Miss Gerda from the Isle of Föhr! But this part of the story is of no interest here.

The whole camp complex was double-fenced, and guard towers had been erected. But the post-war security arrangements at

Rimini, also in Italy generally, had something un-real about them throughout the two years of our PoW existence. It was as if the Allies were not particularly interested to keep us locked up. Many of us, as will become apparent later in this saga, were able to freely move around the country without any guards.

From our refuge in South Tyrol and during the trip to Rimini, anybody could easily have escaped without great risk, but probably nobody did. Half of Germany was occupied by the Red Army, and our aversion and horror of the Russians was deeply embedded in us. The other half was largely destroyed and occupied by the not exactly German-loving Western Allies. We had heard that food was still rationed and, together with everything else, was in desperately short supply. And in both halves of Germany many of the factories and workshops had been dismantled or plundered by the victors, meaning it was highly unlikely that one could find any work.

To start with, we had American Negroes (this was the official terminology at the time!) to serve as camp guards. They often approached the fence and appeared to be friendly towards us. Only later did I understand the underlying reasons for this: the animosity between white and black US soldiers and "Your enemies are my friends". Some of them gave us some cigarettes or bread or the occasional C-Ration. After a short conversation with one of them, whose English was different, and not much better than mine, my father's automatic was exchanged for two cartons of 'Lucky Strike'. A fortune in a PoW camp!

But soon the US troops disappeared, and Polish and British guards took over. We did not realize it then, but it appears that at about this time the two armies had sorted out their respective Zones of Occupation: the British Eighth Army (including the Polish Corps) was to control Northern Italy north of the Apennine Mountains, and the US Fifth Army the rest of the country. This would explain why the US Army left the Rimini district at this time.

We had started to dig out our new 'home' from the sandy soil of some former vineyards, in the form of a pit about two by three meters and half a meter deep. The tarpaulins, which had been provided to us, gave some protection from the occasional rain, but more importantly, from the Italian sun.

We now settled down to a stay of unknown duration. General Fries of the 29th Division was rumored to have been installed by the British as the German commander of the Rimini complex. What had happened to Field Marshal Kesselring and the Commanding Generals of our two armies was not even a subject to the ubiquitous rumors. The German camp administration had now been established for some time, including an official interpreter, scuttling any chance for me of working in this field.

Some large tents had been supplied by the 8th Army, providing consulting and treatment rooms for some German army doctors and dentists. I had to visit one of the latter, before they had proper pain killers available. Not one of my pet memories. Even a theater company started functioning after a while, but this lay outside my sphere of interest. Some other such tents were utilized by fellow prisoners to distribute our rations, and to cook a warm meal once a day.

At least one other such tent was used by some US Army Lieutenants of the CIC, the US Army Counter Intelligence Corps. They were speaking German fluently, including some regional dialects. I suspected that they were the sons of German Jewish emigrants. It was their job to question us as to which units we had belonged, and where and when we had been deployed. By now we former *Brandenburger* were fluent liars and had no problem to pass their ministrations. Years later I found out that the records of these interrogations still were in the possession of the army, and that our secrets had not been quite as secret as we had thought at the time.

When some enterprising (or bored) fellow prisoners offered lectures in German law, I enrolled immediately, because the subject had always interested me. You may recall that in high school I had already formed the intention to study law after the (naturally victorious) war. This opportunity enabled me to dust off my limited exposure to the subject (remember the policeman neighbor in Dresden?) and I enlarged my knowledge of the subject quite a bit. This was something I enjoyed very much, even though these studies were also fraught with problems.

A pencil stub cost three to five cigarettes on the camp Black Market, and the tan-colored cartons of the biscuit rations had to serve as note paper. We had prosecutors, lawyers and judges as lecturers. I still remember quite a few details of case studies they quoted us, and I will never forget the criteria for murder in German law: the intention to kill, base motive and the ability to be criminally culpable. Another thing stuck in my memory was the difference between *dolus directus* and *dolus eventualis.* And as a bonus of these lectures, you could temporarily forget the hunger, and no boredom took hold.

Other offered lectures included advanced English. I enrolled in this one too, I but stopped attending when I had found out that the university professor was an expert in English literature, from Beowulf via Chaucer and Shakespeare to Edgar Allan Poe, but was rather lost, when it came to present-day usage, particularly regarding army language.

Another course I joined taught basic instructions in organization, accounting and administrative systems. This one laid the foundations for the future choice of my profession as a management consultant. The bookkeeping part of these lectures came in handy on several occasions during my later life.

Apart from the courses provided by the German camp administration, the only relaxation we had was to play *Skat*, the German national card game. I had never played it before, but now I had to learn the rules, accompanied by some humorous or abusive comments from my fellow players when I had made a mistake, which happened quite often, particularly in the beginning. Some of these chaps were rather dogmatic in what was supposed to be a friendly game. I never achieved the level of competence and experience the other players had. One of the peculiarities of this card game which I remember is the astonishing fact, that a suite of seven trump cards, out of a total of ten, usually leads to the loss of the game for the holder of such an impressive hand.

Luckily, I still had my father's chess set with me, but without a chess board. A friend of mine, who would nowadays be called a handyman, produced a serviceable one in no time. We spent hours and hours over this board, temporarily forgetting all about our hunger pangs. But to my surprise, there were not too many of the prisoners interested to play, even though this was an ideal past-time. A post-traumatic-stress symptom, maybe?

Our main concern, however, which occupied more or less our

every waking hour, were the daily rations. In the evening we usually received some milk powder and two or three dried figs, together with a few army biscuits. These rations were extremely meager, but we could not blame the British Army for this. To have to feed hundreds of thousands of extra mouths, and at short notice, had to cause huge problems.

We soon discovered that soaking the figs in the dissolved milk powder produced very little nourishment, but something very tasty. As a matter of fact, is it possible that we invented or re-invented the famous Italian milk-shake? We were often dreaming about this mixture, envisaging to consume huge quantities of these drinks, once we were out of the Prisoner of War compound. Fact is that we only occasionally had a milkshake in our later relative freedom in Bologna or Padua.

In the army, and in prisoner camps or prisons, 'kitchen' equates to 'food'. When our Polish guards were looking for kitchen helpers, many volunteered and some of us were sent, without any guards, to their billets outside the camp. After some light work we were given a dish of rich food, prepared with plenty of olive oil. This was marvelous, but for our bodies, starved and deprived of fat for so long, this resulted for two or three days in extensive bowel movements.

The interesting point for me was the fact that I always had hated any kitchen work, and that I was brought up by the Nazis to look down on 'inferior' people like the Polish (and the Russians). The latter point had already been corrected by the II Polish Corps during the fighting. But it was still disturbing to realize, how hunger can influence one's mind. Survival instincts can be very strong motivating factors.

A problem of gigantic proportions was the fact that by now most of us had run out of cigarettes. We received a few with our daily rations, I guess maybe three or four. This was obviously not enough, even for the average smoker. And we were almost all nicotine-dependent! A Black Market had started to operate almost immediately. I tried to smoke in my pipe some dried-up vine leaves I had found between the improvised tents, but the taste and smell were just too awful. Therefore, I did the next best thing and stopped smoking. This enabled me to exchange from then on my tiny cigarette rations for some food.

About a month after we had booked into this luxurious holiday camp, the authorities showed us on a huge open-air projection screen some documentary films, about what the Allies had found when they had liberated some of the extermination camps. The Nazi atrocities during the war, which were shown to us here, had a tremendous and lasting impact on most of us and opened our eyes, because now we could see for the first time what really had been happening in Germany and the occupied countries during the final part of the war.

Front-line soldiers were always the last ones to get information on what was going on inside and beyond the army. This was definitely true for the German army. After having seen these films, we began to understand many things, such as the hatred shown to us by so many different peoples, and why almost the whole world was united against Nazi Germany during the war.

This film screen was also used to acquaint us with the international news in the form of British or American newsreels. These were for us a great awakening, after so many years of clever propaganda and brain-washing. One item I remember very clearly: US Secretary of the Treasury Henry Morgenthau announcing the "Morgenthau Plan". Accordingly, America would ensure that Germany would in future never again be in a position to start a war. It had been agreed among the Allies that all heavy industries in Germany would be dismantled, and he said something like: the German people would be limited to planting potatoes.

What surprised me the most about this outburst by a highly intelligent man was not his hate, fully understandable for a Jew, but the fact that this prognosis, with its catastrophic implications for our eventual return home, raised barely any reaction among us. A clear case of delayed shock, I thought.

In the best of army traditions, we attended every morning a roll call. Why our jailers bothered with this, I never could figure out, because there was never anybody missing. But on the other hand, making sense or not, soldiers and especially prisoners of war had to be kept busy!

Standing there for a long time in the sun, one could observe some wildlife. A lively population of lice was on show. One could follow a procession of the little darlings along the collars of some chaps' shirts. To pass the time, one could also speculate, which one of the competitors would arrive first at a given point.

Surprisingly, I cannot recall whether there was ever any delousing action, but we found our own solution to the problem. We could get rid of these lodgers by locating and killing all of the as well as all the nits deposited in the seams of our clothing. This led to their eventual extinction, hopefully, after two to three weeks. It sure worked for us, after we got the hang of doing it correctly, not overlooking a single one.

Only once, in late summer, were a few hundreds of us loaded on to trucks and carted to Cessenatico, near Cessena on the coast of the Adria. The beach was empty. There we all stripped (the British had forgotten to issue bathing costumes) and we had an extensive bath or swim. That salt water removed what must have been by now thick layers of grime and sweat. But no subsequent pollution of the Adriatic Sea was reported. Did I explain that water for washing ourselves was also in short supply in the camp?

Despite the huge number of idle men in a confined space, I have never seen any homosexual activity or behavior. There must have been hundreds, at least, and quite possibly thousands, of gay men in the complex, but the ingrained army discipline was still intact. All armies in those days had not only outlawed homosexual behavior but suppressed it with *gusto*. Calling a fellow soldier 'gay' was a terrible insult, whether it was true or not. We were programmed to hate, or at least to despise, homosexuality. The present-day wide-ranging acceptance of this behavior was at the time simply unthinkable for us.

Another thing which one could have expected under these cramped circumstances, but which was completely absent, was theft among the prisoners. There was still a small number among us, who had some valuables in their possession, a gold watch or a silver cigarette case, or just some cigarettes, for instance. Another reminiscence pops up here: after my high school wrist watch had been 'lifted', I have been without a wrist-watch for some time. But I think I possessed one later-on. How and when had this come about? Another one of too many open questions. A pity I did not have an Ipad to take some notes!

Our dressing code must have been atrocious by now. At one stage we were issued civilian summer shirts. I received two sky-blue ones. Presumably, I did not own even a single shirt up to this point, since we did not wear shirts with our uniforms, just under-shirts and a cloth-collar. We probably also received a pair of civilian shorts at this point, because I remember wearing a pair later in the camp.

These shorts served an additional purpose for me, as a hiding place of last resort. Their textile belt rested in a sort of pouch, which could, and did, serve as a secret receptacle for some narrowly folded 10 000 Lire banknotes. These very large notes in bed-sheet size (a slight exaggeration) were almost valueless after the war. They served as the currency of the camp black market, together with the cigarettes, of course.

After having stayed in the camp complex for a few months, I 'celebrated' my 21st birthday and 'coming of age'. The birthday party was, by necessity, restricted to me. I did not mention the occasion to my friends, what for. It was a time for me to reflect on what had happened in my life up to this point. But even more so, on what to expect in the near and in the more distant future for my mother, myself, and for Germany generally.

The outlook in the camp was rather dismal and subdued by now. We still had not received any mail from home. From the scarce information which reached us about the situation in Germany, it appeared that there was no future, not for us individually, and not for the country. But I was reasonably confident that I would probably somehow manage to extricate myself from this mess, created by the Nazis and the lost war. After all, I had survived the war!

But did this observation make sense, considering that hundreds of thousands of soldiers in Italy had also survived? Yes, I thought so. Somewhere I had read that for every front-line soldier there were twenty-three in the rear areas, which seemed credible to me, after what I had encountered in Northern Italy shorty before the end of the war. The critical point was: the percentage of the front-line soldiers who had survived. Looking at it this way, I felt sure I had been lucky indeed.

37% (Wikipedia) of my vintage of 1924 had perished. If I project the above observations onto this percentage, I arrive at a guess of a survival rate of much less than 50% for the frontline soldiers of my age-group.

In early autumn, the British were looking for English-speaking prisoners for a new German unit, and I volunteered. Mainly, because I was worried what the winter would be like under these camp conditions, while still remembering the knee-deep soggy snow of January of 1945 at nearby Bologna. I figured that, as an interpreter, I would in any case be spared the worst of the climatic conditions. But I also remembered that in such a position the existence of the mental stimuli of translating was very important for maintaining one's psychological equilibrium. Not to forget the likelihood of all sorts of fringe benefits available in such a situation.

The job they offered was for an interpreter at a German equestrian unit, which was intended to look after the Lipizzaner Horses, which General Patton of the US Army had 'liberated' somewhere in Istria during the final days of the war.

I had to tell the German Major in charge that I could not ride, and jokingly mentioned my one and only bare-back 'ride' organized by our driver in the previous year. This was of no consequence, I was assured, because there would be plenty of time and opportunity to teach me to become a champion rider.

After the monotony of the previous months, the atmosphere within this unit, still inside the camp, was invigorating. I was happy to be part of this adventure and was looking forward to a reasonably pleasant near future. But as so often in the military, things did not proceed as planned. This assignment eventually fell through, before it even got off the ground, for reasons I do not remember, if I ever knew them. The Allied armies also worked on the 'need to know' principle, I guess.

25

BOLOGNA

Shortly thereafter another opportunity came up, to get out of the camp. The British had decided to establish a German engineering battalion to work for the British Army and to do occasional civilian reconstruction work for the Italians. There were enough damaged buildings, bridges and roads to keep this unit busy for quite some time. This unit obviously required an interpreter. I applied and was accepted, probably due to my claimed time with the 29th Engineering Battalion. Within a few days, I was finally out of the camp complex.

Now I found myself in this new battalion headquarters. The commanding officer was in charge of three companies of German engineers, stationed in the British Zone of Occupation of northern Italy: in Padova, Bologna and Rimini. He was a highly decorated Major, wearing the *Ritterkreuz*, the Knight's Cross. He was always in full immaculate uniform, with the swastikas still in view on his medals and tunic. Surprisingly, this did not seem to bother the British.

The Battalion Staff counted about twenty to twenty-five men all told, including a Captain as executive officer, a medical officer, a Sergeant-Major, several drivers and some office staff. We had available to us a number of German and British vehicles, such as two four-wheel-drive Horch staff cars, two or three motorcycles and six or seven trucks, and an American Jeep.

Before leaving Rimini, we had been issued with new German uniforms. Otherwise we would have looked too scruffy for words, and we would not have been presentable to other German units or units of the British Army, nor to the envisaged Italian civilian authorities (and ladies!). Very importantly for us, we also kept our civilian garb we had been issued in the camp.

I cannot figure out where we were stationed at first. Possibly still in the vicinity of Rimini. All I remember is the fact that we were billeted in Nissen huts. These were British prefabricated steel structures, formed by a half-cylindrical skin of corrugated iron. About two and a half meters high in the center, maybe four to five meters wide, and about ten to fifteen meters long.

The battalion staff and one of the companies were housed on the same property. There was also a two-story building on this plot, probably used by the staff. One day, a German film projection truck arrived. They had all they needed in their vehicle, film rolls and a large screen. For the sound they used a wire recording device I had never seen or heard of before. They showed us the film *Münchhausen*, with Hans Albers as the star. We were told that this was the first German color picture, and also the last German movie completed during the war.

By now, I had made friends with two older fellow-prisoners. One had been a butcher before the war, the other told me that he had been a member of the *SS* (no details available). Both had already acquired local girlfriends. How this exactly came about, I do not remember, and my slightly greenish tint had nothing to do with this. The only thing I am sure about is the fact that we were able to leave our quarters at will, and that we had no problems receiving visitors, even if they were staying over-night. Additionally, we had by this time found ways of making some money. Again, details escape me, how we had managed that.

The following events are again more clearly remembered. Probably during October of 1945 our battalion headquarters were moved to our final more central location in the suburb of San Lazzaro, just outside of Bologna. There we were established in a deserted and damaged villa with some substantial outbuildings.

First, I thought that this location was rather a remarkable coincidence, since several months earlier, our German army unit was stationed within a few hundred meters of our new quarters. But then I realized that during the war we had been at so many different places all over central and northern Italy, that it really was not much of a coincidence at all.

As mentioned before, by now the Allies had sorted themselves out, regarding the occupation zones of Italy. The Americans occupied southern and central Italy, and the British established themselves mainly in the River Po valley of Northern Italy. These northern provinces of Lombardy and Veneto were the industrialized heart of the country's economy. The smaller British Zone was more important economically than the vast southern areas, which were largely empty of economic activity, apart from the Mafia, of course. The border between the two Zones of Occupation ran east-west along the Apennine ridge, very similar to the German *Gotenstellung* at the end of 1944.

The previous involvement of the US Army had by now ended. Only our American Jeep stuck out like a sore thumb from this arrangement. But then, quite a few British units also used some Jeeps. This was just such an indispensably useful all-round vehicle for the military.

The location of the billets of the battalion was not selected at random. In San Lazzaro was also stationed the 297th Royal Engineering Company, under the command of a very young-looking Major. The idea had obviously been that this British unit would control and supervise our activities. They provided, for a few days, a guard at the entrance to our 'palace'. But since there was not even a fence, this was a bit of window-dressing in typical army style. In any case, we drove in and out continuously with several vehicles, officially and otherwise, and the poor chap on guard had no idea what went on.

The CO of the 297th summonsed me almost daily to report. Why me, and not our Major? I spent more time with him and his staff officers than with our staff. Which helped my English very nicely, thank you. One of his instructions was, that we had to complete the relevant British Army trip-ticket forms whenever a vehicle was leaving our compound. This at least provided some employment for our Sergeant-Major and his helpers.

And this brings me to another one of the many unresolved

conundrums of my reminiscences about San Lazzaro: what were our officers here really doing? Neither speaking English nor Italian, they required my presence every time they wanted to get some information or take some action, and this did not occur often. Except, of course, when they drove to, or were on the phone with, one of our companies. And as far as I can remember, this also happened not often. If my memory about these things is correct, life must have been very boring for these German officers. It is, however, very well possible that they also had to prepare reports for the German camp commander at Rimini.

Then a peculiar situation developed. During the war, I had learned from the soldiers, who had to deal with them, the *partigiani*, the Italian partisans, had fought our troops whenever they had a chance, and they had caused many losses. And the best of them, and the most successful ones, had been the communist partisans, probably a side-effect of the earlier German attack on the Soviet Union.

Shortly after we were established at San Lazzaro, the first young communist groupies arrived. We were at first suspicious, considering not only the past experience with the partisans during the war, but also thinking of the Soviet Union Communists. But it turned out that they hated the Allies more than us, for whatever reason. Possibly, the "Your enemies are our friends" could have been the explanation, or maybe the begin of the Cold War? Now we understood better the numerous "Ami go home" graffiti (this word did not jet exist then) on many walls.

It suited us, when the guard was eventually withdrawn, because when we sometimes (actually, almost daily!) received some lady visitors in later weeks, a British soldier with a shouldered rifle could have frightened-off our female visitors from spending their time and goodies with us, which would have been a shame (this latter turn-of-phrase was outing me as a South African English-speaker, if one should be interested).

Well, we were not complaining about these changed perceptions! These girls brought us food specialties, cigarettes and newspapers. One of them even offered us some cocaine! I thought this rather odd behavior for a communist girl. But maybe they were not really communists! We refused the 'coke', by the way, but the offeror was using heavily.

My frequent official travels to divers British, German, and occasionally Italian units and offices made it very easy for me to arrange 'unofficial' ones as well. Not to mention the odd moment (most of my time, actually) when I was busy with my own activities, which included exploring the Bologna area and the Emilia province, and to go shopping. Also, I visited a few of the places where we had been stationed during the war. Yes, the life of a prisoner of war can be quite varied.

Things had developed in every respect much better now for us. To start with, we now had a table tennis, and played for hours. I remember my (unsuccessful) attempts to play a straight *Schmetterball*, where one tries to strike the ball very hard, and plays it just over or touching the net, making it almost impossible for the opponent to return the ball. And we also had Italian and English reading matter, so I kept myself busy. Oh yes, we also now had a radio. The boredom of the PoW camp was now finally in the past and had been overcome.

We also had a completely equipped large kitchen, where some of us got busy, cooking and baking all sorts of things. My butcher friend even tried his hand in making German sausages and cold meats. This was the first time in my life that I realized that some men, apart from the professionals, actually knew how to cook and bake, and that they loved doing so. A strange, un-manly infliction, I thought. Animated by all this activity, even I showed off my prowess in the kitchen: I prepared scrambled eggs whenever we expected visitors. Only for my friends, of course, I had no use for such power sustenance.

Among our transport equipment we had a BSA and a Triumph motorbike. I liked riding one of them, to race down the straight Via Mazzini from San Lazzaro into the center of Bologna. There I admired the remaining dozen or so of *Torres* still standing, of the about one hundred eighty (Wikipedia) originally built in the Middle Ages. These towers were fortresses of the leading families of an obviously violent town. However, when I tried to visit the interior of the oldest university in Europe, founded in the 11th century, I sadly was for some reason refused entry.

On the way back to our quarters we used a dirt road, as we say in South Africa, with a ninety-degree bend near the end. Riding quite fast up to this point, and then braking and simultaneously leaning into the bend, and with the rear wheel sliding sideways, one could negotiate the dog-leg without losing speed. Not that we were ever in a hurry, but just for the thrill. The same maneuver also worked with the Jeep, by the way.

This vehicle I had reserved for myself (our officers had their staff cars) and I drove it almost exclusively. One day, one of the youngest members of our team asked me to let him drive. I moved over, and he took the steering wheel. He did all right, until we encountered, in a very narrow country road, a farmer's light delivery truck. Its side panels had been lowered almost to the horizontal, and the truck was packed high with produce, including on the side-panels.

My aspiring driver managed to hit this small delivery truck sideways, not too hard. Unfortunately for the farmer, the flat bonnet of the Jeep fitted like a wedge under the lowered side-panel, and his vehicle tipped on its side, spilling everything all over the road. Since nobody was hurt, we just righted the little truck and went our way. That was the first and the last time that I let somebody drive a car of mine, except my wife, of course. With two later exceptions, but they were family.

One of the members of our staff was a young barber. He insisted to shave me every morning, "to stay in training", as he put it. I must say, this was very nice, saving me the trouble of the daily wet shaving. There was also plenty of time for listening to what our fellows had experienced during the war. There was quite a lot of chatting going on, also with our visitors.

We were now in the middle of the winter of 1945/46, but I remember neither having been cold, nor having had any type of heating facilities in our quarters. This must clearly be another slip of my memory, when I think of the bitter cold of the previous winter in the same area. Our villa was rather drafty, a clear advantage in the Italian summer, but not so 'hot' in winter in the Po Valley. Did we simply keep warm with the help of alcohol? I doubt it, even so this definitely would have helped, but I cannot think of any alternative method, acceptable to public moral standards.

By now we had decided, that some additional money had to be earned to supplement our army rations, to generally improve our living standard and to increase our independence. We were also now thinking about our uncertain future. Since I was the only one to speak Italian, I felt an obligation to help our team in this regard. On top of everything else, by now most of our chaps were bored stiff, because they did not have any hobby, nor any special interest.

We had been told by our groupies that there was a general shortage of flour here in Emilia, the south-eastern province of the British Zone, because most grain mills here had been damaged or destroyed during the war. On the other hand, there was a shortage of grain in Toscana, the adjoining north-western province of the US Zone. A typical free market challenge and opportunity. This dire situation immediately triggered my well-developed sense of civic duty.

I assume that one of our groupies had put me in touch with a local black-market operator. He wanted to move grain from the Emilia to a mill in Toscana, and to bring back the flour to Bologna. His problem was a lack of transport and, as explained already, the border between the two Zones of Occupation, high up in the Apennine Mountains. All civilian road traffic between the Zones was restricted and controlled. The main check point was near Porretta Terme, halfway between Bologna and Florence.

II Polish Corps had operated near the end of the war in the Bologna area, and for some reason or other, Polish uniforms were easily available on the local black market. My new associate obtained a Polish 1st Lieutenant outfit for me, and we were in business. One may recall that during the war I had already had such a uniform, and my first thought was: could this possibly be my old one? No, it was not.

The Polish troops had left the Bologna area before the end of the war and had been re-deployed to the Rimini area on the east coast, which minimized the danger of encountering a Polish officer here. I had organized two of our 3-ton trucks with drivers, and my co-conspirator had arranged to collect the grain somewhere in the Emilia, and the mill in Prato, just past Pistoia. In my Jeep, donning my Polish uniform, I lead our little convoy all the way south and back to Bologna.

We did this a number of times, and usually without a hitch. Only once was there a nerve-racking moment at the Porretta Pass control point, when a non-British (probably a South African) sergeant had difficulty reading our military travel documents, which were perfectly in order, since I had completed them carefully, as always, myself. Such things have to be in perfect order in the army, to obviate any problems.

This free market activity made a lot of money for us, long before Professor Ludwig Ehrhardt in Germany had copied my ideas. But that was all right. My income was sufficient to subsidize my comrades' lifestyle as well as feeding my own piggy-bank. Our officers had to be left out of this, of course, in order not to compromise them, and to avoid upsetting the apple cart, or should that be the 'gray train'?

Apples we did not buy often, but we bought in San Lazzaro other fruit and cigarettes, salami and mortadella, bread and butter, and *Perugina* chocolates. The latter we already knew from war-times as being not good, but there was no choice. Wine was also an important component of our shopping lists, but no beer. The sole *Peroni* brand was not at all to our German taste.

To buy Italian clothing and shoes we had to drive into the center of Bologna. I bought myself my very first hat, a genuine (as the salesman and the label claimed) *Borsalino*. We also converted some of our ill-gotten 1 000 Lire banknotes into Swiss Francs and US dollars. We were now living 'like the King of France', little worrying that he had ended up without his head.

We were now again the same reckless, care-free youngsters of the early part of the war in Italy. Moral scruples were absent. After all, we saw ourselves as victims here, as prisoners of war of the Allies on the one hand, but also as the victims of the wasting of our youth and our future by the Nazis. If you consider this rationalization a bit labored, I won't argue very much. As I have stated previously, I would truthfully report my actions and my true feelings at all the relevant times.

26

PADOVA

In the spring of 1946 we found ourselves in Padova in Northern Italy, near Venice. I am not sure why we had been moved there. The only thing which seems to be clear in my memory is the unexplained fact, that all of a sudden, we were not anymore with the battalion staff, or that our officers were no longer with us, but most likely I got this all wrong.

I have no idea what our functions were supposed to be there, and only remember that we did not undertake anything officially. It appears now as if the British had forgotten all about us. That in itself would not have been a first in military history, but on the other hand, it looked rather unlikely.

We were now comfortably housed, with field beds, chairs and tables, on the first floor of some sort of public building, probably a secondary school in Via Manzoni. I remember the name of this street, because this was our way towards Mestre and Venice, and this author had written '*I Promessi Spossi*', one of the most well-known literary works in Italy. One could find a street or *piazza* named after him in any town, I would guess.

From our window we looked down into what most likely had been the school yard. A dais had been constructed there, where every evening a small *impromptu* band played some dance music. This, of course, attracted young girls, and in turn, us (only partially due to the music). The dancing lessons long forgotten, we were now taught by the girls to dance to cool modern music, like the boogie-woogie and something, which developed later into rock-and-roll. But sentimental tunes were also played, which required unfortunately close contact, but much more inducive to instruction and learning.

At this time, we finally received our first mail from home since the end of the war. My mother wrote that my girlfriend had decided on a career in the *FDJ*, the *Freie Deutsche Jugend*, or Free German Youth, which was the communist copy in the Soviet Zone of Occupation of our *Hitlerjugend*. Actually, this statement about copying is not quite correct, because the Soviets had their own youth organization, long before the Nazis had copied theirs. Copied around three corners! And another example of the soul-affinity of communists, socialists and the Nazis.

I never wrote to my girlfriend after that revelation. Was it the deep-rooted aversion towards the communists and Russia, which the Nazi propaganda had indoctrinated into our minds? Or was it rather wounded pride? Anyway, she was instant history. Served her right!

For almost the first time since the end of the war, except for our life in Bologna, we had a very good time. Food, wine, money, and all the amenities attached to having money. For myself, I rented a furnished room, less than a hundred meters from our quarters, where I now had a private place for my possessions, could read or listen undisturbed to music of my choice in the evening, or could occasionally receive a visitress. I know, the word does not exist, but I like it.

In the evening I usually went into downtown Padova, for a drink or three and a chat with some Italian students. By now I had no problems contacting young Italians, since this was a university town. The younger people mostly had by now written off the vicissitudes of war. And I suppose, they may have even commiserated with us poor prisoners.

Once I went with one of my female acquaintances to see an Italian film. This was a serious disappointment for me, because I had to admit to myself that my understanding of Italian was insufficient in connection with watching a film, even though I had no serious problems with the face-to-face personal conversations.

The three of us from Bologna were still together, and the girl-friends of my two fellow 'prisoners' came one day visiting. The butcher's girlfriend brought her younger sister along, and for a few days we all had a profitable and pleasant time together. My rented room came in very handy.

After they had returned home, I often went to one of the *Casa dei Popoli*, House of the People. These were either municipal or communist affairs. Which did not make much of a difference, because most of the larger northern Italian cities were ruled by the *Partito Comunista Italiano* in those days (the spelling is correct, I looked it up!). These establishments played modern dance music at least once a week and, therefore, there were plenty of friendly girls around. Naturally I went there only to listen to the modern music and to polish-up on my still not good-enough Italian.

Now we finally come to the interesting section of this part. Our financial reserves from our illegal Bologna enterprise looked by now somewhat anemic and needed replenishing. We still had all our trucks, which had to be sent to the British Army filling station in Mestre for refueling. This town could be viewed as an industrial suburb of Venice. An Autobahn-type toll road (the toll was inoperative now) led from Padova via Mira to Mestre and on to Venice.

From our time in Bologna we knew about the huge depot of captured German military vehicles near Modena, where we had at the time cannibalized some trucks for spare parts. More specifically, for spare fuel tanks, which we had installed in our trucks for my grain and flour enterprise to support the Italian economy. Everybody praises quite correctly the Marshal Plan for propping up the economy of this country, but nobody recognizes the role, which hard-working small enterprises like ours have played in this regard.

It did not take me long to make the connection again, from spare part to spare fuel tank. Off we went to Modena, with a regulation trip-ticket composed by me, and came back with a further four spare fuel tanks for the remaining under-equipped trucks. It took our mechanic and the drivers a few days to install them, and we were open for business. By the way, in those days a truck driver was practically forced to be also partially a mechanic.

From now on, we drove one or two of these trucks to the filling station in Mestre almost every afternoon, to have both tanks of each truck filled. Next day it was the turn of another one or two trucks. On the way back to Padova, we turned off the expressway in Mira, entered a small hidden country road, and there our booty mysteriously metamorphosed into a small bundle of L1 000 banknotes. Way under the going rate, I guess, but so what. It was the Allied's petrol we sold, not ours.

Back in Padua we bought cigarettes, salami, cheese, bread, some fruit, a few beers and a one-liter bottle of *Chianti*. Sometimes I splashed out for us on a bottle of *Lacrymae Christi*, the Tears of Christ, a fortified wine from Naples. When we went to town in the early evenings, we occasionally bought some civilian clothes, maybe a shirt, or a smart jacket. All in the interest of supporting the economy.

A sergeant at the filling station noticed either our added fuel tanks, or our suspiciously frequent visits to fill up our trucks, and he made it clear that he was not going to allow these goings-on to continue. It was not too difficult to ascertain what was behind this officious behavior. From now on we had to share our loot with this 'gentleman', as simple as that. Luckily, there was enough money around.

Behavior like that by supply NCOs, and on a large scale, was later encountered in Vietnam by the US Forces, and I also came across this, when I was working in later years for the US Army in Germany. At least we were stealing only from the 'enemy', not from our own (a beautiful rationalization, worth a medal!). But maybe, things were not much better in the German army. Remember the horrible death of the German supply officer in the waste pit in the Rimini camp?

One of my fellow prisoners sold me his camera, a Contax made by Zeiss-Ikon. This product was competing before the war against the famous Leica produced by Leitz and was one of the most expensive 35mm German cameras. How he got this treasure through all the filching after the war (remember the loss of my high school wrist-watch?) was a mystery to me. I took a lot of pictures, but never became a proficient photographer. Between the right type of film, the correct photo printing paper, exposure and timing, there was always something slightly wrong.

I did drive to Mestre not only to chase the lucre, but also to widen my cultural horizons, by occasionally driving the few extra kilometers to visit the fabulous city of Venice. With my Jeep I could drive only as far as the *Piazzale Roma*, next to the railway station. This was the gateway to Venice, where buses and cars had to be parked, because, as everybody knows, there are no streets in Venice, only the *canali*. And as is also very well known, Venice consists of an archipelago of small islands in the *laguna*, including some uninhabited ones.

The water-bus ride along the *Canal Grande* was most impressive, viewing all these old and splendid *palazzi*, which were usually poorly maintained. Right next to the Doge's palace, where the *Canal Grande* met the Venetian *laguna*, was located the British Officers Club, where I usually started and, some hours later, finished my excursions. Why the heck was I wearing my Polish 1st Lieutenant's uniform on these occasions? A completely unnecessary risk! But the visit to the Officers Club wasn't just for the drinks and snacks. Often, I had interesting discussions with British and Allied officers, sometimes even including US air force or navy officers.

Occasionally I hired a *gondola* to explore along the *canali* the sights a tourist would normally never see. I particularly remember on one of the canals a tiny, decrepit-looking church but with a beautiful interior. Later I would have enquired from the *gondolieri* about a good small *trattoria* for a typical Italian lunch, as the locals preferred it.

Subsequently I usually took a vaporetto to the *Lido* on the far side of the *laguna*, where there was also much to be seen. One of the attractions was the palace of the Venice Film Festival or *Film Biennale*. One day I hired, at great expense, a *gondola* to visit some of the many outlying islands, among them Murano with their glass blowers, and the cemetery island, or 'Island of the Dead'. This latter visit was a bit depressing.

Naturally, I took some more pictures with my expensive German camera, but this was not much of a success, because I simply did not know enough about how to properly use such a sophisticated piece of equipment. Or the Italian drugstore operators, developing and printing my pictures, didn't know their job? But no, they were definitely my shortcomings, possibly the use of the wrong type of film, or the tricky relationship between the setting of aperture and timing.

After several months of leisurely and profitably fleecing the 'enemy', our idyllic life took a turn for the worse. Up to now we had been dealing with generally peace-loving so-called business men, meaning Black Market operators, and with the odd NCOs with sticky fingers. But now we had an approach of a different kind.

One day I was contacted in Venice by two smooth-talking, well-dressed and apparently well-behaved gentlemen, who politely suggested that we should sell our petrol in future to a service station near Miro. To clarify the implications of their well-meaning suggestion, one of them casually lifted the corner of his jacket, to reveal a shiny automatic pistol. Even this unsophisticated foreigner got the message first time round.

For a while we stalled, not being convinced that they were serious to act like this. Who wants to give away a well-run profitable business? But then things got a bit out of hand for our taste. Our new would-be friends had heard about a small fuel tanker, which was moored in the harbor of Mestre. They were looking for a way to steal the damn thing, or rather its load. They had already, they claimed, roped in a navy chap of some sort, but they needed road transport. Before they could go into details, I told them not to bother: we were not interested! Icy silence, then the expected threats.

We three came to the conclusion that this was all very well, but that we did not need this kind of aggravation. And we further had the feeling that the time had come to consider our return to Germany and to our families, despite all the problems there. Together with my two friends we all now packed up our valuables and drove up to the Italian/Austrian border near Bruneck in South Tyrol. Did we pinch one of the battalion's vehicles? Don't remember, but it was most likely.

One of our business partners had provided me with a local address there. We paid a tidy sum to some mountain farmer, to take us over the border and to deliver us to his counterpart across the summits of the Alps in Tyrol, Austria. This appeared to work out according to plan. This farmer gave us a hearty supper, rounded off with a few glasses of their local and very potent herbal liqueur, and at nightfall we started on our way.

We had, however, completely underestimated the weight of our two suitcases each and the difficulties of our way across the mountains. After a few kilometers I was forced to lighten my suitcases, which were badly overweight. I threw out expensive smart clothing, but kept my *Borsalino* hat, my cartons of Lucky Strike and Camel cigarettes, and the currency, naturally.

By now we were trudging through deep snow on our way to the border, which we eventually crossed unseen. In Austria awaited us the counterpart of the smuggler from the Italian side and a good breakfast. After having exchanged the remaining bundles of Lire for Austrian *Schillinge* banknotes, we were on our way to Lienz, a medium-sized town not too far from the Italian border. To get there, we wandered along the slopes of the mountain peaks, high above the roads and villages down in the valleys, until finally we could walk safely down to civilization again.

Here our guide left us, and we were lucky to catch a lift with a tractor-trailer collecting early every morning the barrels of fresh milk from the farms along the road, to deliver them to the nearest railway station. We avoided the Lienz one, because we considered this would have been a place too obvious for checking for escaped prisoners of war from Italy, who would try to catch here a train north to Germany. When we arrived at a tiny station nearby, with just one railway employee in sight, we bought our rail tickets to Salzburg, further north in Austria, as a first stage of our return to Germany.

27

HOMECOMING - WITH MINOR PROBLEMS

After our arrival in Salzburg, we were hungry and walked into town to look for some sustenance. At a bakery we were given some fresh bread, without ration stamps having been demanded. We had completely forgotten to buy any, because in Italy there was no rationing. The sales lady obviously saw from our clothes that we had come from Italy as escaped Prisoners of War. That same day we met another nice and helpful Austrian lady, who invited us to her family's home. There we tried *Salzburger Schmarren*, a tasty kind of apple cake. The sales lady in the bakery and this friendly lady were the only Austrians we came in close personal contact with, apart from the paid guide. They reinforced our assumption that our Austrian blood-brothers, co-soldiers and co-Germans would assist us on our way back to our families.

Next day we set off along the River Salzach to the village of Grödig, from where we intended to cross the Untersberg to reach Gross-Gmain in Bavaria. I hope, I have remembered the names and the spelling of these localities correctly.

After walking only a few kilometers, an Austrian border guard spotted and arrested us. After he had summoned reinforcements we were searched, each one of us by only one individual guard. Thus, there were no witnesses to what was taken from us and landed in the big pockets of the border guards. My friends lost everything, whereas my searcher only took my substantial amount of foreign currency, but he left me my cigarettes. I would have preferred it the other way round, because money is more versatile than cigarettes in a tricky situation.

We were immediately brought before the *Landeshauptmann*, the Governor of the Salzburg Province. He suffered from an obvious leg injury. A war casualty, probably collected in the German army? He sentenced us to ninety days in prison, for illegally crossing the Austrian borders. I tried the lame argument that this was only an attempted crossing, because we were caught before we reached the border, but he countered that we must have crossed the Austrian/Italian border to arrive in Salzburg. Well, when a man is right, then he's right!

I bitterly complained to the Governor about how we had been illegally robbed by the border guards. He flatly denied that they would commit such ghastly deeds. His comment: "The war is over, when such things were done regularly, probably by you three as well". Surprise, surprise, since that day certain Austrians are not quite my glass of beer!

Well, that was that, then! After all the crazy and dangerous and more or less illegal things we had pulled, now we had been caught for what we considered our natural right, or a mere misdemeanor, at worse. After all, to get from Italy to Germany, one is forced to cross either Austria or Switzerland. And we had naively thought that crossing friendly Austria would be OK.

As explained already in an earlier part of this story, the Austrians, Nazis or not, had overwhelmingly been on the side of Germany before and during the early stages of the war. Now some of them treated us as criminals, and many saw us as foreigners or, at best, as unwelcome family members. Bloody unfair, but who said that life was fair? However, as recorded above, only some of the Austrians behaved like that. Since then I prefer in their country the people of Tyrol and Carinthia.

On the second day of our involuntary stay at this forbidding establishment we were escorted to the office of some official, probably a detective. He wanted to know, who had helped us to commit our heinous crime of crossing the border illegally. No, sorry, these heinous political crimes, plural, against the sovereignty of this independent, democratic and anti-Nazi country. We had to suppress a feeling of nausea.

Then we had to explain in great detail, where we had been, and exactly when. This friendly gentleman was suggesting that we surely had committed other crimes during our illegal passage through Austria, such as pillaging and robbing. He was generous enough to leave unmentioned rape and arson. After a few hours of grilling, we were escorted back to our cell.

Our stay in the Salzburg prison was educational in more than one way. First of all, we quickly realized that our early hunger period at Rimini had only been a training exercise for the hunger we would experience now. The cell population received daily a small loaf of bread for every six or eight inmates, I would guess. I soon learnt that the two end-pieces contained relatively the most nourishment. The supplementary other food items were of low quantities. One had to acknowledge, however, that food was still rationed, but that was of limited consolation for us.

We were staying in a communal cell, housing an estimated thirty inmates, with an eclectic mixture of offenders. There were Nazis as well as men who had been incarcerated for the possession of weapons. The authorities seemed to consider us as belonging to the hardened and serious international political criminals.

The cellmates were of a very interesting mixture. My bed neighbor, for instance, had been a famous script writer for the film studios of Vienna, before and particularly after the German takeover. I remembered his name clearly from the 1938/1942 period, when he had written the scripts of many highly popular films, mostly comedies. But he had also been a high-profile admirer of Hitler. He appeared to still have good connections, since he had a stack of his film scripts in the cell, all of which he allowed me to read.

Another remarkable inmate was a Gypsy (the correct terminology at the time), only a few years older than me. Why he was incarcerated, and why with the 'politicals', I did not know, and this remained his secret. He was highly intelligent, and we had some lively, and always friendly, debates about everything and nothing, about 'god and the world' (I mean this literally).

His main attitude was an anarchistic one. He predicted that the

Jews would soon achieve their own strictly religious state through the barrels of their guns, while the Gypsies would never achieve statehood, because they were inherently nihilistic and ungovernable. The very near future proved him right.

After the early lights-out, some of the fellow prisoners told stories of things which had happened during the war or gave lectures on one subject or other. These talks were mostly very interesting, and often dealt with former German state secrets. Since the 'referents' remained anonymous in the dark, some peculiar and some disturbing things came to light.

Particularly I remember the story about the submarines of the German navy with the Walter power train. According to what we had heard, this system was revolutionary, but not yet fully developed. Wikipedia tells me, that in the final analysis, the technology did not deliver what it had promised, and that many accidents had happened during the war, causing numerous fatalities among the navy personnel. Needless to say, during the war the German public was never apprised of these facts.

Another contribution came from a fellow member of *Division Brandenburg*, who had served on the Russian front during the final months of the war. When the division had lost its unique character, and had been converted into an ordinary infantry division, he managed to move from the Eastern front more and more southwest, always with proper documentation (this sounded rather familiar), until he landed in Austria as a civilian. His experiences as a specialist forger of documents were hilarious.

Obviously, he must have been before the war an experienced operator (in private practice!), but during the war he produced or forged passports and personal documents of all sorts for the government and the army. He was even involved in the production of spurious propaganda postage stamps. One such 'British' set ridiculing the Empire showed, for instance, King George VI surrounded by 'hammer and sickle' symbols. Another one showed his likeness amidst Zionist and Hebrew characters.

A further contributor was dealing with the hydro-power complex of Kaprun, high up in the Austrian Alps. I do not remember much of what we were told in this instance, except that this massive undertaking had been in the planning stages for decades. But when the work had actually started, they met with numerous unexpected problems. Apparently, these related mostly to the complicated geology of the local mountain massif. The outbreak of war put a halt to all the sandpit games they had played until then. I assume the complex is now in operation.

One day some of us prisoners, unfortunately including me, were ordered down into the yard, to split and stack firewood. The winter of 1946/1947 was extremely cold in Central Europe. We were still wearing our summer and autumn clothes and were not prepared for these extreme temperatures. The cold was so intense that after ten minutes my hands and feet were badly hurting and feeling like solid ice, and I became nauseous.

By the way, as far as I can remember, this was the only time during our jail sojourn that we were in this yard. No such thing as a daily hour in the exercise yard, like what seems to be standard practice nowadays in other jails, judging by what one sees in American TV films.

After our ninety days were done with, and we were down to skin and bones, we were not released by our Austrian fellow Nazis (this is an intentional politically not-correct dig). It appeared that the Governor had thrown away the key to our cell, or more to the point, to our conviction and prison records. Accidentally, and without malicious aforethought, of course. Only when, two weeks after the expiry of our sentence period, an American inspection officer appeared, was I able to get ourselves released. With his apology, but without one from our former Austrian war comrades!

Probably sometime in March of 1947 we were handed over to the British Army, because technically we were still Prisoners of War. As mentioned already, Salzburg was in the US Zone of Occupation, and the British had their Zone in the southern parts of Austria, adjacent to their respective Zone in northern Italy. For about two weeks they locked us up in an army penal camp near Villach, which was also used as a Recalcitrant Camp for escaped and recaptured PoWs. This was correct procedure, and fair enough. How we got there, escapes me (pun intended).

We were handed over to some sergeants and corporals, who treated us fairly. I did not see any British officer there. We learned here something about discipline in a British boot camp. Our beds had to be made not just very well, but perfectly. If not, the whole shebang could be collected from some rafter in the Nissen hut in which we were living. It took us a few days to learn all the tricks, but after that we got on very well with our jailers. After all, these chaps had also been in the front lines, fighting against us in the Italian campaign.

A German prisoner was held in a wire cage, all by himself. We were not allowed to speak to him. When we enquired as to what was the special story about him, all we were told was that he had been a paratrooper. This could impossibly have been the reason for this unusual punishment. There must have been some-thing else, and something rather serious. Maybe another Hannibal Lector? One more of the many unresolved mysteries in my life.

There were also a small number of British soldiers held in this camp. They told me about the 'crimes' they had committed. Most of them had gone AWOL, Absent-With-Out-Leave (a US Army term). Now, after the war, the lure of the local girls was just too strong for them to resist. So, they stayed away from their units for an extra day or two. But all armies are funny that way. They don't like it, when soldiers prefer the embraces of a warm-blooded female over the loving attention the Sergeant Major bestows on them.

The mention of AWOL raised the question in my mind, whether I should maybe try to escape again, to join the young lady I had fancied on my way from Vienna to Villach two years earlier, since the camp was in the neighborhood. But I discarded this tempting idea as unrealistic, because I could not be sure, whether I would be able to find her, and under which circumstances. What, if she had by now a whole kindergarten at home?

After a few days in this camp I started a small retail operation, illegal as always. One of the sergeants exchanged a large packet of cigarette paper for some packs of my American cigarettes. Cigarette paper was vital, if you had tobacco to roll a decent cigarette. Newsprint was plainly unsuitable for the purpose. Only the Russians used it. And not everybody prefers a pipe over some civilized smoking. This was a short-lived enterprise, and not remotely as profitable as the trans-port of grain and flour, or the re-distribution of petrol.

This small British Army post was located approximately halfway between Salzburg and Padua. The fact that we had been shipped to this camp in Southern Austria served as an indication for me that the British intended to bring us back to Padua, the location of our original 'crime', namely our escape.

But, as happened so often with the military, events developed quite differently. Maybe some staff officer had figured out that this would be a waste of resources, if our anticipated release as Prisoners of War was to happen soon. When our time was up, we were informed that we would be repatriated to Germany. To release us now made some (army) sense: we had escaped from their custody - we had been re-captured - and we had been punished by the army. All neat and proper and according to the regulations, thank you very much.

This development induced me to sell the rest of my cigarettes, to have some cash in my pockets, and to lighten my travel baggage. We were placed on a train (actually, I remember nothing about that) and in due course found ourselves in the former Nazi *Konzentrationslager* of Dachau outside of Munich, which now operated as a US release-camp for PoWs.

Here it was explained that we would be released to our last civilian address. To be difficult as always: what about those soldiers, whose families had been chased out of their homes in Poland and Czechoslovakia? Anyway, in my case this translated into the Soviet Zone of Occupation.

I was determined not to go there. Presumably, the Nazi brainwashing about the Soviet communists was still active enough, but mainly I did not trust the communists to be able to properly run the economy with their economic prejudices. Therefore, I expected that life in Dresden would not be rewarding at all and would become as dull as in the Soviet Union itself.

Dachau was only a very temporary sojourn for us. I had befriended a fellow prisoner there from Hessia, and when I told him that I was not going back to the Russian Zone, and that I needed a credible address for the authorities, he gave me one for me to use, in Frankfurt/Main, in the US Zone of Occupation.

Before we were allowed to leave, we were again quizzed as to what we had done during the war, but this was only a half-hearted exercise. The US officers of the CIC, the Counter Intelligence Corps, had all our information collected by their colleagues in Rimini, and they were just spot-checking.

When we were channeled through the offices of the camp, and I was asked about my destination in Germany for my trip home, I gave them my 'imported' address in Frankfurt/Main. Now I was given my train ticket, and probably some travel ration stamps, and maybe even some pocket money, but I remember nothing about any of that.

The time had now come to take leave of the two men I had been together with for about two years. We had, each in his own way, supported ourselves and had lived through good times and some not so hot experiences. But we had not been bored and had lived dangerously and had not been caught (apart from that stupid border incident). We had played our captors for all they had been worth, without any moral qualms.

This was a satisfying feeling, compensating somewhat for the disappointments of the Nazi betrayal of a whole generation of idealistic youngsters. And also for the fact, that family members and friends had died in vain, and that careers had been smothered before they had a chance to begin.

But also, for the trist outlook for our future in a bombed-out country, without neither an economic nor a political future. And, further, in partial compensation for the unfairness of having been locked up for two years after the war had ended.

However, most importantly, for a deep-sitting sense of unqualified and unspecified anger, against everybody and any-thing, a nagging hate of the world.

And off we went to the devastated Fatherland and a doubtful freedom and even more hazy future.

PART VI

FRANKFURT/MAIN, GERMANY

LIFE AS A CIVILIAN (1947 TO 1965)

28

DENAZIFICATION IN A LANDSCAPE OF RUINS

1947 TO 1949

Even before arriving in Frankfurt I knew that this city had also been severely bombed, but I hoped that the destructions were maybe not quite as serious as in Dresden. Immediately after leaving the main railway station, sometime in April or May of 1947, the destruction was confirmed right away. Facing me were the burnt-out ruins of what I later learned to have been the *Schumann Theater*. All other buildings facing the station had also been damaged more or less seriously. Only the main station itself was almost undamaged (same as in Dresden!). But here at least there were some tram lines working, two years after the end of the war.

My first requirement was obviously to contact the family at the address I had been given in Dachau. My enquiries as to where I would find *Hindenburg Strasse* elicited the first raised eyebrows. I was informed, probably by some communist or social democrat, that this Fascist name had been replaced by the anti-Fascist name of *Ludwig Landmann Strasse*. This brought me down to earth quickly. Hindenburg had been the hero of WW1 in Germany, and he also had been the last democratically elected State President. He had, so one could hear, disdainfully categorized Hitler as "this lance corporal". But I had never heard before of Herr Landmann, and I was surprised about how a genuine war hero had been so unceremoniously dismantled by the new democratic dispensation.

A streetcar brought me to *Ludwig Landmann Strasse 110*. There I encountered a small problem: a house number 110 had never existed in this street. Now what? The only contact address I possessed had evaporated into thin air, and since I did not have the name of the supposed occupants, I had reached a dead end. No family, no relatives, no acquaintances, no contacts of any sort! Therefore, I had to fall back on what my military experiences, including the Prisoner of War memories, suggested how any difficulties of this nature could be overcome: don't accept "no" for an answer and go onto the offensive.

I went back to the main railway station, because in passing I had seen there on my arrival from Munich the sign of an US Army office. Since I was now in the American Zone (of Occupation), I figured that working for the US Army seemed to be the only avenue worth following, at least for the moment. After all, I needed a job, some money, but even more so, a roof over my head and a real address. This latter one was vital to receive food ration coupons, and to be registered with the police and the local municipality, which had always been a very important requirement of life in Germany.

My thinking proved to be realistic, when I was given there the address of the Griesheim Ordnance Depot of the US Army. This was located in the partially destroyed factory complex of the Messer–Griesheim firm in Frankfurt-Griesheim. This installation included a camp of huts to house their civilian employees in need of accommodation. It took me a while to absorb the fact that the term 'civilian' now also included me.

At the Personnel Office of the depot I was given a referral slip for the local CPO, the Civilian Personnel Office of the US Army, stating that they would have a job for me. There my PoW camp release papers were checked, my claim of knowledge of English was verified, and I was sent back to the depot with a document. There I signed some papers. I had also been assigned a bed in one of the huts. Now I was, for the first time in my life, an employee.

This hutted camp included a large kitchen and a primitive dining area, where we received two meals a day in lieu of our food ration coupons. Thus, the most pressing problems of the moment had been solved. I doubt, whether I even checked for what kind of work I had been hired. But my hourly wage as a checker was *RM*

0,84. This miserly amount was, however, of no consequence, because the *Reichsmark* had by now almost no value. On the following morning I was to start my first job as a civilian. Quite a peculiar feeling!

The camp had been built during the war for prisoners of war or for 'forced labor' working at a decentralized armaments factory of what was then the Messer-Griesheim group. The name of the company did not refer to the Frankfurt suburb of this name, as I had assumed, but to a synonymous small town outside Darmstadt. The huts were similar to the ones I had encountered at the Labor Service, and they contained about thirty normal field beds each. The sanitary facilities of the camp, however, were atrocious. Every morning the urinals were overflowing. It was disgusting, worse then what we had experienced in the military and Prisoner of War camps and in Salzburg prison.

But even worse, if that was considered possible, were the meals which the kitchen served. Food was still rationed and scarce in Germany, but our meals were monotonous and badly prepared. Red beet was the standard accessory to potatoes-in-their-jackets, which had suffered from frostbite and tasted horribly sweet. Even today, seventy years later, red beet is a no-no for me, even though my wife tries to convince me how healthy they are.

Now I better explain what this depot was all about. Together with a few other such installation the depot stored US ordnance, which had been collected after the end of the war from all over the European Theater. This materiel had to be cleaned, identified and stored, and afterwards re-issued to US installations and units all over the show. Some of its special customers were the US Military Mission at Teheran in Iran, or the US Army procurement section in Yugoslavia, which procured beef for the US troops there. But most of the customers were, of course, US Army units all over Europe.

The depot's personnel consisted of US Army officers of approximately the strength and the grades of a regimental HQ staff, plus a handful of NCOs and DAs, Department of the Army civilians. Additionally, there were more than a thousand LNs, the Local Nationals. Mostly Germans, largely former officers and soldiers, but also some DPs, the Displaced Persons. The whole organization had German executives and managers in charge, from the depot command down to the divisions and branches, working under the direction and supervision of US officers.

The Supply Division accounted for almost ninety percent of the 1 400 civilian employees of the depot. It consisted of the Storage, Stock Control, Plans & Operations and Administration Branches, each with several sections. The division and each of the branches had an officer in charge and an LN executive (except for the P&O Branch), responsible for the day-to-day operations.

My first place of work was in one of the storage areas. My job as a checker was to control the receiving, correct storage and dispatching of boxes of ordnance in and out of this storage area. On my very first working day, my future German boss, the LN Chief of the Supply Division, happened to come to this area (or had he been advised of my hiring?). He shortly interviewed me, and after a few questions and answers, he told me to get my things and report to the wage office in Building 461. Thus, my 'extensive' career as a storage worker and wage earner ended rather prematurely.

Now as a salaried employee, I was kept busy here for the next few weeks with time clock cards and personnel records. One of the female clerks showed me how to manage a modern typewriter, a contraption I had not encountered previously, and my 1-finger-search-typing-system was born. But I was also able to help out some of my new colleagues with translations. Most of them, however, had picked up enough English to get by, usually as former US Army PoWs.

My first-ever working in an office carried on for a few weeks, a typical eight-to-five job. One pleasant novelty for me was the fact, that the US Army did not work on Saturdays. This gave me an additional day-off, to go to Frankfurt or go for an extended walk.

Then, one day the Lieutenant Colonel in charge of the Supply Division asked me into his office. He wanted to know, whether I knew anything about flow charts, as my German boss had probably indicated to him. I had to say no, but that I would be keen to learn, and that I was a fast learner. He sent me to Major Barber, the Depot Controller. I had no idea what a Controller was, but he explained this function to me, and I think he simultaneously checked me out. He was very friendly and helpful. Maybe also a bit bored with his job? Naturally, he mainly showed me what flow charts looked like, and how they should be prepared. Amongst some little tricks of his trade, he taught me cross-multiplication (why did we not learn such a handy thing at high school?) and showed me how to write down sums from the front, instead of as usual from the back.

Coming back to our Colonel, I explained that I now would be able to prepare a flow chart. He ordered me (he was, after all, an officer) to prepare one for each one of all the documents handled by the division, but first to deal with the shipping documents. He hoped that I would be able to finish this first and most important task within a month.

The Stock Control Branch operated a dozen or so of the huge IBM tabulators (remember them from the Dresdner Bank?). They had a full-time job to print mostly the shipping and inventory documents. One of the side-effects of preparing this flow chart was that I was able to recommend some changes to the SOP, the Standing Operating Procedure for these documents.

This would result in the saving of an extra copy for the hundreds of daily shipping documents, which translated into an annual saving of about one ton of computer paper. Additionally, in saving of some days in total processing time of the shipping documents, the most critical and voluminous of the depot's paperwork. It took me a bit less than a month, and the boss was pleased with the results and he forwarded my recommendations up the military hierarchy.

After this successful and particularly satisfying job I was assigned some similar smaller special tasks in the field of organization and management, which type of work I found interesting and liked very much. Later I was asked to see the Controller again. The Major told me that new instructions had been received from the Washington War Department. Governments were then still honest about their jobs, and the PC, the 'politically correct' label had not been invented yet.

The Depot had been ordered to introduce a new modern decimal filing system, globally applicable to the US Army. After he had shown me the documentation from Washington, he wanted to know whether I would be able to implement this, because he himself would have to leave, since he had been temporarily seconded, due to the Berlin crisis, to General Clay's staff, the US Supreme Commander, Europe.

This system would still use the traditional American way of filing documents by using hanging folders, as opposed to the European one of using standing Leverarch files, but it would be based on a standardized decimal filing schedule.

Then he made a comment, which I would never again forget: "many Anglo-Americans have problems working with percentages and with the decimal system", which later experiences confirmed when I was working for the US Army and afterwards in South Africa. But I found that this did not apply to Scotsmen! I saw no difficulty in managing this, because it was just a question of applied logic. And since it was something new, it did not require any specific experience.

This temporary secondment of the Controller turned out to be a game-changer for me. Without this event I would never have had the chance to speak to the depot commander, because he would simply have dealt with the very competent Controller.

My next task was also triggered by a directive from Washington: to establish a Work Measurement and Work Simplification Unit in the depot, to be housed in my Plans and Operations Branch within the Supply Division. I was told to see the Depot Commander. It became quickly clear to me, how this assignment should be handled. Since this also was new, no specific prior experience was needed, only common sense.

He had given me a list of people (all male, naturally, in those days) which he had received from the CPO. They were all former (?) Nazis, who were black-listed and were not allowed to work in their professions. The list contained university professors, a judge, prosecutors and such-like professionals. Theoretically, they should have been the perfect candidates for this type of undertaking, but when I started to interview them, I encountered a difficulty.

This assignment started out problematically. They were obviously all intelligent and knowledgeable in their fields of expertise. But because this was an entirely new subject, past experience did not count for much. What I was looking for was, in addition to intelligence, an open mind and the ability to think 'out of the box', and above all, for common sense.

This latter term, as I had found, was one of the many typically English 'false friends' in their language. Like the 'rest room' (who wants to rest there?), or the 'cloak room' (equally unsuitable for keeping your overcoat), or the 'bathroom' (do they piddle into the tub?). In my later experience as a management consultant, I learned that common sense is neither common, nor is it necessarily connected with intelligence.

When I told the Colonel that this list was not going to work, but that I had available in my Branch a suitable assistant, he confronted me with the angry question, whether I intended to sabotage the US Army's efforts at improved efficiency. But after I had detailed the results of my interviews with each of the candidates, and how I had searched for 'open minds and common sense', he accepted my decision and seemed pacified. He felt, like many US officers at the time, a deep distrust towards academics.

After this was done to the satisfaction of the top brass, I was promoted from clerk to LN Chief, Plans and Operations Branch, jumping several salary brackets. Now I also received a low-level security clearance, which I needed to deal with classified Army Regulations, for instance. And all this after only four or five months of employment. Here I experienced for the first time the 'American way of doing things'. As a civilian in the German military or in any large German firm it would have taken me many years, and many individual steps, for such an advancement, if it would have ever happened. Without the formal qualifications of a university education, one did not have any chance of becoming an executive, and definitely not almost overnight.

Now I had established a new unit in my Plans and Operations Branch, the Work Measurement and Work Simplification Section. For this unit I had found a few suitable young investigators, by ignoring all formal qualifications and experiences. Their ability to quote a string of prime numbers was more important to me than a PhD.

Among our laborers were some who were prevented from working in their usual field, due to the denazification rules. Also, those men, like myself, who had been prevented by circumstances to study after the war. Refugees from Eastern Europe, for instance, or employees of firms which had been dismantled or bombed-out were other examples.

Going through the new Army Regulation for this unit, the first thing I noticed was an omission. I indoctrinated my new co-workers: "Before you even start to look at the details of any organization, the first question you must ask, whether it was necessary to exist". In later years I found that my gut reaction had been correct, and from the start of my future professional work I followed this rule successfully.

Another new unit, the Reports and Statistics Section mainly dealt with progress and status reports which controlled the workflow, from the Stock Control Branch through the various sections of the Storage Branch to the Shipping unit of the depot. My assistant for this section had a brother, who was the driver of Ludwig Erhard, the man in charge of Economic Affairs of the *Bizone*, the combined Anglo/American Zones of Occupation in Germany. Later he became the first economics minister of the *Bundesrepublik*. He resided in the *Fürstenpalast* in the center of Frankfurt, an imposing and almost undamaged building. Once, when my assistant visited his brother, I met this important man, but just to say hello. I considered it unprofessional to tell him how to run the economy of West-Germany since he did very well on his own.

The German Depot Director, who knew about my Rimini sojourn and what I had studied there, and who also knew that I was living in the hutted camp, asked me to have a look at reported problems at the camp kitchen. I found out quickly what the reasons had been for the terrible food provided in the camp. The camp administrator and the man in charge of the kitchen had both been concentration camp inmates. Together they skimmed off much of the money provided by the depot for feeding the camp inhabitants. Many of the more valuable food items were stolen by them as well and sold on the Black Market. One of the main reasons, why this was possible to go on for quite some time, was the absence of a bookkeeper and of proper administration systems.

One of the things I had studied in the Rimini PoW camp was the basics of record keeping, bookkeeping and accounting. To start with, I felt a bit out of my depth, but soon got the hang of things after I had found a middle-aged lady who was a good bookkeeper with general office experience. Together we introduced proper double-entry bookkeeping systems with a decimal accounts schedule. Receiving and Stock Control, and a decent filing system (decimal, obviously) were the other planks to a transparent administration. I kept far away from the actual kitchen, of course. After the criminal activities of these two 'upright anti-Fascists' had come to light, they had been arrested.

The shortage of practically everything in post-war Germany was crippling. Almost all goods were rationed, or they had to be procured at horrendous prices on the Black Market. Sometimes one would get something from a friendly soldier or officer, which was greatly appreciated. Even a single Lucky Strike or Camel cigarette was welcome. A whole pack of twenty was like Christmas and Easter falling on the same day, as we say in German. I still remember the wife of one of our officers asking me, whether we had enough soap. After telling her that this was now a luxury, she produced three bars of the red Lifebuoy soap. Most welcome, for sure, but then I wondered, why she had given me carbolic soap. Was she telling me something? Yes, we were a miserable bunch!

Together with my registration with the local police came the necessity to obtain my denazification document, certifying that I was not a fugitive or criminal Nazi. This was issued by an office in the Frankfurt *Polizeipräsidium*, the Office of the local Chief of Police. I do not remember, whether the simple membership of the Party was considered a crime. Normally, the members of the *Hitlerjugend* were transferred automatically into the Nazi party at age 18, but I seemed to have fallen through the cracks. This I only found out now. Good for me, that I never became a member of the Party!

One of the great mysteries of this period was the enigma of the Nazis metamorphosing to Antifascists. Before 1938 practically all good Germans were Nazis. After 1945 most good Germans were Antifascists, or at least had never been Nazis. An amazing illusionist performance! At this time, not a single Nazi was to be found! All right, a few surfaced over the years and admitted their past, and some even stated to be sorry that the Party was not in power anymore.

Prior to my arrival in Frankfurt, many important developments had taken place there after 1945, as I now discovered when talking to people and perusing the local newspapers, which I was now reading regularly, as I have done always in my life, whenever possible at all.

Right after the end of the war twelve million (Wikipedia) German refugees, most of them expelled by Poland and Czecho-slovakia, had arrived in Germany and had to be integrated into the local population. This worked reasonably well in the cities and towns, but it created many problems in the rural areas. Addition-ally, thousands of Displaced Persons, or DPs, were still living in Germany. But these foreigners, displaced by the war, usually either eventually returned home, or they emigrated over-seas with the help of the Allies, so they were not a big problem.

It was a common occurrence in the villages, even before this influx, if a youngster from a neighboring village had chatted up a girl, next Sunday after church a serious battle between the young men of the two villages was inevitable. If the amorous lad happened to be a refugee or a DP, a more or less bloody skirmish was pre-programmed.

Another challenge were the inmates of the concentration camps, which had been released. The Allies were either not aware of (rather unlikely!), or they did not care much about the fact that there had been two distinct groups of prisoners: political and crimi-nal. The political ones found immediate employment in elevated positions of the Administration, of course. But many of the crimi-nals also managed the same feat.

In Frankfurt we had a number of those cases. Whether these men had been criminals to start with, or only became such after their release, I did not know. There were the likes of Herr Morgenbesser, a stamp dealer, Herr Klibanski, a lawyer, the Chief of police at this time (name forgotten), etc. They and many others too were all rumored to be rather shady characters. When I tried to check the spelling of these names in the German-language Wiki-pedia, I noted that they were not listed. A case of selective amnesia, perhaps?

Now I wanted to start my doubtlessly illustrious legal career by studying law at the Frankfurt university. But I was rudely told that I did not qualify because my home was in the Russian Zone (of

Occupation). "Why don't you go back to Dresden and study there, instead of wasting our scarce resources here?" I decided to remain an un-studied democrat, rather than becoming a communist legal eagle, and I decided to stay in Frankfurt in the US Zone.

There were a few other problems to be resolved. Because of my stay at the Griesheim Depot camp, I was now able to get my first ID card from the police. I also could now obtain from the municipality my permit to stay in Frankfurt. This was then a legal requirement in Germany, to control the tremendous upheavals within the population. But I still did not have a permit to rent a room or apartment in Frankfurt.

If I wanted to get out of the camp, I had to get this document as well, which required a visit to the municipal Accommodation Office. This final task was accomplished easily enough. I had been told that a carton of Lucky Strike would speedily remove any obstacle, and the cigarettes quickly disappeared into a drawer of the official's desk. If you have formed the impression that post-war Germany was drowning in bureaucracy and corruption, you would be spot-on.

Finally, in possession of all the vital pieces of paper, I was now able to leave the camp, and to rent a furnished room in a private household in Schwanheim, the suburb on the opposite side of the River Main from the depot. The bridge between the two suburbs had become a victim of the war (bombs or explosives?), and the British Army engineers had replaced it by a Bailey Bridge. This allowed a short walk to my office.

As I soon found out, many of the maybe two hundred old-established families there had the same few surnames. This was quite common for small villages in Germany before the war. In this connection the influx of dozens of refugee families was a good thing for the suburb. It brought fresh blood into the community, and it helped to curb the previously widely encountered rural in-breeding.

My new quarters (I was still thinking in military terms) allowed me now for the first time something like a social life. Sunday was a big day there, with live dance music in the afternoon in the local sports hall. For a thick wad of almost worth-less *Reichsmark* one could sometimes even buy a bottle of the local plonk.

There I met my first wife. She had been given a single room of sixteen square meters to rent, where she lived with her out-of-wedlock daughter of two years. The room contained a crib for the girl, a sleeper double-couch for her and an electric hot-plate. With a toilet and washing facilities on the landing.

After I had moved in, we got married, probably in early 1948. There was no love involved, not even any particular liking. Just the need for some company and mutual support, by sharing the daily miseries of post-war life in Germany. This was clearly a recipe for disaster which, not surprisingly, manifested itself in due course. It is impossible today to under-stand such a psychological situation, if one has not personally experienced these times.

By now I often used the number 21 streetcar to go to town. The streets in the city center had now been cleared of the rubble, and the public transport system was working almost normally. Generally, the ruins of the burnt-out buildings were still untouched, but some had been partially repaired to create some primitive accommodation. There were no building materials easily available and those recovered from the ruins had to suffice. Watching photos and videos from present-day Syria conveys a realistic impression of the picture that German cities presented then.

I remember, looking from the main entrance of the central railway station into the three main pre-war shopping roads leading to the city center, that in neither of them was there a single undamaged building to be found.

Kronprinzenstrasse, which had suffered under the anti-Fascist fervor and had its name changed to Münchner Strasse, sported one single small shop on the ground floor of a burnt-out building, selling *Kunstgewerbe*, a euphemism for not very artistic wood carvings, crocheted little things and such, because there was not really anything worthwhile to sell. Oh yes, they also sold some postage stamps for collectors.

Taunusstrasse looked even worse, if that would have been possible. Here some underworld figures had established themselves in some of the rudimentary improvised bars and dives, mostly frequented by colored US soldiers, and heavily populated with 'working girls'. A special feature of this street was the number of the so-called 'dollar taxis', which parked in this street and which charged their fares exclusively in US dollars.

Kaiserstrasse had also been renamed in remembrance of the first post-WW1 German president as Friedrich-Ebert-Strasse, to follow the new democratic dispensation. The usually dysfunctional public spirit of the locals since the beginning of the Nazi time had forced in this case the reversal of this unpopular decision. In this street stood, amongst all the other ruins, an also partially destroyed apartment building. The upper floors and the roof were burnt-out, but on the first floor could be found the improvised shop of a stamp dealer.

The owner was the former cycle champion Rudi Reilländer. Collector's stamps were just about the only commodity into which one could invest one's useless money, in the hope of somehow salvaging some value in the future. Rare stamps were valued at exorbitant prices then, due to reduced supply (caused by the many destroyed collections and dealer stocks) and strong demand as a result of the weak currency. They were out of my reach, with my executive salary being paid in this almost worthless money. 'Monopoly Money', we would later call it.

By this time, I regularly advertised in the local papers that I wanted to buy stamp collections. I was lucky and made some good purchases. This was then a hit-and-miss affair, because there were no current stamp catalogues available to look up the stamps and their prices. On one such occasion I bought a small stock book with, among others, sixteen so-called submarine stamps. They looked rather primitive, and the collectors, who had never seen or heard about them, suspected that they were bogus products. This dealer offered me, on spec, a carton of 200 American cigarettes for each of them. Obviously, he knew more than I did!

Only after the June 1948 currency reform, when stamp catalogues were published again, it turned out they had been issued in early 1945, not by the German Postmaster, but by the German Navy, to control the numbers of field post letters to be transported by submarines out of the Hela peninsula, which had been encircled and cut-off by the Russians. The new catalogues showed that their value was now a multiple of the 1947 prices of a carton of US cigarettes. A matter of luck!

Late in 1947 I could finally visit my mother in Dresden for the first time since we had to bury my father. But first I had to apply for a travel authorization, which was mandatory if one wanted to visit another Zone of Occupation, provided one could furnish a convincing reason for such a dangerous and suspicious undertaking. These passes were issued, or the issue was supervised by the Allies, who controlled the borders of the Zones.

The situation in Dresden was even more depressing than in Frankfurt. Everything gray in gray, including the people. My mother told me the Russians, through the local communists of the *Volkspolizei*, had been looking for my father, and had enquired about my whereabouts as well. I was not unduly worried about that because they had nothing on me, because I had neither been a member of the Party, nor had I fled from their Zone, which action was later officially declared a 'crime against the state'. I had simply not returned to the 'worker's paradise'.

After my arrival I realized that this was the time when I should have asked my mother certain disquieting questions, but I did not do so. Was I afraid I would discover unpalatable facts? When my grandparents had lost their home in Dresden, I would have expected that my mother would have offered them my room. Instead, they had to lodge with my uncle and his wife in the neighboring apartments. Why?

My paternal grandfather took his life, after having lost his only son, his business, his apartment block, his wealth and maybe later his wife. I was told that my mother's father had died due to medical complications, which could not be attended to properly during the post-war shambles. How and when did my two grandmothers pass away?

Once I went to a dance in a Dresden suburb, which had been only partially incinerated during the February 1945 'fire storm'. The ratio of female to male young people must have been at least 10 to 1. It became clear to me only later what the reasons for this imbalance had been. The Russians had held back almost all their prisoners of war until well into the 1950s, and many of the released prisoners of war of the western Allies, like me, had refused to go back to their home towns in the Russian Zone.

When I visited my great-cousin Miss Severin, I tried to

persuade her to come back with me to Frankfurt. An absolutely crazy and ridiculous idea. In the first place, she would never have received permission to leave the Russian Zone and I had neither enough money, nor adequate accommodation to offer her. She fortunately turned down my stupid idea. But instead she gave me a sweet kiss when I left. So, the trip to Dresden had been worthwhile after all!

I had already obtained the necessary rubber stamps of the police and the Russian *Kommandatura* stating my date of departure, twinning the same stamps of my arrival. Then something came up on my last day in Dresden, but I forgot what. And because of this I left a day later than was noted in my travel document. When I arrived at Gutenfuerst, on the border between the Russian and the American Zone, the East German *Volkspolizei* confiscated my travel pass, because of my one day's late arrival there, and arrested and detained me in a small room on the first floor of an office building next to the waiting train.

Remembering what my mother had told me about the Russian's interest in me, and also considering that my employment by the US Army might now be considered hostile by them, I decided on a tactical withdrawal, opened the window and jumped down into the yard. Figuring, it would be the first place they would look for me, I stayed away from the train and re-entered the building, hiding in the ground floor toilet.

For twenty minutes a dozen police officers were searching every coach and every compartment of the train. When I figured that they were almost done, I left the building, which was on the offside of the train, and unseen from the platform I re-entered my carriage, which still held my luggage. Obviously, nobody had alerted the police about my absence. Almost immediately afterwards, the train pulled away on its way to Hof in the US Zone.

When we had almost arrived at the Hof railroad station, I started to worry about the possibility of the Americans detaining and sending me back to the Russian Zone. You never knew then about the cooperation of the Western Allies with the Russians. Sure, there were serious tensions between them, but then again, some deals were occasionally made, if that suited both sides. The interests of the German people were no issue!

To be on the safe side, I jumped off the slow-moving train and ran at least a hundred meters across the tracks towards the wall bordering the rail yard, climbed over it, and finally felt safe. Entering the station from the town's side, like any law-abiding citizen, I bought a ticket to Frankfurt, and the rest of the voyage was uneventful.

About two months later I was summoned to the by now well-known Frankfurt police headquarters. There I was confronted with my *Interzonenpass* impounded by the *Volkspolizei*, and I was questioned about the circumstances of my return trip. Luckily my, as always, truthful explanations were accepted, and the offending document landed unceremoniously in the detective's wastepaper basket.

My mother presumably had given me the address of my uncle Walter, the husband of my mother's sister, in Mühlheim/Main near Frankfurt. This was the man, who many years later was outed in my photo album to have been a member of the Party, the only one in the family. After my return from Dresden I visited him and realized that he was staying with a woman. It was typical for the times that neither of us bothered to talk about that this married man, with wife and daughter in Dresden, was living with another woman near Frankfurt. We were still more or less shell-shocked by the collapse of Germany and the ruptures in all our lives, caused by this catastrophe.

In the early 1950s my mother also committed suicide, probably for similar reasons to those of my grandfather. One of the neighbors had tried to have her evicted from her apartment, arguing that a 3-bedroom abode was excessive for a single person, considering the scarcity of accommodation. Did her realization that I would not, and possibly could not, ever return to Dresden trigger this desperate act? Another thing for which I simply did not have an answer.

When I learned of her passing, my first wife went to Dresden to wind up the meager estate, because I could not afford the risk of going again myself. The escalation of the Cold War and my employment by the US Army had substantially increased the risk for me. She was only able to bring back some oil paintings of my grandfather, which have been with me since then, and some of my schoolbooks. By the way, has anybody ever calculated the total number of German suicides caused by the war and its sub-sequent hardships?

After the war I preferred to listen to the 'Merely Music' program of the AFN, the US Army radio network in Europe. And nowadays, I very seldom listen to any music, even on long trips in our car. If I listen to music at all, it is either to something contemporary but melodious, or the Liszt and Chopin pieces of my teenage piano playing times. Only very occasionally do I listen to some other suitable classical composers.

The attitude of the Americans and the British towards the Germans had changed by then to a more realistic level. They were now prepared to gradually accept Germany back into the company of civilized nations. Surely, primarily motivated by the ever-increasing threat of the Russian intentions. The Anglo-Americans eventually had persuaded the French, after some horse trading (Wikipedia), to join their French Zone to the already previously combined Bizone, creating the Trizone, effectively the forerunner of the *Bundesrepublik*.

This development resulted in quickly deteriorating relations with the Soviets, particularly after plans became known that the Western Allies wanted to introduce a new and stable currency for their Zones of Occupation. The tensions rose even further when it became clear that they intended to convert their zones into the democratic country of West-Germany.

This was naturally seen by Russia as a confrontation with their own dream of a united, but communist Germany, to start with in the form of the *DDR*, the *Deutsche Demokratische Republik*. By now it is common knowledge how to interpret the 'democratic' sobriquet, as used by the communists.

In the background there was always lurking a further complicating factor: the undefined but strong subliminal wish of most Germans on both sides of the boarders for the re-unification of the country. This was partially driven by the fact that many families had been separated by the war and the borders of the Soviet Zone, and also by the millions, who had fled this Zone and wanted to return to their home districts, but without the Soviets! Finally, also by the slowly re-awakening feeling of the German national identity.

In June of 1948 the introduction of the new West-German currency was imminent, and when the Western Allies announced that this would also be introduced in their Sectors of Occupation in West Berlin, the Russian reaction was immediate and decisive: they blockaded all military and civilian access for the Western Allies to and from their sectors in Berlin. General Clay, the Supreme Commander, US Forces, Europe replied to the blockade, which was in violation of Allied agreements, by establishing the only possible supply line for the troops and the civilian population, the Berlin Airlift.

A satellite section of his General HQ Staff was established at Rhine-Main-Airbase outside Frankfurt, and some German civilians working for the US Armed Forces in Germany were also seconded to this office. Most were from Wiesbaden, the HQ, US Air Force, Europe, and a few, including myself, were seconded from the Griesheim depot.

The task was formidable. Up to 9 000 tons had to be moved to Berlin by up to 550 daily flight movements (Wikipedia) from the Rhine-Main and Wiesbaden US Airforce bases. Major General Tunner was the brains behind this logistical nightmare. He organized and continually improved operations, and he became my idol regarding systems, organization and management.

June 28, 1948 was the day of the *Währungsreform*, the currency reform, when the almost worthless *Reichsmark* were exchanged, normally 10:1, for the new *DM*, the *Deutsche Mark*. At first, only up to forty *DM*, in the next month another amount of up to twenty *DM* was paid out in brand new banknotes, printed in the USA. Bank balances were converted in a similar fashion. This was the start of the *Wirtschaftswunder*, an unbelievable explosion of economic activity in West-Germany. The German architect of this miracle was Professor Ludwig Erhard, in conjunction with Allied advisors.

Within three to four weeks the shops, which had been empty up to this time, were full of goodies the consumers had not seen, except maybe on the Black Market, since well before the war. Factories, shops and offices opened like mushrooms after a warm rain, and people found now for the first time since the end of the war meaningful employment. All of a sudden, my monthly salary of DM 517 was a princely remuneration, when one month before, all it would have bought me was five packs of Lucky Strike.

Another main plank of this development was the insistence by the Americans of dismantling the encrusted German professional and economic structures, and by the enforcement of competition in the economy. Obviously, the Marshal Plan played a decisive role as well. The economy started to blossom, liberated from the restrictions of the monopolies and the privileges of the professions and bureaucracies.

The country was confronted with formidable obstacles, but also with huge chances, after the many years of the 1930s re-militarization, the war years and the immediate post-war time:

- the influx of millions of Germans from Eastern Europe
- the gigantic demand for habitation and other buildings
- the backlog of infrastructure investments
- the damned-up hunger for goods and services by the economy and the consumers.

During the first years after the war, the Allies, above all the Russians, had undertaken the partial or complete demontage of many factories and had sent these back home. They had confiscated industrial equipment, patents and registered company names, and sometime even key personnel. The example of the German V1 and V2 rocket systems and the person of Dr. Wernher von Braun illustrates this convincingly. They took what they considered valuable for themselves. All was claimed as compensation for their losses and as punishment for the Nazi crimes. The US had even enforced the dissolution of industrial groups like *IG Farben*, which were in competition with their own conglomerates. Same procedure as after WW1!

One of the unintended consequences was that the German economy was now forced to replace the confiscated machines with new and therefore more advanced and more efficient equipment. This was one of the key points of the 'economic miracle'. Coupled with this was the disciplined attitude of the organized German labor force at the time. They had decided to forget for the moment about strikes, and instead concentrated to first re-build their workplaces.

Only now West-Germany started with the *Wiederaufbau*, the reconstruction of habitation, infrastructure, commerce and industry. Up to this time only the rubble had been cleared from the streets, and just the most pressing of repairs had been done. Now began in Frankfurt the clearing of the rubble and the ruins of the destroyed or damaged apartment blocks and other structures. The debris was transported to an outlying area in the eastern suburbs, were it was heaped to a height of about fifteen meters. Covering, I would guess, an area of about ten soccer fields. The locals were quick to call this *Monte Scherbelino. Scherbel* meaning 'rubble' in English.

The construction of desperately needed new apartment buildings began, generally as social- or low-cost-housing, but soon also on a commercial basis. New factories appeared, and the destroyed ones were renovated or rebuilt. Commercial buildings also started to rise. One of the first high rises was the West-German head office of the *Dresdner Bank.*

When I opened there my first-ever bank account, I also went to see one of the directors, introducing myself as the son of the head of the internal audit unit of the Dresden *Stammhaus*, who had died in February of 1945 on fire watch. I was hoping for some assistance, maybe even a job. But all I was able to achieve was meeting my father's former secretary, who appeared to be a bit uneasy about my visit.

In 1949 the Western Allies agreed (mainly due to the Soviet threats) to establish the *Bundesrepublik.* In June the first German Parliament had elected Konrad Adenauer of the *CDU*, the Christian Democratic Union, as first *Bundeskanzler*, and Ludwig Ehrhard became the Minister of Economic Affairs.

Early on, a number of important laws were promulgated, including the Constitution and those regulations, which the Americans had already earlier created in their Zone, dealing with competition in a free economy. Press freedom and other measures were legislated, to kickstart not only the economy, but also a viable democracy.

Another early law dealt with compensation for losses of real estate and property in Eastern Europe (but not in the Russian Zone!). This covered the expulsion of the German people, not only from the newly 'acquired' parts of Poland and Czechoslovakia, but also from their historical living areas. These included mainly East Prussia and Silesia. Also covered were the losses in Germany proper, caused by bombs and other war damages.

These compensations were to be financed by those property owners in West-Germany, who had not suffered such losses, and who had to accept that a debt charge was hypothecated against their properties. I do not remember what, if anything, was done about bank balances and shares and bonds. The task to administer the collection of these moneys and their distribution was given to the state-owned *KfW, the Kreditanstalt für Wiederaufbau*, which had been created for this specific purpose.

Bonn was chosen by Parliament, against fierce opposition, as the new West-German capital. To vote for Berlin was politically impossible at that time, but Frankfurt would have been much more suitable, especially regarding infrastructure and communication networks. The official responsible for the choice of Bonn, *Staatssekretär* Wohlfahrt, used all the tricks in the book, and then some, to please Adenauer, who happened to live close to the new capital. In any case, he could not subject his stoutly catholic boss to live in the most liberal and protestant city of the country. Probably just one of those coincidences.

The Berlin Airlift ended in May of 1949, when the Russians finally lifted their blockade. WW3 had been narrowly avoided. The US Armed Forces had been substantially reinforced in the follow-up to the Soviet threat. But the German fear of the overwhelmingly strong and nearby Red Army remained deep-seated until the collapse of the Soviet Empire in 1990. It was not difficult to see that my job at the depot, satisfying as it was, had no great future. The work done at the depot would sooner or later come to an end. Therefore, I resigned in the middle of 1949 and looked around for some improvement to my prospects. But none which were promising anything worthwhile for the near future were immediately discovered.

29

LOST YEARS ... AND STAMPS

1950 TO 1958

Soon the first moves were made by the Allies to bring Germany back into the fold. The war in Korea had shown how serious the global communist threat was, and German Armed Forces were considered essential to counter the dangers from the Soviets, but on the German side this was opposed vigorously for ideological reasons by the German opposition, the SPD, the Sozialdemokratische Partei Deutschlands and, not surprisingly, by the tiny *KPD*, the communist party. NATO had been formed, not only as a bulwark against the Russian threat, but also to provide a controlled environment for a future German participation in the defense of Europe and the Free World.

The early post-war period also saw a number of shady deals, smacking of corruption in high places. To start with, there was the selection of Bonn as capital for the new West-Germany. Shortly afterwards came the *Leihwagenaffäre*, when Mercedes-Benz made available luxury 'rental' cars free of charge to Adenauer and his ministers, under the bare-faced guise of unselfish support for the new democracy.

This was followed by several affairs of the most controversial Franz Josef Strauß, the leader of the *CSU*, the Bavarian sister party of Adenauer's *CDU*. He was accused by the press (there existed only state-owned TV then!) of having had 'sticky fingers' in the contracts to build housing complexes for the families of the Allied troops living in Germany. These expenses had to be borne by the German taxpayer, as our contribution to the occupation costs of the Allieds.

The news magazine *Der Spiegel* had exposed his involvement in the housing scandal, as well as the further irregularities pertaining to the German purchases of the 'Constellation' and the 'Star Fighter' planes. Strauß had tried to undermine the brand-new German press freedom, trying to prevent these dis-closures. His handling of the highly explosive *Spiegel Affäre*, including the arrest of Rudolf Augstein, the editor of the news magazine, was the beginning of the end of his ambitions in Bonn and eventually broke his political neck.

A parliamentary commission, under the chairmanship of the *CDU*, had white-washed his activities, but the next cabinet reshuffle saw him gone. It was typical for this period that none of this affected his political standing in Bavaria.

What had happened to the revered Prussian and German mentality, the sense of duty, and of correctness in all things, as well as all the other German virtues we had been brought up with? The war had not only caused tremendous human, material and political losses, but the immediate post-war years showed that public morals were also severely damaged.

After my return to Germany I had never participated in politics or elections. My distrust and abhorrence of all politicians, guilty or not, was so engrained by then that I just did not want to have anything to do with politics. And I was not alone. My age group was often called the *Ohne mich Generation*, the 'without-me generation'.

It has just occurred to me that in those days I thought to have finally overcome my deep-seated anger and despondency about my stolen and wasted youth. But with the benefit of hindsight I now realize that all I had done was to bury these emotions even deeper into my subconscious. The fact that I had not been able to shed any tears when I buried my father, or when I had learnt about the passing of my mother, seems to confirm this observation.

These emotional blockages started to change only ten years later, after I had met my second wife. When we had to put down our dog, my eyes had filled with tears for the first time since child-hood, and I was unable to speak for a moment. Since then, my emotions have surfaced to a certain extent, but I still feel short-changed in this important department.

For some months I was floundering around in this unaccus-tomed private economy. I even tried to sell *Bertelsmann* book club subscriptions and encyclopedias, but without success. But I had been selected to drive a *VW Bus* for the team of desperadoes, which I was allowed to take home.

Nothing much happened while we were standing on the pave-ment of the *Zeil*, the main shopping street in Frankfurt, looking for likely victims. This high street was then open to vehicles, and it was easy to find parking. Until a young man approached me one day. He asked me whether I could sell him a *Bertelsmann* encyclopedia. Just like that! A few days after this impressive but undeserved personal sales achievement, the 'well-earned' commission was collected. But without having any further success, I decided that selling of any sort was definitely not my glass of beer.

Then in early 1950 an opportunity presented itself, when some-body offered me a partnership in a small wholesale business for magazines and periodicals. I had a closer look, and the challenge of something new was appealing, particularly since this did not include any selling. Because I rejected the idea of a partnership, I offered instead an outright purchase. This was accepted, and I now had a small business to run. I regret to say that this never turned into a real success. All it did was to keep me reasonably alive and in beer-money.

Two large and well-established newspaper and magazine wholesalers existed already in Frankfurt, started back in 1945 or 1946. One of them was created to distribute the national news-paper *Neues Deutschland*, newly licensed by the Americans. Other local titles of the post-Nazi newspapers were the *CDU*-leaning *Frankfurter Neue Presse* and the mouthpiece of the *SPD*, the *Frankfurter Rundschau*. Later they were joined by the *Frankfurter Allgemeine Zeitung*, one of only two conservative national papers in West-Germany. By now the local newspaper wholesaling market was sewn up, which automatically included all other periodicals.

The following years saw the rise of '*Bild*', the 10 Pfennig national boulevard paper, with the overwhelmingly largest print run of all German newspapers. This was published by Axel Springer, the legendary founder and owner of '*Die Welt*', the other conservative national daily published in Hamburg and later in Berlin. The other outstanding publication of those days was the *Stern*, an investigative weekly illustrated magazine, published by Henri Nannen in Hamburg. A similar one was *Quick* in Munich. By far the most influential was, however, the sole news magazine *Der Spiegel*.

My tiny distribution firm came much too late to the party. The cake had long been cut and distributed. We suffered a further set-back in 1951. Because of the war in Korea, there was all of a sudden no coated printing paper available anymore. Naturally, this led to the immediate opening up of a Black Market for this essential commodity for most publications. Only the largest and most profitable magazine titles could afford to continue publication. I guess that these few very large titles probably received a helping hand from the government, or maybe even from the Americans?

Most of the titles I distributed simply had to stop publication for a while, my turnover plummeted and I was forced to cut-back on personnel. This forced me to re-assess my situation again, and I tried to expand into the book distribution business. I had been offered an interesting book manuscript and, in my desperation, I was tempted to try my luck. But this insufficiently considered step was also no panacea for my little business undertaking, because this endeavor also suffered from the shortage of printing paper.

I bought for the firm a 1938 *Opel Super 6* car, which had seen service with the German army during the war. This was a six-cylinder, a big (for German cars) and thirsty sedan in reasonable condition. Only the tires were worn to pieces, showing in many places the white canvas where the rubber profile should have been. Consequently, I became proficient in changing tires. Not in changing wheels like nowadays, because I only had one spare wheel and sometimes five or six flats during one single trip. But I had ample tire repair materials!

The steering was also a tiny bit suspect, requiring a full turn of the wheel to get any traction. The six ignition cables, consisting of carbon rods, had many breaks, which were 'repaired' by me with

Scotch tape. When the engine mis-fired it was entertaining to determine, which of the cables was broken, and exactly where. But I still managed to move my chariot at its top speed of 60km/h (40 miles/h), when the chassis started to wobble and screech. This obviated the need to have the speedometer repaired. My previous statement 'in reasonable condition' obviously has to be seen in connection with the prevailing situation at the time in post-war Germany.

This is hard to believe: one day my super-car was stolen in the middle of Frankfurt! I searched high and low for my precious transport, but I had to resign to the inevitable and walked to the nearest police shop. The officer had the ridiculous idea that maybe I had forgotten where I had parked. He loaded me into the cop car and started the waste-of-time exercise to look for it. All right, all right, can happen to anybody. I tried to imagine, who had moved the blasted thing!

After a substantial delay, in comparison to the general economy, the new currency had also established itself by now in the auto market. New tires became available and proper repairs could now be done. I battled financially to buy five new tires (bliss!), and I also had some repairs done. It took some time to lay the ground for proper price calculations for the German service industries, because for too many years prices had either been degreed by the state, or they had simply been thumb-sucks during the times of scarcity of everything, when one took what one could.

Now, new cars came slowly on to the market as well. Private people and small businesses had no cash reserves. To buy on credit was out, due to the general lack of securities. Without these the banks did not want to know. They applied the old and sound principle to lend money only if fully secured, or to those who did not need it. As I remember it, a new *Volkswagen Beetle* cost about *DM* 5 000, completely out of reach for most. But on one of my drives on the *Autobahn* I was overtaken by one of the newfangled *Porsche* cars, and I realized this car was doing at least three times my maximum speed. Obviously, some were better off already then.

The *Autobahnen* were in the same run-down state as all other infrastructure. Wherever a bridge had disappeared, a deviation had been improvised, leading the sparse traffic down an embankment, over a rickety emergency bridge, and up again on the other side. Apart from bomb craters and blown-up bridges, we had another problem. The edges of the individual concrete slabs had begun to move up or down against their neighbors, creating raised ridges between the slabs. These produced a monotonous strong noise while driving, similar to a train riding over the gaps on old-fashioned railway tracks.

For a while I battled along and used my ample free time to further my studies of accounting, economics and management by way of distance learning. I even subscribed to a course to become a qualified management consultant, only to find out later that this qualification was largely ignored by the status-conscious German business establishment, which looked down on anything below the level of *Herr Doktor*, or at least *Herr Diplomkaufmann* with proper university degrees.

One of the many loose ends in this story is connected to the mystery of my eventual disposal of my first car. I don't have the foggiest of what has happened to it. May it rest in peace, or should this be 'in pieces'?

On June 17 of 1953, the workers who were building apartment blocks in the *Stalin Allee* in East Berlin went on strike, protesting against the increased work norms ordered by the communist party's Central Committee. It is easy to see, how such action in a socialist/communist dictatorship would rattle the state. This spontaneous uprising spread to many other cities of the *DDR*, the so-called *Deutsche Demokratische Republik*, thereby affecting also many people living outside the original problem area.

My future father-in-law was, for instance, advised by friends that the Secret Police had started watching him. He decided there and then to prepare to leave his home town of Rosslau with his family and try to reach West-Germany, like hundreds of thousands had done by this time.

My wife's younger brother was already working at age fourteen, which was normal for the time, and wanted to stay in the communist state, but was persuaded to change his mind. He had, together with the majority of his age group, already been successfully brainwashed, just like my age group by the Nazis. In 1956 the family finally left on the first stage of their flight from the 'worker's paradise' for the Western sectors of Berlin. From where the fugitives could reach West-Germany. They bought rail tickets to the village of a phantom relative living on the far side of Berlin but left the train in the Soviet Sector of the city. They passed the police controls there, entered a Berlin subway train and debunked in the US Sector. This was then still possible but was blocked later.

From Berlin they were sent at their request to Frankfurt. My wife does not remember whether they travelled by train or plane. Her eldest sister was living there already, as well as her older brother. She herself had already been sent to a married sister living in Reutlingen, who had left East Germany with her husband even earlier. Only one sister remained with her family in the 'worker's paradise'.

At this time an effort was made by government to fight the perceived threat of pornography in West-Germany. A special law was promulgated, but the courts and public opinion over-reacted hilariously. A Catholic priest in a town near Frankfurt, for instance, had 'ordered' that people on the lawns of a municipal swimming pool had to maintain a minimum distance of 30cm, and touching was explicitly *verboten*.

In one of the magazines, which my tiny firm had distributed to the newsstands, appeared the photo of a fully clothed young woman. The High Court ordered the confiscation of all copies, fines of DM1 000 for me and other amounts for the news agents, for distribution of 'immoral publications'. The stated justify-cation: "the sensual expression on her face". To my simple mind, the lady looked more like being bored than sexually aroused, but what did I know?! No comparison of this prudery with today's porno web pages is possible. They are from different worlds!

The publication situation had settled down somewhat by now in West-Germany. My struggling business had been bought out by the *PVG*, the *Presse Vertriebs Gesellschaft*, the largest of the established Frankfurt wholesalers. The acquisition of firms was then a useful way of obtaining scarce personnel, but I do not know whether this applied in this case. The other usual reason, to get rid of competition, clearly made no sense at all.

Now I was again an executive employee in the private economy, this time in charge of the newly created Subscription Branch, a motley selection of small-scale activities outside of the core business of wholesaling. This position was answerable directly to the owner and chief executive of this large firm.

The main section was a team working in Bonn, which originally had been supplying newspapers, magazines and special reports to departments of the *Bizone* administration and to large firms in Frankfurt. The section had followed the move of the West-German administration after 1951, when the new government had been established in Bonn. They supplied the new government departments, embassies and consulates, banks and large companies with all their periodicals. A new section of the same type was formed to service the few official entities which had remained in Frankfurt and many of the bank head-offices and large firms domiciled here.

By now, this city had become the financial center of Germany. The head offices of the three largest banks were now established here, plus the *Bundesbank* and the *Kreditanstalt für Wiederaufbau*, the KfW Bank. This, in turn, attracted more and more head offices of commercial firms to the city. All of these were potential clients for our new Frankfurt publication distribution section. Over the next few years I visited all of these potential customers and was able to sign up most of them for our service. Luckily, no sales talk needed, just the presentation of the advantages to them.

One of the largest clients in Frankfurt was the US Army. When I visited Major Page of the Admin Unit of Northern Area Command at the *IG FARBEN HOCHHAUS* in the north of Frankfurt, it felt as if I was back in the Griesheim depot. The same large offices with dozens of office workers, the same huge IBM tabulators, and the same army jargon as before. Major Page was the first female US Army officer I had any dealings with. She was very good at her job, a tough and fair administrator. At first, I felt somewhat apprehensive in her presence, because in our army we did not have female officers. I decided to consider her simply as any other officer. "Yes, Ma'am!"

The section supplied this unit with all the newspapers and magazines from the East German state. A very profitable order for all address-books of the *DDR* indicates, what the true mission of this Admin Unit was! We even subscribed on their behalf to all technical and scientific publications we could get hold of for them, which were distributed by the *Mezhdunarodnaya Kniga* agency in Moscow.

A further section administered postal subscriptions for periodicals for various subscribers. Here we corresponded in English, French, and occasionally in Spanish and Italian. The English and Italian letters I attended to, and I was at least able to read the Spanish correspondence. The lady in charge of the section was fluent in French and Spanish.

For a few years we had also taken over from 'Stars & Stripes', the US Army, Europe newspaper, the civilian distribution of Pocket Books for Hessia, which gave me a chance to further my literary education via James Hadley Chase and company. A final unit dealt with the distribution of the NY Herald Tribune to newsagents and subscribers in West-Germany. This later one necessitated over the years two or three round trips to the more important stockists.

The newly formed *Bundesamt für Verfassungsschutz* was tasked with the protection of the democratic constitution against communists and the Far Right. Otto John, the first head of this immensely important office, was a former member of the July of 1944 anti-Hitler conspiracy (Wikipedia). He caused in 1954 another political scandal, the background of which, as far as I know, was never entirely cleared up.

Together with his friend Dr. Wohlfarth, another anti-Nazi but very shady star of the immediate post-war period, he suddenly turned up in communist East Berlin. For years, the West-German press had debated, whether he absconded as a traitor, or whether he was lured by his friend into a trap and was abducted. Eventually, I seem to remember, he returned to West-Germany, but this apparently did not throw any new light on this affair, which was so typical for these troubled times.

The social-democrat *Bundeskanzler* Willy Brandt had reached a political settlement with Poland and Czechoslovakia, based on the German acknowledgement of the permanence of the expulsion of the German population from vast tracts of land these two states had 'acquired' or re-occupied after the war. This settlement was violently opposed by the war refugees.

Later he suffered from the political fallout between communists and democrats, when his right-hand man was unmasked as a communist mole. Consequently, he was forced to resign, even though he was not at fault himself. Thus, a very gifted politician was lost to the nascent West-German democracy.

The *CDU* was not much better off. Uwe Barschel, their governor of Schleswig-Holstein, was accused of having led a dirty election campaign against his *SPD* opponent Björn Engholm. He denied everything and gave the nation his word of honor that he had done nothing wrong. Doubts emerged, however, and he was forced to resign. Nine days later his corpse was found in a hotel suite in Genève, Switzerland. As far as I remember, the details of his death were never resolved or publicized.

During this time the Russians finally started to release the last of their prisoners of war. They also allowed, for the first time, tens of thousands of German families, whose ancestors had settled in Russia during the eighteenth century, to return in dribs and drabs to Germany. These German immigrants from Russia spoke an antiquated form of the language, some of them barely able to speak any German at all. All of these people arrived and were processed in the transit camp of Marienborn, near Helmstedt, on the border between West and East Germany.

This brings me to the most important event of 1954 for Germany: the Soccer World Championship played in Switzerland, which Germany had won against Hungary. There were a number of firsts involved: 1st official Soccer World Championship, 1st won by Germany, and 1st shown on German TV. This was accomplished due to heroes like Fritz and Ottmar Walter, Helmut Rahn, Werner Liebrich, Toni Turek etc. Most Germans, standing for hours in front of the windows of the television shops, saw this as a symbol of the newly awakening Germany, after the horrors of the Nazi crimes and the lost war.

Connected to this event was the typical treatment of this epochal event by the most conservative newspapers in Germany, the *Frankfurter Allgemeine Zeitung*: they published a short article somewhere in the middle of the paper. And that in a soccer-mad country like Germany!

The *IG Hochhaus* accommodated not only NACom, Northern Area Command, and the earlier mentioned shadowy 'Admin Unit'

(Military Intelligence or CIA?), but also V Corps of the 7th US Army. One day in 1956 the S2, the staff officer in charge of intelligence and counterintelligence for this command, asked to see me. I had been in contact with him before, in connection with Major Page's unit.

It turned out, that he not only had my records from my time with the Griesheim Ordnance Depot and my stint at General Clay's Berlin Airlift staff, which was only to be expected, but also the CIC report from Rimini, mentioning among other things that I had been with *Division Brandenburg*. This latter point without any further details. I was naturally somewhat shocked and worried, but he just went with me to his boss, the G2 of V Corps.

There I was told that some not identified persons (in the meantime declassified as the CIA) in Camp King at Bad Homburg near Frankfurt were interested to temporarily hire men to go to Hungary as advisors to support the local uprising against the Soviets. The way he explained things the proposal was interesting, particularly the fact that this was not a fighting assignment, but simply a support and training mission.

And when the remuneration was explained, the situation developed from 'interesting' to 'persuasive', and he had a sale. From his office I phoned the owner of the *PVG* and asked to have my three weeks annual leave, plus another unpaid week. He was at first not too happy, but he agreed when I explained that I was helping our big US customer, on whose turnover, as he very well knew, we had a particularly healthy profit margin.

From the Brigadier General's office, a staff car brought a captain from the 10th Special Forces and me to Rhine Main Air Base, and off we went with the daily military courier flight to Munich. From there we drove to the sister set-up of Camp King for the VII Corps at Bad Tölz.

This was conveniently close to the HQ of the 'Organization Gehlen' of the former German General Reinhard Gehlen, who had during the war been in charge of "Foreign Armies, East" in the German Supreme HQ, and who was now the head of the German Secret Service at Pullach, just outside Munich. It is not clear in my memory, whether at this stage this organization was still private or already official.

There a small group of fellow adventurers joined us, and we received the necessary clothing, hygiene articles and such for a few weeks, also maps, a Hungarian dictionary and a bundle of banknotes. On the road east, the captain explained our function in some form, but it was all rather vague and fuzzy. I guessed that we had not flown direct to Vienna, which then was a European espionage hub of the first order, to avoid announcing our arrival and intentions. The city had taken the place which Lisbon occupied in WW2. The Soviets had withdrawn from Austria only the year before, and they had left many 'sleepers' and agents in place.

Another staff car brought us across the Hungarian border, which by then was like a sieve. It was without the Hungarian border guards, and the Austrians acted disinterested. A typical Cold War exercise in futility, as it had become clear by now that the Hungarians simply wanted to get away from the Soviet Empire, as had been achieved previously by Yugoslavia's Marshal Tito, but with no intention of shedding communism. By now, the anti-Soviet uprising had started to fizzle out, and on our way to Budapest we only got as far as Győr. Clearly, our services were not required anymore, and we returned to Frankfurt the way we had arrived. The Army (or the CIA?) paid up as promised, and quite generously, and no questions asked.

Together with all the other branches of the West-German economy, the world's oldest profession also flourished. When the well-known call girl Rosemarie Nitribitt cruised along Kaiserstrasse in Frankfurt in her black Mercedes 190SL with the red leather upholstery, many heads turned (enviously?). After she was murdered in 1957 (Wikipedia), she became not only famous, but a sex symbol all over the country.

Many famous people and rich businessmen were on the list of 'persons of interest'. Her murder was never solved, probably due to bungling (or complicity) by the Frankfurt detectives (Wikipedia). But brushing this embarrassing and potentially explosive story under the carpet has always been considered likely by the public and the media.

Shortly thereafter, another sex symbol was also murdered. He was the 'Queen' of the Frankfurt gay community. A name like Neubert comes to mind, but I could easily have this wrong. He owned a small newsagent, and his shop was one of my firm's customers. Because of this I even became 'a person of interest' myself in this investigation, fingerprints *et al.* I seem to remember that this crime was also never solved. There existed possibly a connection here between these two murders and a protestant pastor, who was raving and performing against sin in general, and prostitution and the homos in particular.

Nothing else of much importance happened to me during the following years. Now I had time to concentrate intensively on my stamps. After my early school years, I had soon intensified my collecting interests, and I was now on my way to advance from a stamp collector to a serious philatelist. More money was spent on specialist literature and equipment than on stamps, for instance to detect forgeries and repairs. When I did spend on stamps I went for collections, because that was where I could find rare postmarks, varieties, forgeries, postal stationery items, revenue stamps and other specialties, which generally did not cost me anything extra.

A highly interesting and then largely neglected field of philately were the German Private Posts of the 1887 to 1900 period. Almost none of the stamp collectors were interested in this field, and I was able to buy small quantities of their stamps and postal stationery for next to nothing. After joining a specialist group studying these Posts, my interest was concentrated towards their postal stationery items.

Because none existed, I started a selling and buying service for these envelopes, postcards etc. with imprinted postage stamps, which helped me to not only enlarge my collection substantially, but also to widen my knowledge of this highly specialized collecting field. After the most important stamp dealer in Frankfurt had offered me a large accumulation of these items for DM 400, I probably had one of the most representative collections of the stamps and postal stationery of the German Private Posts then in existence.

During the long winter months, I had a recurring fantasy in this period: to lie in the warm sun on the beach of a South Sea island. I knew of course that this would never happen. But little did I know, that forty years later I would lie in South Africa in the warm sand of a Natal South Coast beach of the Indian Ocean.

Not the identical image, but even better than my dream of the 1950s, because now I was not alone to enjoy this *fata morgana* come true!

By now I missed the opportunity to play occasionally an interesting game of chess. Until I discovered a chess café in Moselstrasse in Frankfurt. Whenever I had some spare time, I went there and played, or watched the experienced players. One of the regulars there was a young man from, I think, Bamberg, who later either became German Master, or at least one of the leading German players. It was a pleasure to watch his brilliant and daring combinations.

To watch the dark side of this game was rather disturbing. Two dangerous- and rough-looking regulars played ten-minute *Blitzschach* or Lightning Chess with chess-clocks, at DM 100 a game, then a substantial sum. With double this stake if *Contra* was given, and again doubling this with *Re* being announced. The DM 100 banknotes stacked up, first on one side, then on the other one. I wondered who could afford to lose such sums. The card players in this café also wagered rather large amounts.

Talking about gambling: My friend Gerd, the son of one of my former customers, acquainted me with the game of roulette. True to my mental makeup and inclinations, I tried for a while to figure out a way to make some money by beating the bank. Better brains have tried this, and they failed. It did not take me long, however, to prove to myself that mathematically the casino will always win in the long run.

But I found an admittedly theoretical way how the odds could be beaten. In practice this would have required a large starting capital, which I did not have, and an even larger number of man hours. As is well known, individual roulette results are subject to the 'Monte Carlo' law and cannot be accurately forecast because they happen at random, as I knew very well. If, for instance, Red had appeared twelve times in a row, the chances that the wheel would produce a thirteenth Red were exactly 50:50, ignoring for the moment the Zero.

In those days the results of the roulette wheel of table number one were published monthly by the Bad Homburg casino, just outside of Frankfurt. Using this and drawing a curve of the appearance of the *simple* chances of *Rouge/Noir, Impair/Pair* und *Manque/Passe* over a full month or two produced a curve which rose above and dipped below a median x-axis.

If this curve had risen to a certain high level above or below the median axis, the odds were in favor of winning at least a net twenty or so games from this point onwards, as the curves tended to move again closer to the median line. Betting DM 2 000 a throw should have netted the gambler a tidy sum for the evening, but no guarantees given!

But constellations like this, of extreme deviations from the median, are rarely found, even if one checked the results for all the even chances on all the tables. And there was also the minor problem that the casino management would be likely to politely throw you out, as soon as they cottoned on to what you were doing. A later chat to a 'pit boss' confirmed that they were quite aware of the possible danger to their 'meager' profits by punters utilizing this system. Thus, this attempt at high finance also came to nothing.

My friend, who had been aware of the fact that my marriage had for many years been irreparably on the rocks, confided one day that he had had an affair with my wife. Now I decided to seek a divorce, to escape from an unhappy marriage for both of us. This promised to be a costly undertaking, after my lawyer explained that he would have to engage private detectives to obtain independent proof, since my friend's admission would be attacked by the other side as a 'sweetheart deal'.

Luckily for me, the detectives found proof of a further lover-boy and the painless divorce went through quickly, but I did not consider myself completely innocent about the situation. I was released from our unhappy marriage, without having to pay alimony. If my memory serves me right, the court even ordered that my ex-wife would have to pay alimony to me, if I should in future be unable to support myself.

By now I figured that the time had come to get out of what I felt to be my rather wasted life. I moved out of the apartment we had finally been allocated in Frankfurt-Nied a few years earlier by the *Wohnungsamt*, the Accommodation Office. Using my friend's *Mercedes 170D*, I moved my moderate belongings to the single furnished room I had been able to rent in Kronberger Strasse in town, near my place of work.

I had to pay a *Baukostenzuschuss*, contribution to the building costs, of DM 2 500 for renting this room. This was a proper racket at that time, because after the bombings and the huge influx of refugees, any living quarters were in desperately short supply. The owners could quite legally demand a ransom for a single room or an apartment which had been built long before the war. Remember what I have said in a previous chapter about the solidarity among the German people at the beginning of the Nazi era and during the war? But by now the charitable attitudes were largely *passé* in Germany.

To finance this expensive undertaking, my friend, who was now driving a taxi, had helped me to obtain a taxi drivers license, which was a pre-requisite to be allowed to drive a taxi in Frankfurt. In order to get this document, I had to study for many hours, to prove to a police official that I knew my way around the streets of the city and the suburbs.

The laws and regulations governing the industry were for me no serious problem. Among the many things a taxi driver had to know about were the rules governing the handling of a drunk person, or a hunter with a rifle over his shoulder, wanting to enter the taxi. Or what legally could be done, if a fare did not or could not pay up, or if he had thrown up in the taxi. And there were a few more potential problems to deal with.

After I had managed all of this, my friend gave me a contact number for a taxi owner to enable me to earn some extra money, besides my daytime job. Every second night from six to six I have driven a taxi. Amazing what the human body can endure if the inducement is strong enough, such as financing a divorce, for instance.

I made a lot of money by not doing the obvious, namely standing in a taxi parking queue and waiting for a fare to show up, like the professional drivers did. Instead I specialized in cruising the places the off-duty GIs were frequenting. These were predominantly GI bars and nightspots, but also places, where they went to just socializing. My English was obviously helpful in this connection. It was then still not as common as nowadays for Germans to speak any foreign language. Because I also accepted US dollars, the fares were more generous with their tips in this currency than normally.

I remember one incident, regarding the size of a tip, which was rather below the belt. I had brought somebody to the airport, and normally we had to return empty to Frankfurt, because we were not allowed to take on passengers at the airport, since they had their own taxi association there. But on this occasion an American couple had entered the taxi and I took a chance to have a paid return trip. Back in Frankfurt the meter showed something like DM 40, and the fare gave me 45 dollars instead of 45 DM. When I pointed out that he only owed me something like ten dollars, he muttered about "these bloody stupid Krauts". Well, we all know: "the customer is always right"!

But the main source of my above-average income was the arrangement with the owner of the taxi which I drove most of the time. The normal procedure in the industry was that the driver handed over the fares he had collected, and he received a weekly wage in return. This was naturally open to crooking, if fares were not recorded and were pocketed by the driver. Since I already was employed, we needed a better arrangement.

My suggestion was that I would pay the owner a flat fee of DM 0,50 for every kilometer the taxi had been driven that night, without any documentation. That meant, any cheating was eliminated and often I did not have to activate the meter but could negotiate instead the fares with my clients. A very profitable arrangement for all concerned.

Not surprisingly, there were a number of interesting events happening while driving a taxi at night in a big city. One obvious expectation was that one would encounter a large number of 'night owls', and many of them would become regular clients: waiters, escorts, working girls, strippers, bouncers, gays and party goers, as well as people, who simply wanted to spend part of the night in company. One acquired certain regulars, whom one would pick up at a given time, at home, their place of work or their regular watering-hole, if the taxi was free at the time. Such arrangements provided a solid base for the turnover. These regulars, if they were solo, almost always occupied the front passenger seat.

Out of the hundreds of homosexuals I encountered over the years on the job, not a single one ever tried to proposition me. They somehow knew that I would not have been interested and left me alone, and so did I, thus guaranteeing a sound working relationship. I can safely say that I never harbored any judgmental feelings about their sexual orientation. Furthermore, almost all were interesting men. Somewhere I read that the average IQ of gays was above that of the 'normal' population.

A somewhat closer relation was established with a stripper of the New York City bar, one of my female regulars. After I had picked her up late at night, meaning very early in the morning, she had only a short way home. Being in a hurry to get into her bed, I guess, she started on the way undressing in the back of the taxi. By the time we had arrived in front of her apartment building, she was buck-naked like a new borne baby, and she calmly walked the few steps to the entrance of the apartment block.

For reasons I do not remember, I omitted to file a complaint about her illegal behavior, regarding my impaired dignity and my violated human rights, not to mention my constitutional rights. But I forgot for a moment that we were not in the 21st century yet. In those long past days, we suffered such atrocities silently. Another regular fare, female as well, asked me one morning out of the blue for sex. I forgot what my answer has been. Yes, the tough life of a taxi driver in the glorious 60*s in Europe!

One of the things I learned as a taxi driver, which was confirmed by my colleagues, was the fact that driving during the night could induce a sort of coma. One knew one had to go from A to B, and this B was sort of programmed into one's subconscious. Often, I did not know afterwards how I had arrived at my destination, but arrive I did, and without any problem. My guess would be that being permanently over-tired had a lot to do with this useful phenomenon. Driving on autopilot may have happened even more often than I was aware of.

The most impressive example of this tiredness-induced condition happened in *Eschenheimer Landstrasse*, which then had tram lines running up north, which now have been replaced by the underground subways. These tram lines necessitated overhead electric cables. One very early morning, an excavator machine was trundling along this street, with the beam carrying the huge bucket proudly raised above. The operator was likely also half asleep, same as me.

Suddenly, there was a tremendous bang, and the bucket was lying in the street, the empty beam still high up in the air. When the bucket had come into contact with the cable, the electric current had created a light-arc and had cut through the mounting of the bucket like a hot knife through butter. I was rudely awakened from my dozing, and it took me a moment to realize what had happened. My fare, on his way to the airport, started performing because he was afraid that he would miss his plane, due to the street temporarily being blocked, and us being witnesses of this mishap. He was proven right, poor chap. And what had happened to the machinist?

I used my spare time and the weekends to dabble in some stamp dealing. After I had bought a rather valuable collection of the stamps of the German Colonies, my advertising in the *DBZ*, the *Deutsche Briefmarken Zeitung*, solicited among others an order from Wicks Stamp Agency of Pietermaritzburg in South Africa. This was the only order ever received from Africa. It is almost ridiculous that we eventually landed up living for more than twenty-five years less than sixty kilometers from that town, and that I would later often personally visit their auctions.

After selling some of the better items out of this collection, I was able to sell the still substantial remainder to the owner of a newly opened Frankfurt stamp auction house for some more than I had paid for the stamps. He soon afterwards went broke, because he was often over-paying. In those days, the values of stamps soared continuously, since investors and speculators got involved. Most of them must have burnt their fingers.

This part-time activity brought me again in contact with the leading Frankfurt stamp dealer. When out of the blue he offered me a job, I did not hesitate long. Stamps had been in my blood, so to speak, from early on and I was keen to learn more about the commercial side of things. And I did learn a lot from this knowledgeable dealer, which later served me well in my retirement undertaking of running my own stamp auctions.

Murphy's Law: anything which can go wrong, will go wrong! One day I suffered rather severe pain in my belly and during my lunch break I saw a near-by doctor. It took him just a check of my eyes, and he phoned for an ambulance to take me to hospital for an emergency appendicitis. As I learned later, the others in our hospital room had written me off already, because I did not show any sign of life after I came back from theater.

But as a certain Mark Twain has put it so succinctly before, the notion of my passing away was slightly exaggerated, even if not wholly unfounded. My ruptured appendix had infected my bowels, and my doctor was forced to take the emergency measure to tear the operation wound open with his fingers. I was told by a visiting specialist that this had probably saved my life.

After I had left the hospital, I found a letter from my stamp dealer that he had to terminate my employment, because I had simply left without giving notice, nor advising him of the reasons. In fact, I had asked the admitting doctor to notify my employer, but obviously this had not been done. I could have fought this matter but decided that by now I had learned all I was going to pick up about stamp dealing. After explaining what had happened, he agreed. We parted amicably and kept in touch.

My friend knew the manager of the *Medallion Mode* mail-order firm, who was looking for an administration manager. I accepted his offer and was, among other activities, in charge of an office, where a lady was supervising about twenty typists completing shipping documents. It was immediately obvious to me that they were more talking, polishing their nails and browsing in fashion magazines than working.

The reason for that was that the lady in charge was working herself to death, and therefore had no chance to do her job as a supervisor. My simple solution: the introduction of a system of a controlled workflow of the documents from desk to desk. Then I fired the lady in charge and almost half of the typists, and there were no more problems.

This firm was unusual for me, because I had never before worked in an office where smoking was forbidden by the boss. At this time, I blew daily three packs of twenty in the air. Here I encountered the ADREMA system of metal plates, also for the first time, used for addressing envelopes or for the sorting of data. In principle the same idea as the **IBM** punch cards, which I had met earlier in the Griesheim depot. Both these systems appear nowadays terribly outdated, but this was all we had then for work our computers now easily accomplish.

30

US ARMY AND A NEW BEGINNING

1959 TO 1965

Sometime in 1959 I had decided that it was now high time to finally settle down for good. My best bet for an executive position would still be, I guessed, to make use of my English, and my inclination towards management. Systems, methods and organization had become my main work-related interests. The US Army appeared to be the obvious choice, because of the American more relaxed attitude regarding my lack of a formal tertiary education. I knew from experience that the ability to get the job done counted with them for more than reams of formal qualifications.

A visit to the US Army personnel office in the *IG FARBEN HOCHHAUS* proved to provide the quick solution to my problem. They had my 301 file with my previous employment record right there. When I stated my work preferences, combined with the characteristics of my previous work with the Army, this secured me a job offer I could not refuse. My previous pay grade in the Griesheim depot was elevated by two notches which, together with the effects of the moderate German inflation in the meantime, had doubled my previous salary.

An additional bonus of my new job was the involved substantial traveling. I knew that allowances for extensive travel could easily double one's take-home pay. Even more important was for me that this extended traveling would create more distance from my ex-wife, who had repeatedly pestered me for a reconciliation. This had turned into a harassment I could do without.

Originally, my place of employment was the Management Services Section of Northern Area Command, NACom. This rather large section consisted of a number of specialized units, dealing with internal audits, general management and manpower control. Our head office was at USAREUR, US Amy, Europe in Heidelberg where, as we discovered later, no fewer than eighteen US Generals were stationed, including our boss. Our mission was to survey all army posts in the area of the northern and western parts of Germany controlled by V Corps of the 7th Army. This included BPOE, the Bremerhaven Port of Embarkation, and a few outlying special army installations.

After a few months the section was divided into the three more manageable constituent parts which became independent units. I chose to stay with the Manpower Control Unit, which had the mission to control the civilian and non-combat military personnel of all service elements within NACom and V Corps. Considerations of management and organization tasks and the traveling involved, played a big part in this decision.

A Lieutenant Colonel was placed in charge of our unit. He was no expert in our line of work, and he was assisted by two Department of the Army (DA) civilians, one very competent, the other one incompetent in this function. The Colonel was to protect us from commanders, who tried to pull rank on us civilians. The Local Nationals (LN) held equivalent ranks of army captains. Amongst the LN were not only Germans, but a few other nationalities as well. In our unit we had a British Captain (Royal Navy), (Ret), a former Israeli Air Force Captain and one or two other nationalities.

Our main job was to evaluate the manpower requirements for each section of each of these military organizations, and to recommend the appropriate minimum staffing needed for them to perform their designated functions. These recommendations covered not only a head count, but included specifics such as details about military or civilian spaces, but also ranks or pay grades and job qualifications, etc. Excluded from our mission were combat units, but Officer Clubs, hospitals and supply functions like depots were covered by us.

An important tool of our trade was a Monroe calculator. This was a mechanical forerunner of the later electric and electronic calculators. Most functions were conventional, but the division function was complicated, requiring the handle repeatedly to be turned forward and backward. Early on the results were sometimes ridiculous, but in time we figured out the correct way to use this machine.

Our most important tool, however, was the US Army Staffing Guide, with hundreds of pages indicating the numbers and types of personnel required to perform specific workloads in the USA, such as at the numerous US Army Forts. The workload statistics established by the units to be surveyed provided the basis for our assessments, under consideration of the local conditions and any other pertinent facts.

One of the trickiest aspects of our work was the fact that we as outsiders had to recommend how many personnel spaces, of what type (military, US or local civilian), at which rank or pay grade and with what type of qualification would be required to deal with a specific work load, based on the local conditions at the respective Army Post or unit. Given the general attitude of military commanders towards civilians, and to make it worse, to German civilians, it is not surprising that tempers sometimes flared, when it was perceived that we were telling them how to do their job. For good reasons we had our Lt. Col. in charge of the unit, who out-ranked most of the troublesome local officers.

If shove came to push, we also had, as mentioned already, our General at USAREUR to support us, who was in charge of all units such as ours in Europe. But his intervention became necessary only once in all the time I worked there. This happened when we were dealing with the highly strung Major General commanding 3 Infantry Division in Würzburg. Further-more, our reports went via USAREUR to Washington, to what is now politically correct called the Department of Defense, the DoD, instead of the War Department, the WD, as it was originally named. We had all the backup we needed.

My first assignment was a survey of the Kaiserslautern Post, the largest in our area of operation. It was probably the largest, because this had until quite recently been the HQ of the now defunct Western Area Command, WACom. We worked there for two or three months, in order to cut back the 'fat', which commonly accumulates around any HQ, just as at any head-office complex in the economy. Much detail is given here as an example of our work at other Army Posts.

The first problem we encountered was the determination of the Post Commander that the personnel of the Post Engineer should perform preventative maintenance on buildings and grounds. While a case could be made for this approach, as opposed to fixing things only once they have broken down, current DoD policy did not allow staffing on such basis.

Buildings & Grounds Branch was one of the sections of the survey which was assigned to me. According to Army Regulations, I had to recommend the deletion of about thirty LN civilian spaces which had been established for this unit. This was bad enough, but worse still had to come. Another one of the Post Commander's pet ideas was to give the extensive lawns of 'his' Post a pedicure like that of a luxury golf course in Hollywood. He insisted that throughout the summer months the grass had to be cut weekly, because of the claimed special local growing conditions.

When I contacted the local municipality and questioned this claimed special situation, they advised that all public lawns and road verges were cut during summer once a month. Based on that information, I recommended, not to be too much of a pain in the you-know-where, staffing for fortnightly cutting, resulting in a further cut of another ten spaces. Strictly speaking this was an infraction on my part, but our Colonel had suggested this (politically correct) leniency.

Not surprisingly, I never received a Letter of Commendation from the Post Commander, who unsuccessfully had rebutted my findings with USAREUR. However, I did receive one such letter from our General in Heidelberg, which looked pretty good in my 301 file, the army personnel record.

One of the sidelines of this particular survey were Officer Clubs and other non-combat activities in this densely by US Army units populated area, with inter-continental rocket units, a strategic Air Force base and the 101 Airborne Division, among many others.

During our lunch breaks we frequented a Milk Bar in town. A special reminiscence centers on a gentleman in his forties, who looked like a cross between a Gypsy and a Mexican high-way robber. The amazing thing was that he always had a number of young girls, clearly the proverbial 'groupies', hanging on his every word. No further comment about my pinched greenish face!

In our next deployment (still the Army jargon!), the Army Post of Bad Kreuznach, we were not able as usual to move into rooms at the BOQ, the Bachelor Officers Quarters, for $1 a night. Large scale maneuvers were taking place at Baumholder, a huge training ground for the US Army. My colleague and I attempted to rent a cheap room in town for the duration and discovered, just before moving in, evidence of a healthy population of bedbugs. Panic stations!

Our work had us on the road most of the time. All the team members except me used their private cars, and I was paired for transport with one of my colleagues. He asked me one evening, when we went out to have a drink or three, to drive 'our' *VW* Beatle. I was not much into drinking, but he wanted to go to town that night. I had never before driven this make, which did not have a petrol gauge, but had instead a lever to switch to the reserve tank. With modern cars none of these things exist anymore, of course. Typically, he had neglected to fill up the car, and nor did he tell me that the lever was already set for the car to run on reserve.

Halfway to the pub, the car stalled. This happened just on the far side of the high point on the steeply rising road out of the valley where we were quartered, to the pub in the next town. Using the reverse gear, the starter and the battery, I managed to reverse back to the high point. From there, free wheeling got us back to our point of departure. If nothing else, this mishap saved us a bit of *lucre*, and taught me something about how not to manage things.

Another one of my early assignments illustrates the wide scope of our work. We had just done our surveys of the US Army Procurement Centers in Frankfurt and in Paris, France. At that time some US military units were still stationed in this country, even after General De Gaulle had pulled France out of NATO. I was sent back to Paris, to tidy up some details of the previous survey which needed further investigation.

My report noted that the Paris center largely duplicated the work done in Frankfurt, except for a section dealing with the procurement of French rocket systems and their launchers, plus some aeronautic parts. My recommendation was, to dissolve the Paris unit, with the rocket section becoming a satellite of the Frankfurt office. If accepted, this would result in very substantial savings, because the Paris center employed not only military personnel to the equivalent of a regimental HQ staff, but also many highly paid civilian specialists.

Our top brass and Washington concurred, and I collected, in addition to another Letter of Commendation, an 'efficiency suggestion' cash bonus of DM10 000. This was invested immediately in a secondhand but almost new Karmann Ghia cabriolet for DM7 000. The balance became the first installment in my investment in German government bonds with a 6% interest coupon, which started over the coming years a very healthy breeding program, based on the age-old profitable compound interest principle. When we stayed in between assignments in our Frankfurt offices, I still occasionally made some extra money as a taxi driver, to supplement my income and to build up my financial reserves.

Splashing out, like I did with buying this almost-sports car was not exactly my normal behavior, but I was now a free man, with a well-paid job. And for the first time I could afford a car. The fact that I was now free of my marriage had certainly some bearing on the matter, because I figured (subconsciously?) that driving this type of car could only be supportive to my intention of looking for some companionable permanent female company, which I had missed for many years.

A further chore to attend to was to convert my military driver's license to a civilian one. Without having a car, I had not bothered to have this done. This task, surprisingly, was accomplished in two minutes flat, and did not even require the consent, signature and rubber stamp of the State President. I was even allowed to keep my cherished military driver's license, which I used occasionally during checks by the traffic police. This raised a few eyebrows but avoided possible problems. Once in Wiesbaden, visiting the US Air Force

HQ, Europe, I was accosted by a German traffic policeman for parking in a restricted area. When he saw my military driver's license, he just laughed and let me go.

My favorite assignment, apart from Paris, was undoubtedly the staffing survey I undertook of BPOE, the Bremerhaven Port of Embarkation. The fact that I, as a German civilian employee, was sent there all on my own without any US chaperone, was a rewarding experience in itself. After all, BPOE was of extremely sensitive strategic importance to the US Forces in Europe. In case of a Soviet offensive towards Western Europe, the US Army would not have been able to do much more than to slow down the Warsaw Pact steam roller, at least during the first few days.

As we all realized, the Russians could reach the Rhine within a few days, at least in some places, thus blocking the way from Southern Germany to Bremerhaven. The main problem the Army faced, were their more than 100 000 civilian dependents living in West-Germany at the time. to be evacuated, they all had to be moved to this North Sea harbor. The safer way, through France to the Atlantic harbors of Le Havre and Brest, had been blocked by de Gaulle's brinkmanship in leaving NATO.

After having received the necessary additional temporary security clearance for this assignment, off I went, enjoying the ride in my 'top-less' cabriolet, and the certain knowledge of a substantial boost to my bank account via mileage and travel allowances. As mentioned earlier, these perks were rather generous and tax free. What I did not explain before was the fact that all such payments, including our salaries, were paid for by the German taxpayer. This was another part of the agreements about the stationing of the Allied troops in West-Germany, hopefully as a deterrent against any Soviet aggression plans.

The survey was uneventful generally, apart from some very raised eyebrows by the brass there. I had to recommend a few minor cuts and adjustments, but the CO of BPOE did not even rebut my recommendations. Before I returned to Frankfurt, I used the opportunity to eat my first shark steak, offered as a local specialty. But I do not even remember what it tasted like, except that I was not exactly overwhelmed by the experience, which I never repeated.

Let me describe a final example of the types of surveys we conducted. This one was the result of the conversion in about 1963 of the US Army infantry divisions into so-called ROAD divisions, reducing their strength from almost twenty to about sixteen thousand men. Simultaneously, the US wanted to increase their troop numbers in the European Theater. The solution they found was to ship all the equipment and weaponry of two additional divisions to Germany and to store these stores behind the Rhine, together with some knocked-down river bridges ready for quick assembly. Thus, everything was prepared for the troops to be quickly airlifted into their readied-in-advance positions, for their immediate deployment.

The personnel to attend to the storage and maintenance of these weapons and pieces of equipment for these fallback reserves consisted of some Polish labor companies. A reminder for me of II Polish Corps in Italy, but I did not find out whether there was any connection. These men, who did not want to or could not return to their homeland, were employed by the US Army in a semi-military status.

To survey this function and the manpower requirements under these circumstances was obviously sensitive, militarily and also politically. To be able to do this work, I had been given an additional security clearance. And after successful completion, another Letter of Commendation landed in my 301 file, and probably still is there, if V Corps did not take their mountain of records with them to Iraq.

Here I must re-introduce my colleague, who had provided me with a lift in his VW Beatle, prior to me buying my own car. He was a few years younger than me and had worked for one or another US Army unit more or less since the end of the war. Starting as a kitchen helper, he worked his way up to his present type of position, which one had to admire.

He suffered, however, from the obsession that he had to have a different girl in his bed every night. Naturally, he did not achieve this exactly, but surprisingly often he did succeed. Because of his lifestyle, he was permanently short of cash, later aggravated by the fact that he had bought an expensive Mercedes 250 (to impress the young girls he was seeking), which was way above his means. Since

I was in a position to help him out occasionally with his financial difficulties, we formed quite a close team relationship.

To add insult to injury, he had just bought a motorboat and a trailer. Naturally, he wanted to experience his new acquisitions, and he invited me to join him. We went together on our annual summer holiday in his VW Beetle, with the boat on its trailer. We trundled slowly through the night and half a day through Bavaria and Austria, via the Grossglockner toll road, our first such experience. Then through the Hohen Tauern railway tunnel, on board a special car train, another first for us.

Completely bushed, we finally arrived in Opatija, Yugoslavia. Before 1918, then part of the Austrian-Hungarian monarchy, this town was called Abbazzia in the Italian language of the inhabitants of Istria. This seaside holiday resort near Rijeka, the previous Fiume, provided a splendid example of the European building style of the turn of the century. But now the communists ruled this country, and everything was sadly neglected. The contrasts between the splendid architecture and the decay was depressing to see.

My friend successfully set sail (he started the in-board motor) in his seduction toy and gloated in anticipation of the results his acquisition would produce in the acquisition (poor grammar intended) of young ladies, locals or tourists. Details of his amorous adventures are surely of no interest here.

On my own, I explored the shoreline and tiny islands nearby in a historical motor launch I had rented with its skipper. The Diesel engine carried a plaque, stating that this 'ship' was part of the Austrian-Hungarian Navy, which had been stationed in this harbor up to 1918. The reason for operating such a relic was the simple fact that we were in a communist country, with an encrusted and deprived state economy. On these excursions I discovered many submarine springs, feeding ice-cold water, as I found out when swimming, from the surrounding Karst Mountains into the warm Adriatic Sea.

On our way back to Frankfurt we used for crossing the Alps the Katschberg Pass, with a steep incline of the winding road of about twenty-five percent. Naturally, at this time we still had to suffer the indignities (and costs) of border passport controls and changing currencies back and forth. And there are still people in Europe, who pine for their national currencies and for borders everywhere!

Having just now watched an episode of NCIS, Navy Crime Investigation Service, I wondered whether our team members (and myself!) exhibited the same type of idiosyncrasies and foibles as displayed by the members of this TV series. Generally speaking, the answer would be a very definite "yes".

In addition to my over-sexed friend, we had a non-smoking colleague, who regularly raised his hand when on American high holidays our Colonel handed out cigars. Or another one, who had been on the training staff of Sepp Herberger, the manager of the German national soccer team, who on each and every Monday morning insisted on giving us his expert commentaries on all the top team's soccer games of the previous weekend. And still another one, who continuously regaled us with the gardening prowess of his girlfriend of twenty year's standing. Have I missed anyone? No, I do not want to talk about myself all the time. This would not be polite.

One day in 1962, shortly before the Pentecost long weekend, my friend persuaded me to accompany him on a blind date. The obvious reason for his care-taking was that his newest relationship would have another young lady in tow, which was bound to present a problem for his carnal intentions. Partially to help him out, partially because I was looking for company myself, I went with him on the 2nd Pentecost holiday. AND THUNDER STRUCK!!!

I knew immediately what had happened to me, and I never since looked back! The fact that my wife does her excellent proof-reading job on this story has nothing to do with these statements and is purely and only coincidental.

My blind date was then living with her cousin (my colleague's *amour*) in a small room under the roof of an apartment block in Frankfurt. Her parents worked for a German government developmental agency in Persia/Iran. She had stayed with them for some time in Tabriz, had some English lessons there and acquired some basic office experience when she worked for a time at the local Siemens establishment. She liked the style and experience of living abroad. Now my future wife worked as an accounting clerk for the film distribution company MetroGoldwynMeyer in Frankfurt.

German salaries were rather low in those days, especially for people who had just started out in life. She was often as short of cash as I had been until recently. After I had helped to find her a small room of her own in Neu-Isenburg, just outside Frankfurt, we were able to spend some time together in-between my regular travels on surveys. I remember I was able to buy her a small Italian refrigerator, which gave me great and unaccustomed pleasure, because I had been able to help her out a bit. Her two brothers lived there as well.

When I was stuck in the office in Frankfurt in-between assignments, we sometimes went on little excursions of our own. On Easter Sunday of 1963 we drove with my wife's brother and his wife to a lovely old town on the river Main (Wertheim?), which sported a historic ruined mediaeval castle, and similar buildings in the center, but in well-preserved condition. It was freezing cold, but we enjoyed ourselves.

While on assignment at Bamberg Army Post, I took her with me and we visited the nearby historical fortress of Coburg, and I enjoyed a very happy time with the young lady. In due course I met the members of her family living in the Frankfurt area: an older sister in addition to the two brothers.

In the summer of 1963, we went to Yugoslavia on our first holiday together. We left Neu-Isenburg on a Friday in the early evening. As we only had two weeks leave together, every hour counted! We drove in our little cabriolet right through the night, with a stop-over somewhere on the marketplace of a little town in Austria, where we slept for two or three hours in the car. After having traversed the Eastern Alps, we stopped at a large stream to wash. The water was milky-white, saturated with dissolved limestone. Late in the afternoon we had finally reached our destination in Croatia, Yugoslavia.

We had booked a place on a naturist camping site on a small island just outside of Poreç on the Istrian peninsula. Our car was parked near the docking site of the small ferry, and we transferred our tent and paraphernalia to the boat. Because there were only minutes left before the ferry was scheduled to leave, I locked the car, but left the soft top down, because of the time pressure.

No big deal, I figured, because for some reason I had to return to Poreč the next morning, when I would attend to the closing of the top. Anyway, it was well known that it practically never rained in summer in the Mediterranean area. I was right, as always: it did not rain, but instead we had a tropical cloudburst that night. The next morning the water was standing several centimeters high in the open Karmann Ghia. These communists were just not capable to get even the simplest thing right, like their own weather!

Minor catastrophes like that mustn't spoil one's fun. We enjoyed our brand-new house-tent, with two field beds and air mattresses, and even a small kitchen alcove. Hours were spent in the beautiful unaccustomed sunshine, with a bit of a sunburn thrown in for good measure. The water of the Adria was marvelous, but the waves had to be treated with care, if one did not want to be pushed against the rough limestone rocks.

But we also dabbled in culture, by driving to Pola, or Pula, as it was now called. The old towns of the Croatian coast were full of history and charm, but badly neglected. Driving in our cabriolet was huge fun. Somebody even stood up and rode top-less for a while, enjoying the warm breeze. In the course of exploring the interior of the mostly Italian-speaking peninsula of Istria, I realized with shock that my once good Italian was already largely gone and forgotten.

On our way back, we visited the unforgettable caves of Postojna in the Karst Mountains of Slovenia. An extended rail trip in this cave system created a lasting impression. We also had a look at the highly unusual blind 'Grottenmolche', which have made these caves world-famous. On the way back, we stayed a short while in and about Venice. It was a funny feeling for me, the Canal Grande, the Lido, Mestre, the British Officers Club, which now was a tourist restaurant, and the other places which I had left only quite recently.

Finally, the crowning event came, and on August 30 of 1963 we were married in a civil ceremony. A church wedding would in our case have been the height of pretension! The date was significant, because if in Germany a couple married before the end of August, both their salaries were taxed for the whole year at the lower 'married' scale. If one earned a good salary, this represented a nice wedding gift. One had to look out for any legal possibility to reduce income tax, which was heavy in the higher tax brackets. But it would be a defamation to say that this was the only reason for our marriage, or that I had waited to the last possible moment.

Later in 1963 we were finally able to lease the ground floor of a typical German 2-family double story cottage in Spessartstrasse in Dietzenbach-Steinberg. Again, I had to pay the extortionist *Baukostenzuschuss*, because accommodation was still very scarce in the Frankfurt area. Our new abode allowed us for the first time a civilized life together.

During my wife's pregnancy I decided to stop a habit of about fifteen years' standing: smoking sixty cigarettes every day. The original inducement for this drastic change in my lifestyle were health considerations for our unborn child, my wife and myself. Many years earlier I had been able to stop my then desultory smoking overnight, no problem. This time things were different. For weeks I battled to kick the habit, but without sustainable success.

Reducing the daily consumption seemed to work for a few days, but there was no permanent result. Until I worked out what the continued horrible smoking habit was going to cost me over the next fifty years (I 'knew' I would reach my nineties). The moment I saw the amount in front of me, I threw away the current pack of twenty, and that was that. Years later I lit a cigarette for a lady friend of ours, and this had no effect on my abstinence (from tobacco).

June of 1964 saw our son born. When I first saw the somewhat crumpled-up baby in the Frankfurt hospital ward, I was immediately convinced that I held our rightful baby in my arms. The resemblance was obvious to me (even though I look crumbled-up only now). A very happy event for both of us. Our son, surprisingly, did not react to my question of how he was feeling. But I knew he was at least approving of our Karmann Ghia, because the first word he pronounced later was "Auto". Thus, he was showing an early appreciation for what is important in life.

Shortly after our son was born my wife's parents came from Iran to visit us. I do not remember much about this event, because most of this time I was on the road on my job. They offered to give us a TV set, but my wife pointed out to them that a washing machine (for the diapers) would be more urgent. They gave my wife both, the TV and the much needed, and much appreciated, *AEG* washing machine. It was a god-sent for the next almost thirty years: it could wash more than just diapers.

One of my wife's grandmothers also stayed with us for a few weeks. Because of her age she had been granted permission by the East German government to come and visit. Normally, nobody was allowed to leave the 'worker's prison', sorry, the 'worker's paradise'. The rumored real reason for such unusual *largesse*, unaccustomed by a communist country, was the hope that these oldies would stay and not come back and later cost the state money. These charitable chaps were real charmers, with the subtlety of a vicious butcher's dog!

To our surprise, our new apartment had neither any heating, nor running hot water. To solve the former problem, we had to buy an oil heater, with a huge double-walled storage tank in the basement. The annual filling of this tank, for the heating season of nine to ten months, ate up something like one and a half of my monthly substantial salary. It was frightening! The hot water was obtained the traditional way, by putting the kettle on the kitchen range or the electro plate. Primitive by today's standards, but still a huge improvement over the Neu-Isenburg situation.

One of the few luxuries in our rental apartment was our black-and-white television set. Availability of TV programs in Germany was still on the parsimonious side, despite it having already started in earnest in 1954, when the World Soccer Championship had been won by Germany. We received only two channels, both state-run. One of them showed a series *'Kommissar Maigret'*, based on the books by the famous Belgian author Georges Simenon. The lead was played by Bruno Cremer (Wikipedia). The younger brother of my wife came visiting once a week with his wife to view this detective series with us.

It was revealing about the state of the German economy at the time that he, who owned a small but sound business, could not yet afford to buy one of those black-and-white television sets. Living standards were still very low, in comparison to those in the States, for instance. Wages and salaries were painfully inadequate in comparison to today. Our money was valued at *DM* 4,20 to the dollar, which later corresponded to about Euro 2,10. Everybody knows the current ratio.

Later in 1964 we discussed what our future would look like if we stayed in Germany. My father-in-law had offered to finance the purchase of a small house for us. Nothing came of this generous offer, because at this stage we had already, I guess, half-way decided to try to emigrate. The political, and especially the military future appeared to be too ominous.

We were then at the height of the Vietnam War, and a spill-over into armed conflict with the Soviet Empire was seen by all of us as a very real possibility. The Russians had a few hundred or possibly a few thousand atomic bombs and rockets in readiness, and uncomfortably close by! The hysteria about such a development was all-pervasive in Germany in those days. An indication, how deep-seated these fears were, could be seen by how the present aggressive Russian posturing was strongly re-awakening these almost forgotten worries.

In addition to these important considerations there were other aspects to consider as well. My wife, after living for some years abroad, had acquired a taste for living outside of Germany, and did not fancy the prospect of staying here. As an accomplished rebel and anti-establishment man, I felt likewise.

Based on these considerations we applied for immigration permits for the USA. For quite some time nothing happened. After several months of waiting for a reply, I answered a job advertisement for management consultants, which a colleague of mine had discovered, who had already sent off his application. This job offer was to work for INEFEN, Industrial Efficiency Engineering, a Dutch company with offices in South Africa.

Both our applications were accepted, and we were advised to apply at the South African embassy in Cologne for immigration permits. Here the positive reply was quick and acceptable, particularly since it included the offer of a free passage to Johannesburg, including the charges for a small container with our goodies.

As far as I remember, the only condition for this generous paid-for passage was an undertaking to stay for a minimum period in the country. By now it is obvious that this generosity by the South African government came about because they were desperate to attract European immigrants to bolster their endangered Apartheid system by increasing the White population of the country.

Our status in South Africa would be that of "Permanent Residents". Meaning that we would not leave Germany for a temporary job abroad, but that we would be gone for good, or at the very least, for many years. In about June or July we had confirmed our acceptance of their conditions and had signed our applications for immigration papers and for the Permanent Residence permits. We then dispatched everything to Pretoria.

We were now mentally prepared to burn our German bridges, and to exchange our life in Europe for the unknown fate and conditions of Africa. And then we waited, and we waited, and we waited. We were now in the autumn of 1965, and we experienced and suffered the coldest October in Germany of our memories. Just before we turned into icicles, the letter of acceptance finally came, with our Permanent Residence permits, air tickets and documentation for our small container with all our worldly possessions.

Now I made one of the worst mistakes of my life. Instead of selling the Karmann-Ghia at a loss to a less than honest dealer, I should have taken a deep breath and should have splashed out to have the car shipped to Durban, the main harbor in South Africa. The costs would have been worth it, because being a cabriolet, the car would have been ideally suited for the climate. It broke my heart to let this beauty go, with all our special reminiscences attached to it.

Our television set and the oil heater were taken over by my wife's younger brother, who had visited us for the weekly TV shows. He was unlucky with his purchase, when some months later they made some mistake and the oil heater overflowed and drenched their apartment with stinking oil. Other things we were forced to leave behind must have included some furniture as well, but details are forgotten.

Another cleaning-up operation was also necessary, the unwinding of my wife's accrued pension entitlement with the State Pension Fund. Since she had worked only for a short time, and at a meagre salary, her pension at 60 would have resulted in a tiny monthly payout. This liquidation did not exactly make us rich, it was actually only a pittance, but at this financially critical stage anything helped.

When the time came for my colleague and me to leave the US Army we were invited by our Colonel to a fare-well lunch at the Officers Club, attended by a number of staff officers we had been in contact with during the last few years in Frankfurt. I must say that I had really felt at home with my work for the Army and, in a way, was truly sorry to leave my job, my team and the officers we had worked with.

My wife missed a probably smashing fare-well party thrown by her boss and her colleagues at MGM, because she had stopped working already a year earlier, due to the arrival of our son. Which reminds me of a previous office party, when she had been fed too much drink, and we had a whale of a time to prevent her losing her inner self next to our car.

We quickly packed, or rather stuffed, our belongings into the container, and dispatched the lot with not only our personal things, including my books and my stamps. But also, with the previously mentioned small Italian refrigerator (disposed-off only a few years ago), the *AEG* washing machine (which served us well for another twenty-six years), an extendible kitchen table and my office desk (both still in use now), and many more or less important household items.

On October 28th of 1965 we proceeded, as the Army would have formulated this undertaking, to the *Rhein-Main Flughafen*, and were finally on our way to South Africa. If I remember correctly, the South African Airways plane was a four-engine turbo-prop machine, which brought us first to Nairobi, the capital of Kenya, for the necessary re-fueling. In those days non-stop flights from Frankfurt to South Africa were not yet possible. We had to leave the plane in the middle of the night, and a cleaning crew started to disinfect the cabin with some white powder. It escaped me, why a plane coming from Germany to Kenya had to be treated like it had come from some disease-ridden tropical hellhole, but never mind.

We were shocked about the heat and the humidity of Nairobi at night. We had read-up a bit about the climate we would encounter in Johannesburg and I was able to console my wife that conditions there were quite different, mainly due to the substantial elevation above sea level, and because we would be quite a bit further away from the equator.

The flight of more than fifteen hours, including the stop-over, was rather cumbersome. Without any sleep for us, particularly for my poor wife, because her son was crying more or less non-stop all the way. My son would most certainly not have behaved like that!

—

The continuation of this story, first in South Africa under Apartheid, and then in the land of Mandela and Zuma, can be read in For Better Or For Worse: A Memoir of South Africa - During and After Apartheid (AMAZON, 2019).

PLEASE LEAVE A REVIEW

Thanks for reading *FOR ALL IT WAS WORTH!* Your support makes it possible for this author to continue creating.

If you liked what you read, please **leave an honest review** wherever you bought this book. Your feedback is invaluable, and reviews help new readers discover my work.

To get in touch with me directly, please use one of the various contact methods listed by BIOCOMM PRESS at http://biocomm.eu/press

ABOUT THE AUTHOR

Bernhard R. Teicher was born in Dresden in 1924 – the year Hitler's "Mein Kampf" was published. Growing up during the pre-war Nazi years, he joined the Hitler Youth before he turned 9. Later in the army, following harsh basic training, he was sent to the Eastern front where he saw combat near Kursk. Captured by the Russians, he escaped and was transferred to the Italian campaign.

With his acquired knowledge of Italian, he volunteered for the special forces Division Brandenburg, where he was trained in sabotage and intelligence gathering. Operating with his comrades behind enemy lines, he wreaked havoc with the enemy's command, communication and logistical structures.

After the war, he returned to Germany where he worked in various management positions. In 1965, disillusioned by prospects in post-war Germany, he moved with his family to South Africa where he continued to work as a management consultant.

BOOKS BY BERNHARD R. TEICHER

For All It Was Worth: A Memoir of Hitler's Germany - Before, During and After WWII. AMAZON, 2017.

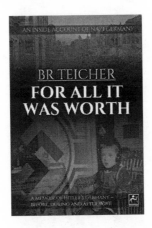

For Better Or For Worse: A Memoir of South Africa - During and After Apartheid. AMAZON, 2019.

Parallel Developments: A Geophysical / Paleontological Timeline from Big Bang to 3000BC. AMAZON, 2016.

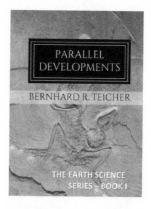

Rock Identification: A Compendium of Classifications. AMAZON, 2019.

Made in the USA
Middletown, DE
17 April 2020